PRAISE FOR *DIGITAL MARKETING STRATEGY,* SECOND EDITION

W9-AQV-974

'A strong resource that covers all of the key digital marketing disciplines and how to build them into a winning strategy. Essential reading for beginner and expert alike.'
Matt Owen, Director, Oban International

'A well-structured and insightful guide to building an effective and practical digital strategy.'
Daniel Rowles, CEO, Target Internet

'The first edition of Simon Kingsnorth's *Digital Marketing Strategy* was a great resource for digital marketing students, and the update in terms of content, structure and case examples makes the second edition an essential read and key companion as they start their marketing careers.'
Dr Emma Louise Slade, Lecturer in Marketing, University of Bristol

'A thorough and highly readable summary of everything marketers and business leaders need to know as they navigate our complex digital world. Kingsnorth pulls off the difficult task of balancing theoretical summary with both actionable steps and clarity in a vital book for marketers.'
Jon Mowat, Managing Director, Hurricane Media

'An excellent all-in-one text for today's digital entrepreneur.'
Jonathan Gabay, keynote speaker, lecturer, brand psychologist

*This book is dedicated to my parents who gave me the
foundation that provided me with the opportunity to work on
some of the exciting projects I've been involved in.
To my wife Ali for her support during the long evenings
of endless typing and to everyone I have worked for and
with to date as you have all helped to shape this book.
It is also dedicated to those people who will create
the future of this planet (and beyond) including my two
wonderful children, Oz and Dexter.*

Second Edition

Digital Marketing Strategy

An integrated approach to online marketing

Simon Kingsnorth

KoganPage

First published in Great Britain and the United States in 2016 by Kogan Page Limited
Second edition published in 2019

2nd Floor, 45 Gee Street	122 W 27th St, 10th Floor	4737/23 Ansari Road
London EC1V 3RS	New York NY 10001	Daryaganj
United Kingdom	USA	New Delhi 110002
www.koganpage.com		India

© Simon Kingsnorth, 2016, 2019

The right of Simon Kingsnorth to be identified as the author of this work has been asserted by him in accordance with the Copyright, Designs and Patents Act 1988.

Hardback	978 0 7494 9808 5
Paperback	978 0 7494 8422 4
eBook	978 0 7494 8423 1

British Library Cataloguing-in-Publication Data

A CIP record for this book is available from the British Library.

Library of Congress Cataloging-in-Publication Data

Names: Kingsnorth, Simon, author.
Title: Digital marketing strategy : an integrated approach to online
  marketing / Simon Kingsnorth.
Description: 2nd Edition. | New York : Kogan Page Ltd, [2019] | Revised
  edition of the author's Digital marketing strategy, [2016] | Includes
  bibliographical references and index.
Identifiers: LCCN 2018057298 (print) | LCCN 2018058718 (ebook) | ISBN
  9780749484231 (eBook) | ISBN 9780749498085 (hardback) | ISBN 9780749484224
  (pbk.)
Subjects: LCSH: Electronic commerce–Management. | Internet marketing. |
  Strategic planning.
Classification: LCC HF5548.32 (ebook) | LCC HF5548.32 .K566 2019 (print) |
  DDC 658.8/72--dc23

Typeset by Integra Software Services, Pondicherry
Print production managed by Jellyfish
Printed and bound by CPI Group (UK) Ltd, Croydon, CR0 4YY

CONTENTS

Online resources including lecture slides, activity sheets and implementation guides are available at:

www.koganpage.com/DigitalMarketingStrategy/2

ABOUT THE AUTHOR

Simon Kingsnorth is an award-winning digital consultant, strategic marketing expert, influencer and futurist who has worked for and consulted to many leading businesses across the world.

He has delivered highly effective strategies in digital, marketing and related fields and helped both global corporations and start-ups to scale and succeed.

He is a regular speaker at business and marketing events and trains companies on a range of marketing, digital, leadership and business disciplines.

He is also known for delivering many accurate predictions of future trends in technology and consumer behaviour.

If you would like to get in contact with Simon you can connect with him on any of the below social channels or through Kogan Page.

Twitter: TheKingsnorth
Facebook: Simon Kingsnorth
Instagram: simonkingsnorthdigital
LinkedIn: Simon Kingsnorth

ABOUT THE CONTRIBUTORS

Daniel Gilbert

Daniel Gilbert is founder and CEO of Brainlabs. As the self-proclaimed superhero of PPC, Daniel's mission is to change the future of advertising, whilst creating the best place in the world to work.

Using data and automation to drive remarkable results for clients, Daniel has grown Brainlabs from 1 to 170 people within the short space of six years. Daniel was named Number 1 in PPC Hero's Most Influential PPC Experts in the World list (2018), and one of the most influential people in digital by Econsultancy, and was a finalist for the Ernst & Young Entrepreneur of the Year Award (London, 2018).

Daniel is often invited to talk at events such as HeroConf, SMX and the Festival of Marketing. As a strong advocate of media transparency, automation and embracing future technology, Daniel writes regularly for Campaign, Econsultancy, The Drum and City AM.

Glen Conybeare

Glen is Chief Commercial Officer at international digital marketing agency Stickyeyes, specialists in SEO, biddable media, display, social, content, design and development, marketing automation and digital consultancy. A member of the executive board, Glen oversees client services, business development and marketing. He also works closely with Stickyeyes' parent company, IPG Mediabrands, the digital division of the global media group Interpublic Inc.

James Bourner

James is a digital advertising expert who works for the international independent agency Jellyfish. James has worked for many companies in a range of sectors and his expertise includes online advertising, digital marketing, content monetization and e-commerce. His current passion is programmatic buying.

James Mayhew

James Mayhew is Commercial Director at digital marketing agency Codehouse (codehousegroup. com), where he is fortunate to work with an exceptional team who create remarkable digital experiences. He has spent his career working with industry leading software vendors, systems integrators and agencies, where his passion for aligning technology, marketing and sales has delivered transformative results. He lives in Buckinghamshire with his wife and two boys, who benefit from his outstandingly good taste in music and brilliant cooking.

Murray Cox

Murray Cox is a digital strategist with deep and diverse experience. He is particularly interested in how design thinking and service design techniques can be used to more effectively drive digital transformation. He has worked both agency and client side to get differing perspectives on the challenges of change and making the customer voice heard. Murray's experience spans many sectors, and he began his digital transformation work in media.

Richard Hartley

Richard has 12 years of paid search experience, managing strategy for hundreds of clients down the years across all industries, as well as running training courses across paid media. He is currently Technical Paid Search Director at Jellyfish, heading up their internal and external PPC tech stack.

Tim Hughes

Tim Hughes is a social selling innovator and pioneer and has been mentioned by Forbes as one of the Top 100 Social Sellers globally. Tim was involved in rolling out one of the most advanced social selling programmes across 2,000 salespeople in Western Europe. He has advised and helped many organizations achieve their social selling and influencer marketing objectives.

Introduction

How will this book transform your digital marketing strategy?

Welcome to the second edition of *Digital Marketing Strategy: An integrated approach to online marketing*.

My inspiration to write this book came from the fact that I have struggled to find supporting material and helpful tips when I have been constructing my strategies over the years. I have always been able to find guides and tips on each digital channel, on user experience, digital transformation, customer service and many more relevant subjects but there are few that bring it all together and also consider how the digital strategy should fit within your organization, no matter what it might be. I hope this book goes some way to filling that gap.

Firstly, it is worth looking at what we mean by digital strategy.

What is a digital strategy?

This is perhaps best answered with a question. Can you sum up in one sentence what you will be trying to achieve over the coming years? If not, then you don't have a strategy. If you can articulate that but you don't know how to get from where you are to your end vision, then you don't have a strategy. If you have a vision and a path to get there then you have a strategy but if that is not based on research, bought into by your leadership team and with clear deliverables then your strategy will almost certainly not be a success.

If you were to Google the word 'strategy' you would find definitions such as 'A plan of action designed to achieve a long-term or overall aim' (**www.oxforddictionaries.com**) and 'A method or plan chosen to bring about a desired future, such as achievement of a goal or solution to a problem' (**www.businessdictionary.com**). Both of these definitions are of course true, but we need to go deeper.

What we look at in this book is how to turn your great ideas and those of your team and business into one strategy that is robust, agreed and aligned with your wider business. This strategy needs to go through some clear steps to becoming something you can believe in, clearly articulate, gain advocacy for and work to as a clear plan to deliver you vision. This needs to be accomplished through these core areas:

- knowing yourself;
- knowing your customer;
- managing change;
- reaching the customer;
- converting the customer;
- retaining the customer;
- measuring success.

Once you have these in place you have a strategy and so this book is designed to address each of these steps.

What's the story of this book?

As mentioned above, this book will talk through each of the key steps to creating your strategy.

In Chapter 1 we look at the background of digital marketing, wider marketing and business models to ensure that the strategy you develop is based on proven techniques and models. This gives some academic perspective that is very useful in ensuring that your methods are robust.

From here, we explore the digital ecosystem to understand today's landscape and give some perspective to the early formation of the strategy. Then we move on to look at how your strategy must align with your business if it is to perform effectively. Working in silos is a challenge that many large businesses face but whether your business is large or small it will need to be aligned. A business that pulls in different directions runs the risk of pulling itself apart.

In Chapter 4 we will look at the digital consumer. Let's be clear here: almost all consumers are digital consumers today and so we need to understand consumer behaviour broadly alongside the idiosyncrasies of these consumers in the digital space.

Chapter 5 looks at some of the challenges that face digital marketers today. There are many challenges that can completely change the shape of your strategy and so understanding these early on is vital. Data, privacy and regulation are increasingly key considerations and we will look at those alongside others.

To finish the early shaping phase of your strategy we will look at transformation, an area that is vital to taking your business to the next step on the digital journey. This includes transformation from a technology perspective but also, more importantly, from a cultural perspective.

Once we have the background from these first six chapters, we will look at effective planning processes and how to ensure your plan is solid and logical before we get into the detail of each channel.

In chapters 8 to 12 we will look at some of the key channels. This book is not designed to be a 'How To' guide to digital marketing and so we don't go into every channel and the detail of technical set-up (you can find a great deal of what you need online) but we do focus on strategic and tactical approaches to each and what that means to your digital strategy. For the second edition I have included a chapter on marketing automation, messaging and e-mail marketing.

Following this, we will look at content strategy and personalization. These two areas are vital to understand in today's digital landscape as getting them right can make a significant difference to the performance of every channel as well as to your customer satisfaction, lifetime value and retention.

From here we look at effective user experience and website design as this is the ultimate destination of most users.

We will then look at retention techniques in areas such as CRM, customer service and loyalty, and how these apply to your digital strategy.

Measurement has never been more important and the wealth of data enables us to gain deep insights into performance; we will examine that in Chapter 19.

Finally, we will bring it all together and shape your plans into the final strategy. By this point you should know what you want to achieve, the best channels to achieve it and how to get there so this exercise is cementing that into a robust and clear strategy that you can effectively communicate and manage for the coming years.

Online resources including lecture slides, activity sheets and implementation guides are available at:

www.koganpage.com/DigitalMarketingStrategy/2

How to get the most from this book

One thing I have always found when reading non-fiction books is that I just want to cut to the chase. In fact one thing I talk about in this book is that culture and technology have moved us towards a place where we demand the key information quickly.

So, whilst I hope you read the whole book and enjoy it, I have also tried to include helpful tips throughout that will help you to pull out the key elements of each topic. Below is a quick overview of some of these and how you can use them.

Chapter goals

At the beginning of every chapter you will find a set of goals. The purpose of this is to help you to understand what the chapter is trying to cover. By the end of the chapter you should have a solid understanding of all of these key points.

Key terms

At the beginning of some chapters I also include a list of the key terms used in that chapter. There is a lot of jargon in digital marketing and it is increasing all the time, but these 'key terms' sections simply help you to understand some of the more jargon-heavy chapters.

Chapter checklist

At the end of chapters you will find a checklist that is effectively a way of checking that you feel you have a good understanding of all of the key points that were listed in the chapter goals at the start of each chapter. If not, you can flick back to specific sections of the chapter to refresh your memory.

Further reading

This feature contains my list of recommended reading should you wish to conduct your own deeper research into any of the specialist models, techniques or ideas discussed in this book.

Case studies

Throughout the book you will find case studies on various subjects. These really help bring the point to life (either good or bad) and I find are a great way to understand just how effective (or disastrous) digital marketing can be.

Implementation guides

As digital marketing is a constantly evolving field I have not included practical implementation guides in the book. Up-to-date implementation guides can be found at **www.koganpage.com/DigitalMarketingStrategy/2**

I hope these help you to get the most out of the book and you find it useful and enjoyable. Thanks for reading.

Simon Kingsnorth

The foundations 01
of digital marketing

What we will cover in this chapter

Building a digital marketing strategy cannot be delivered effectively if built independently of business or marketing strategy. We will therefore first need to ensure we have a broad understanding of the underlying principles. To do this we will look at established business and marketing models and how they apply to digital marketing. The models we will review are:

- The 4 Ps of marketing
- Porter's five forces
- Brand or perceptual positioning map
- Customer lifetime value
- Segmentation
- Boston Consulting Group matrix

Chapter goals

By the end of this chapter you should understand some of the key marketing and business models that will help to shape your plans and, most importantly, how to integrate them into your strategy.

As with any book, and indeed any marketing strategy, the best place to begin is at the beginning. Digital marketing is an ever evolving and growing beast and one that continues to spread its tentacles deep into the processes that organizations have lived by for decades. That all sounds very dramatic but the truth is that it is simply aligned with the direction of travel of the modern world. Digital marketing is (or should be) a part of almost every key business decision from product development and pricing through to public relations (PR) and even recruitment. We touch on why throughout the book.

Now is an exciting time to be in digital marketing.

Digital marketing is often confused with online marketing. As we moved into the 21st century most businesses had, or were in the final throws of, developing a web presence. E-mail was commonplace and there was technology allowing people to manage this fairly easily. Customer relationship management (CRM) systems had been in place for some time to manage databases. Some companies were placing banners on websites with a similar approach to press advertising. Forward-thinking companies were working on their search engine strategy and even working with some affiliates. All of this was online marketing and, in time, online marketing teams and specialists would begin to appear.

So what has changed? The social media revolution has completely changed the internet and consumer behaviour. The penetration of broadband has increased speed, internet usage and user expectation with over 54 per cent of the world now online and over 90 per cent in many countries (Internet World Stats, 2018). Analytics has grown to the level where we can understand our consumers' behaviour in real time, including not just their usage statistics but also their demographics and even interests. Mobile has gone smart and tablets have stormed onto the scene and both of these changes have brought along apps. Touchscreen is becoming increasingly common across all devices. Google has become an enormous organization and owns search in most countries across the globe. TVs have gone smart and Bluetooth opens up another level of possibilities. With a naturally ageing population there is now only a very small percentage who are technophobes simply due to age. I could go on, but it is clear to see that digital is now much broader than the online channels of the late 1990s and must be embedded into everything we do. We will discuss the modern digital marketing channels in more detail in Chapters 8 to 14.

One key point that needs to be made at this early stage is that the focus of this book is on digital marketing and that the word marketing is as important as the word digital. Many organizations have moved towards creating digital marketing departments and digital departments that are separate from their marketing departments. It is crucial now, more so than ever, that digital marketing is an integral part of all marketing activities. This includes PR, creative direction, brand, CRM, retention, product development, pricing, proposition, communications – the entire marketing mix. Creating a silo for digital activity is very dangerous and only through truly understanding the strategic benefits of fully integrating your marketing from day one will you succeed.

To gain a good view of the strategic side of digital marketing we review the following models:

Table 1.1   Marketing strategy models

Model	Summary
The 4 Ps	The established marketing model
Porter's five forces	A view of competitive positioning
Brand positioning mapping	Analysing your perceptual positioning
Customer lifetime value	Understanding true customer value
Segmentation, targeting and positioning	Understanding the customer
Boston Consulting Group matrix	Product categorization

The 4 Ps of marketing

- Product
- Price
- Place
- Promotion

There have been quite a few variations on the Ps of marketing, including the 4 Ps and 7 Ps, but for this book we focus on the core 4 Ps of marketing – often referred to as the marketing mix. They are product, price, place and promotion. So let's look at what each of these means and how they apply to digital.

Product

This may be a physical product or it may be your service proposition. The key here is that something is developed that people actually want to buy. Some businesses begin with a product and then try to force that on an audience. If there is no demand for your product and no one is interested then you will not be able to create demand.

What does this mean for digital marketing? The key considerations here from a digital perspective are around whether your product can/will sell online. What channels are open to you for your product or proposition? Are there opportunities to make it flexible to be more appropriate for the online or mobile audiences? Does it provide real value for the consumer and is it differentiated from your competitor offerings? Is it being updated, serviced, maintained effectively to keep it strong? Are there features of it that can be added or should be excluded for the digital customer and is it fair to do this?

An example might be a music album. Three people buy an album. John buys a CD, Maria downloads the album and Robin streams it. All are different consumer behaviours and each person will use your music in a different way. John may proudly display the album on a shelf as he is a loyal fan. Maria may delete some other music from her phone to free up space for the new album. Robin may put the tracks into separate playlists in order to cultivate his collection according to genre or mood. Understanding the different motivations and usage habits for these products is vital to getting your marketing right in the digital age.

Price

Pricing is the second P and one that can be more of a science than an art. Understanding price elasticity and competitive positioning are angles to consider but we won't go into the economics of this here – the key factor is whether you are asking for a price that people are willing to pay. The 'willing to pay' element of that does of course have many factors behind it such as your brand value, online reviews, product quality and others but there are also numerous tactics that can be employed here.

What does this mean for digital marketing? Discounts and offers are certainly not new to digital marketing but the concept of fast price comparison and the introduction of cashback and voucher sites have certainly changed consumer behaviours. Businesses can take advantage of this through affiliate marketing programmes. Affiliate marketing is where you promote your products through a third-party website in exchange for paying a commission or fee to the website when an action is taken. This is very common in the comparison, voucher and cashback space as it is very easy to directly track sales and therefore attribute value to the relationship. Commissions are often paid on sales but can be paid on click-throughs or other actions.

There is also an expectation in some sectors that prices should be lower online as there are no overheads. It is considered by many that selling online should be cheaper than selling from a retail outlet. One counter to this of course is that there is no need to post products from your retail outlet.

Deciding how this fits with your business strategy is key. Another factor to keep in mind is that it costs less to keep a customer than to acquire a new one so retention, CRM and lifetime value are a vital part of your strategy. We examine the digital side of those in Chapter 17.

Place

Location, location, location. Building your shop in the wrong place decreases footfall and ultimately means fewer sales. Having your shop in the right place but not having the stock in the shop is even worse. Having your product in the shop in the right location but then not displaying it correctly – so people cannot find it – is also a factor of 'place'.

What does this mean for digital marketing? All of these apply to digital marketing. You may not have a physical shop but your online shop must be easy to find – this relates back to SEO, paid search and most other digital acquisition channels. Once someone arrives is it easy to navigate and find the information and products that they want? Do you have the items in stock and is your site working correctly to dispatch them? Ultimately, if people cannot find what they are looking for then you can expect them to go elsewhere. If this happens online then you can expect them to go elsewhere much faster as speed is much more of an expectation online.

Promotion

Promotion is what most people think of when they hear the word marketing. Your TV campaign, your press advertising, your display banners. This is often the first time that people will have any relationship with your brand and sometimes, certainly in below-the-line marketing, this can be a personal relationship. As we all know, first impressions are very important so getting your promotion right is vital.

Above and below the line

Above-the-line and below-the-line marketing are terms used to differentiate between broadcast and targeted marketing techniques. Above-the-line marketing refers to mass market advertising that is often used to push specific promotional messages out to large audiences or to build your brand. Below-the-line is used to tailor your communications to individuals or segments to ensure a more powerful message. We explore personalization in more detail in Chapter 15.

Through-the-line is a term often used and this simply refers to creating an integrated approach by using an appropriate blend of above- and below-the-line marketing. This is of course what we are advocating in this book. To help you further understand the split, given below is a list of marketing channels that would fall into each bracket:

- *Above-the-line*:
  - TV;
  - radio;
  - press;
  - display advertising;
  - outdoor.
- *Below-the-line*:
  - SEO;
  - direct mail;
  - paid search;
  - e-mail;
  - direct selling.

These days promotion has moved far beyond simple advertising and into dialogue. Smart marketing is much less about shouting about your product and much more about taking customers on a journey. That journey does not end at purchase either. There are many standard approaches to good-quality promotion, including being single-minded, insight-driven, integrated, communicating the features and benefits, creating a clear call to action and many others. All of these apply to the digital acquisition channels.

What does this mean for digital marketing? One of the challenges with the digital space is that we often have limited space or time to communicate the product promotion. Where a TV advert or press advertisement may have 30 seconds to get a point across, digital will often have 100 characters or less than one second. This therefore creates a real need for impact messaging and, more importantly than anything else, a test-and-learn philosophy. No matter how much you know (or think you know) about your consumers you cannot predict every possible outcome and so being in a constant and evolving test cycle is vital to a culture of continuous improvement – something that is a key value of effective marketing.

Porter's five forces

The next model worth reviewing is the five forces analysis model by Michael Porter. This is used to analyse the level of competition within an industry by utilizing industrial organization economics. The purpose is effectively to ascertain the competitive landscape and potential profitability of an industry. Any changes to these forces can directly affect an industry and the companies within it and so it is important to understand them and react to them in order to retain or gain competitive advantage. Michael Porter goes into a greater level of detail than we have space for here in his book *Competitive Advantage*, which has been used by students and businesses alike for many years in order to understand competition.

Porter's five forces are as follows:

- Horizontal competition:
  1 The threat of substitute products or services.
  2 The threat of established rivals.
  3 The threat of new entrants.

Figure 1.1   Porter's five forces

- Vertical competition:
  4 The bargaining power of suppliers.
  5 The bargaining power of customers.

Threat of substitute products or services

This first force is the existence of another similar product in another industry. An example for the digital age might be landline phones versus mobile phones or, more specifically, mobile phones versus smartphones. Were a new smartphone to be launched that charges via a pod in the home and that has specific benefits for home use, it may attract customers who have always been landline users and so this is a substitute product threat to landline providers.

There are a number of factors to consider when determining if a product is a substitute threat according to this definition. Those factors are:

- Switching cost: if the switching cost is low then there is a high threat.
- Pricing: if the other product or service is relatively low in price then again the threat is high.
- Product quality: if the potential substitute product or service is of superior quality then the threat is high.
- Product performance: if the other product is superior in performance then the threat is again high.

What does this mean for digital marketing? This threat is ever present in the digital age as companies continue to innovate. Tablets have threatened the laptop market and phablets have in turn threatened the tablet market. Holograms, drones and many others continue to impact on more traditional and established industries.

Threat of new entrants

This threat is fairly obvious. A new entrant to a market can be direct competition and therefore threaten the success of an established business. There are many examples of this from the digital age, not least Google, Amazon, eBay and Twitter. Google entered the search market and quickly became the leader above many established players due to the accuracy and speed of the results. Amazon grew quickly, defeating more established players through excellent customer focus and introducing innovations in personalization that gave them a distinct advantage. Although eBay was not the first auction site it was very simple and easy to use. Finally, Twitter entered the social media space with a new micro-blogging approach that created a very simple method of sharing new thoughts and insights. It has been relatively easy for online-only businesses to enter many markets in the last 10 to 15 years. Many of the old barriers, especially capital, have been removed.

Some of the factors that can dictate the threat of a new entrant are:

- *Barriers to entry*: for example patents, regulation. High entry barriers are attractive to established businesses as they stop new businesses entering easily. Also low exit barriers help businesses to leave the industry, which is also attractive. In other words, it is easy for your established competition to leave but difficult for new competition to enter.

- *Economies of scale*: new entrants are highly likely to be smaller than established businesses and so may not be able to profitably compete on pricing.

- *Brand equity*: established businesses have brand equity – a level of trust that comes with being a recognized brand. Although it is true that new entrants do not have this, it can be quickly established with significant above-the-line marketing spend.

- *Industry profitability*: if the industry is generally highly profitable then it is likely to attract a large volume of new entrants and vice versa.

- *Government policy*: there might be government policy in place that limits the ease with which new entrants can join specific industries.

There are many other factors such as location, expected retaliation, technology and distribution and these should all be thoroughly researched and understood in order for strategy to be robust.

Barriers to entry – two examples

Financial services is a good example of an industry that has high entry barriers. There are many regulatory bodies and licensing processes in this industry and these are different around the world. It can therefore be very challenging for new businesses to gain these licences and understand all the regulations and requirements. Also staff need to be hired who have the expertise in the industry and they need ongoing training. These are all additional costs. Photography is an example of a business with very low entry barriers. To demonstrate this you could ask your friends and colleagues if any of them have a photography website and you will almost certainly find that at least one of them does. With the move to digital photography, equipment can be bought easily, techniques learnt at home and studios set up in your spare room. Anyone can become a wedding photographer or corporate photographer with minimal investment and effort.

What does this mean for digital marketing? Specifically for digital marketing it is certainly true that new entrants are common to most markets and disruption is commonplace in the 21st century. Factors such as location, economies of scale, brand equity and technology are far less relevant for entering many industries now, for example technology businesses. Technology businesses have grown at pace in recent years and have attracted a great deal of investment as businesses look to disrupt the existing industries. In 2014 for example, funds worth US$1.4 billion were launched by London-based venture capital firms in just six months (London and Partners, 2014). Many of the businesses being invested in offer digital solutions such as marketing automation, analytics and social media. This results in the digital marketing industry being in a constant state of flux – and ensuring you keep pace with these changes is important. Attending events, maintaining strong relationships with agencies and tech companies and reading the tech news are all important ways of doing this.

Intensity of competitive rivalry

Competitive rivalry is one of the more commonly understood competitive factors and is sometimes considered the most dangerous. The distinct features and behaviours of your competition directly affect your ability to gain competitive advantage.

Alongside digital transformation there are many other factors, including:

- *The competitors themselves*: the number of competitors and their relative strength are key factors. If your industry has no industry leaders the playing field is fairly level and so competitor rivalry is increased.

- *High exit barriers*: if it is difficult to get out then more businesses will stay in, even if they are only breaking even or even losing money. Competition therefore remains high.

- *Slow industry growth*: if an industry is growing fast then all players can grow through acquisition without necessarily directly affecting the competition. All those new customers can be shared out. If growth is slow then there are no more customers but just as many companies, so to grow you need to acquire customers from your rivals.

In markets where competitive rivalry is high, we move towards 'perfect competition' or in other words a situation where everyone competes at an even level with no 'price makers', only 'price takers'. Price makers have the power to influence the price they charge, whereas price takers have no effect on the market. I would recommend more reading on Porter's five forces and generally around economic theory to understand this in greater detail.

What does this mean for digital marketing? There are many factors to take into consideration here and the recent trend towards modernization in the form of digital transformation is one of these. Moving your business into the digital age can be a slow and expensive process for established businesses. This can certainly create a change in the competitive landscape as younger businesses are more agile. On the other hand it is equally true that the larger businesses, which of course tend to be the more established (although not necessarily), can potentially invest money and resource into creating something at scale with advanced technology that may be less available to less established businesses. Digital transformation can gain you competitive advantage and therefore reduce rivalry.

Bargaining power of suppliers

Suppliers of products or services to companies are another factor in the competitive nature of an industry. The bargaining power of suppliers directly affects the ability for companies to make a profit and therefore compete. Strong suppliers are able to control pricing and product quality, which lessens a company's ability to make profit. Weak suppliers on the other hand can be controlled or influenced more by the buyer and so the buyer can retain competitive advantage.

Some of the factors that can lead to high bargaining power for suppliers and therefore increased competition are:

- *Few suppliers*: if there are fewer suppliers than buyers then suppliers retain more bargaining opportunity.
- *Buyer switching costs*: if changing supplier is expensive then the advantage again lies with the buyer.
- *Forward integration*: if the supplier is able to produce the product or service themselves then again they are in a position of strength.

What does this mean for digital marketing? If you are running an e-commerce operation with physical products then you may be working with a wholesaler for the supply of your goods. It is possible that your supplier may be one of very few or the only supplier of the goods that you are retailing to your customers. In this situation the wholesaler has strong bargaining power as you have limited options. This can lead to an increase in costs and therefore your profit margin. This may in turn lead to a necessity to increase prices, which may result in a decline in sales. Should more wholesalers enter the market then the competition for your wholesaler increases, which passes some of the bargaining power back to you. Another option is to look at producing at least some of the products yourself in order to remove further power from the wholesaler.

Bargaining power of buyers

The bargaining power of buyers is the final force and is simply the ability of consumers to put pressure on companies to lower prices, change their products or improve customer service. Businesses can take a number of actions to reduce buyer power: for example, engagement strategies and loyalty programmes.

Some of the factors that influence buyer bargaining power are:

- *Buyer concentration*: if there are few consumers and many companies then the buyer effectively has their choice of company.

- *Switching costs*: as with most of the other forces, switching costs are a factor. If it is easy for a buyer to switch then they retain the bargaining power.

- *Backward integration*: if buyers can produce the products themselves then they again retain the power.

What does this mean for digital marketing? One of the best examples of how buyer bargaining power has changed in the digital age is the increased use of social media and review sites to openly rate and discuss products, pricing and customer service provided by businesses. Many consumers will include reviews within their decision-making process and will not buy products that match their requirements if the reviews from their peers are negative. This has even extended to search engines with star ratings openly displayed within results for searches such as restaurants and products, which can increase or decrease click-through rates as a result. The power of the buyer has significantly increased since Web 2.0.

Brand or perceptual positioning map

It is useful to use a brand positioning map to develop your market positioning strategy for your products or services. These maps are not, however, built from your views of your marketplace but from the perceptions of consumers and so are sometimes called perceptual maps. These maps give a clear view, albeit a little subjective, of where your brand or products sit versus your competitors, thus highlighting any gaps in the market and demonstrating where there are areas of intense competition.

Most perceptual maps are drawn with two axes, X and Y. They intersect each other in the centre and so form a cross. This is not the only way to draw a positioning map but it is by far the most common. What you choose to place on the axes is up to you and you therefore need to consider the variables in your industry and what is the goal of your research. If we were to draw a map of automotive brands using the scales of practicality and affordability (see Figure 1.2) we can see quite clearly where the direct competition lies in terms of perception and where there may be gaps in the market. This is also useful to determine where your brand is perceived to be and can help you to construct your strategy for moving your brand to where you want it to be.

As well as reviewing where your business or brand is positioned today, perceptual maps can also help you to identify opportunities for launching new brands. If the map of the automotive industry shown in Figure 1.2 were to be the output of actual research, you could decide that launching a brand that stands for sports and performance but is in the mid-price range would have little competition and so might be an opportunity. On the other hand you need to combine this thinking with the size of the market. For example, in Figure 1.2 no brands are perceived to be very sporty and very cheap so there is a gap there, but is this because that is not a profitable opportunity or because when people buy sporty cars they expect to spend money and would not trust a cheap sports car?

What does this mean for digital marketing? In relation to positioning maps there is no specific difference between digital marketing and any other form of marketing. As mentioned at the start of this book, marketing is the key word. Brand is one of the areas where having an integrated approach is absolutely vital to success. Considering how your brand performs across all marketing considerations is essential, and whilst it is important to include digital within this, it should not have its own separate approach.

One thing that is worth bearing in mind here is that it is much easier to launch a brand today than it was in the 20th century. You can fire up your laptop at home, design a logo in Photoshop, create a website using Wordpress,

Figure 1.2   Automotive perceptual map

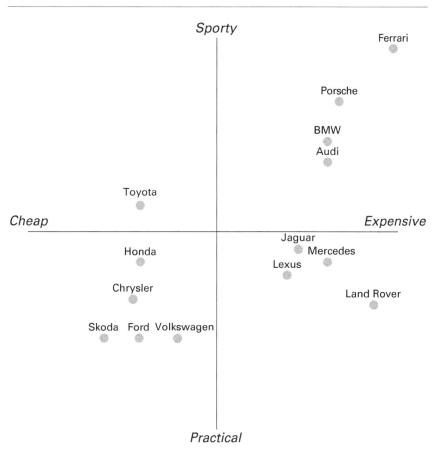

NOTE The above figure is an example only and not the output of a research paper. It should not be used for decision making within the automotive industry.

create a Twitter account and build a Google Ads account all in one evening. You then have a brand and it is being seen by thousands and potentially millions of people almost immediately. Whilst I would never discourage someone from launching their business or moving fast to do so, I would encourage some thought around your customer perception and competitors and this is where perceptual mapping fits in.

Customer lifetime value

Customer lifetime value (CLTV or sometimes LTV) is quite simply the value or profit attributed to a customer for their entire customer lifecycle. This can be relatively simple to calculate in some businesses and incredibly complex in others. Either way, one thing is true: there are many factors that influence it and many levers that can be pulled to alter it. Cost per acquisition (CPA) has long been used as a key metric in marketing and especially so in digital marketing due to tracking technology and the transparency of data. However, this has certainly been criticized as too simplistic a view. For example, if you know that a customer spends $100 buying a product from you that has a margin of $50 and it costs you $40 to acquire that customer then you can be happy that you have acquired them profitably. If that customer then leaves and never comes back then we have a simple model. If, however, the average customer comes back another 3.2 times and phones your call centre twice per purchase then you have additional income and expenditure for this customer that is not taken into consideration.

The CPA model continues to be used in channels such as affiliate marketing as it enables businesses to remove the risk of cost-per-click payments where conversions are not guaranteed. It would be far too complicated in most instances to ask affiliates to abide by your CLTV model as so many of the variables would be out of their control. CLTV can be used to determine which customers are the most profitable and to define segments based on this, which can then be targeted appropriately. We will look at segmentation and targeting below.

Calculating CLTV

There are several different ways to calculate CLTV but for the purpose of this book we focus on the simple approach. I would recommend understanding the different models in more detail to fully appreciate the complexities of CLTV and ensure you have a model or combination of models that is appropriate for your business. In order to calculate your CLTV using the simple method you need to have an understanding of the following two variables: 1) number of periods that a customer remains with you (customer lifetime); 2) average margin per customer in a period.

In order to help understand these variables there are some common factors that need to be understood and these are therefore also the levers that can be pulled to improve your CLTV:

- Length of customer lifetime:
  - CRM programmes;
  - member-get-member schemes;
  - loyalty schemes;
  - service levels.

- Average margin per customer:
  - repeat purchases;
  - cross-selling and up-selling;
  - returns and refunds;
  - pricing and discounts;
  - operating costs;
  - conversion rates;
  - segmentation.

The formula in simple terms is therefore as follows:

$$CLTV = Lifetime \times Avg\ Margin$$

To give an example of this we can look at a retailer.

This particular retailer manages to attract each customer to its store 3.9 times per week on average and those customers spend $21.69 on average during each visit. We therefore know that the customers are spending $21.69 × 3.9 = $84.59 per week. We want to understand our CLTV in terms of years so we can simply multiply by 52 to get an annual customer value of $4,399. We know that each customer has a profit margin of 10 per cent so we know that our profit per customer is actually $439. On average we know that customers stay with us for 15 years and so our CLTV is $439 × 15 = $6,585. That gives us a target figure to acquire customers. We know that we can spend up to $6,585 to acquire a customer over their lifetime.

What does this mean for digital marketing? There are many models in digital marketing that are forced upon us. As mentioned above there are cost-per-acquisition and cost-per-click models that are very common. There are also cost-per-impression (sometimes cost-per-mille), cost-per-action and cost-per-lead models, amongst others. Whilst we are forced to use these as payment methods it is often all too easy to relax into using these as the key performance indicators (KPIs) for running the channels. CLTV is not something that can be implemented purely within one area of your business, but if this model is appropriate then it should be integrated within digital marketing as much as anywhere else. Digital marketers are blessed with exceptional amounts of data (we will look at big data in Chapter 19) so we have the opportunity to understand our customers and the variables involved in greater detail than other areas of the business. This opportunity is golden and should not be wasted.

Segmentation

Later in the book (Chapter 15) we will look at personalization, which is the ultimate goal of tailored communications and is far more possible than it was just 10 years ago. It is, however, still vitally important to understand segmentation as well. Consumers will always have similarities in their behaviours, demographics, buying patterns and other factors that enable you to group them into segments. This enables smarter, more appropriate targeting and messaging within your marketing communications. These groups will have different uses for products and varying perspectives on services. Their lifestyles will be inherently different as will be their needs, aspirations, opinions and much more.

Five common forms of segmentation – geographic, demographic, behavioural, benefit and psychographic – are listed below, including the advantages and disadvantages of each alongside how businesses use these methods.

Geographic Perhaps the simplest of all segmentation strategies, this is quite simply the location of the individuals being analysed. Businesses that have regional retail outlets will have some focus on this but it can also prove a useful tool to understand where to target your marketing. That could be outdoor or press advertising but from a digital perspective it may inform your geo-targeting or data selection for your strategy. The disadvantage is quite simply that this is very basic and tells you next to nothing about the individuals themselves.

Demographic A very common form of segmentation, demographics includes factors such as age, race, gender, education, employment, income and economic status. It is therefore an area of segmentation that gives a reflection of the characteristics of a group of people. Demographic segmentation is used by governments and a very broad range of organizations as it can answer questions such as 'Who can afford to buy my product?' and 'Will this group of consumers be the right age range for my product?'

The disadvantage of this type of segmentation is that there is a large assumption that people with similar characteristics will behave similarly, which is far from the truth. If someone is a French, 45-year-old factory worker who has had a poor education will they behave the same way as all their colleagues in the factory who are of roughly the same age? No. They will have different passions, hobbies and much more. To understand this in more detail we need to understand behavioural segmentation.

Behavioural Behavioural segmentation is becoming increasingly possible. It has historically been difficult to understand consumer behaviour but in the big data world we are able to understand consumers a lot more, especially those in the digital space. This method groups consumers by buying patterns and usage behaviours. This is an excellent way of talking to individuals in a way that is highly likely to resonate with them. It is useful when talking about specific products or use occasions.

Behavioural does not of course give such a black-and-white view as demographic segmentation and therefore is not an exact science. For example, behaviour can change with your lifestyle. Divorce, children and retirement are key examples of when life changes could result in behaviour changes. It is therefore vital to be working with data that is up to date. With behavioural segmentation you have the advantage of being highly relevant to your audience whilst also running the risk of missing the mark completely.

Benefit Something that is vital to understand in marketing, and in fact business in general, is that perception is key. How you are perceived will impact your career – we all know the clichés about first impressions. Well, this form of segmentation is based around consumer perceived benefit. Many businesses use this to understand the consumer base and to inform product development and marketing opportunities. A good example of this is the fashion industry. If you imagine retailers of coats and jackets: some consumers will look for warm winter coats for their ski holidays, some for all-weather jackets for their outdoor lifestyle, some for lightweight jackets they can wear whilst exercising, some for smart coats for work and some purely for fashion. The perceived benefit of your coat will appeal differently to each different segment, so perhaps you need to change the perception of your coat or bring out a new range to appeal to a new segment.

Psychographic Psychographic segmentation sounds exceptionally complex but it is simply an understanding of a consumer's lifestyle. This includes studying activities, opinions, beliefs and interests. Understanding these elements can, similarly to behavioural segmentation, result in messaging and products that truly resonate with the individuals. For example, individuals may be environmentalists, Buddhists, body builders or movie lovers (or any combination of these). Creating segments on this basis creates a more 'real' view of the individuals than geographic or demographic segmentation ever could.

Personas

By pulling together the above five forms of segmentation you can create personas, as per the example shown in Figure 1.3. These are effectively descriptions of your segments. Most businesses will create between five and ten of these, as too few results in large groups that are too generic and too many can result in segments that are too small or overcomplicate the targeting approach.

Boston Consulting Group matrix

According to Bruce Henderson, founder of the Boston Consulting Group, 'To be successful, a company should have a portfolio of products with different growth rates and different market shares' (Henderson, 1970). This model is similar to the brand perceptual model mentioned above – in that it uses a matrix. However, the Boston Consulting Group (BCG) matrix is used for a very different purpose. The model categorizes products in a portfolio into stars, cash cows, dogs and question marks (Figure 1.4) by looking at market share and market growth. This is why it is sometimes called the growth–share matrix. It is used primarily to maximize long-term value creation in a business by maximizing high-potential areas and minimizing poor performers.

Figure 1.3   An example of a persona

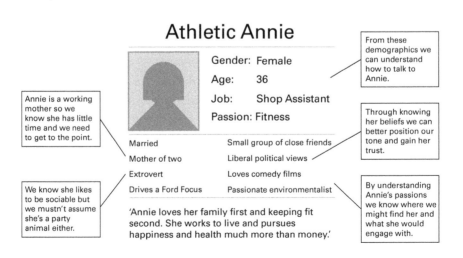

Athletic Annie

Gender: Female
Age: 36
Job: Shop Assistant
Passion: Fitness

Married   Small group of close friends
Mother of two   Liberal political views
Extrovert   Loves comedy films
Drives a Ford Focus   Passionate environmentalist

'Annie loves her family first and keeping fit second. She works to live and pursues happiness and health much more than money.'

From these demographics we can understand how to talk to Annie.

Annie is a working mother so we know she has little time and we need to get to the point.

Through knowing her beliefs we can better position our tone and gain her trust.

We know she likes to be sociable but we mustn't assume she's a party animal either.

By understanding Annie's passions we know where we might find her and what she would engage with.

Figure 1.4   The Boston Consulting Group matrix

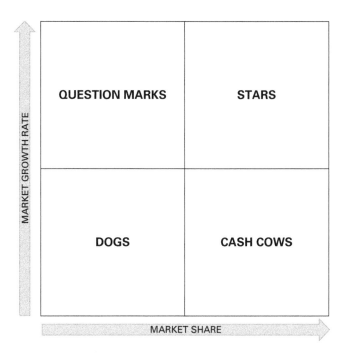

Cash cows – high market share in a slow-growth environment

Cash cows are strong and safe products. They generate money steadily in a market that is not growing at any pace and, as such, do not require much investment. As a result they are highly profitable.

Dogs – low market share in a slow-growth environment

Dogs are not the strongest part of the portfolio and can in fact be damaging for a business. They tend to break even and so do not offer a great deal of benefit to the business. Businesses will generally look to reduce dogs or sell them off and should be very wary of investing money into them as returns are unlikely.

Question marks – low market share in a high-growth environment

Question marks are aptly named as they can go in either direction. They are growing rapidly but have a low share so they consume a lot of cash and do not generate a great deal. A question mark can become a 'star' if it gains market share and then even a 'cash cow' if the market slows, but it also has the potential to be a 'dog' if the market slows before it has gained momentum. Decisions around what to do with question marks must be based on extensive analysis – to invest or not to invest.

Stars – high market share in a high-growth environment

Stars generate cash due to having a strong market share but they also swallow up a lot of investment due to the high growth environment. Once the growth declines, stars become cash cows; therefore, having a range of stars in your portfolio that can become the next cash cows is an important strategy.

The matrix itself shows not only the position of each product but also, by utilizing the area or size of each category, the value of each product. This therefore gives a snapshot of profitability and cashflows of an organization. Ultimately, cash cows and dogs are at either end of the scale and so all business units will move to one end or the other eventually and there is a common path: question mark – star – cash cow – dog. Of course it is not the situation for most companies, or indeed the aim, to have a set of products that simply fall into one of these categories – and in fact a blend of these is important to be able to describe your portfolio as balanced:

- Cash cows exist to supply funds that can be used to invest in the future of the company.
- Stars, due to their high growth potential and high market share, are the products that build this future.
- Question marks are items to steer into your next set of stars.
- Dogs should be removed.

One key thing to remember is that the BCG matrix has complications and has been misinterpreted and misused many times, so understanding the intricacies of it and how to apply it (and indeed *when* to apply it) is crucial.

What does this mean for digital marketing? The BCG matrix will inform which products you should be selling through which methods and channels, which will influence your overall digital strategy. You can also use it to assess your digital channels themselves and understand, therefore, whether you are applying your focus effectively. For example, is paid search a cash cow or a dog? The value of this channel is often debated and so being able to substantiate where your channels fit on the BCG matrix is a great way to communicate how your channel strategy will be managed. Moving SEO from a question mark to a star is a common goal of businesses that have poor natural search performance but understand the steps to make improvements. We will look at these channels and how to maximize them in Chapters 8 to 12.

Summary

Many marketers agree that marketing has changed more since 2015 than it did in the 30 years before. The above models, however, have remained consistently true and relevant so whilst it is vital to stay close to the changing landscape and consumer behaviours, it is also critical to understand these models and build them into your strategy.

Chapter checklist

- The 4 Ps of marketing ☐
- Porter's five forces ☐
- Brand or perceptual positioning map ☐
- Customer lifetime value ☐
- Segmentation ☐
- Boston Consulting Group matrix ☐

Further reading

- *On the 4 Ps of marketing:*

  Perreault Jr, W D (2004) *Basic Marketing*, McGraw-Hill Higher Education. This book covers modern practical examples and best practices and pulls together the theory of the marketing mix with the strategic planning approach we discuss in this book.

- *On competitive rivalry:*

  Magretta, J (2011) *Understanding Michael Porter: The essential guide to competition and strategy*, Harvard Business Review Press

  Porter, M (2004) *Competitive Strategy: Techniques for analyzing industries and competitors*, Free Press

- *On brand positioning:*

  Riezebos, R (2011) *Positioning the Brand: an inside-out approach*, Routledge. This book discusses brand positioning in detail and looks at the different stages of positioning your brand. It is well worth a read to understand the stages of corporate identity, brand architecture, target group analysis, competitor analysis and choosing a market position.

- *On segmentation:*

  McDonald, M (2012) *Market Segmentation: How to do it, how to profit from it*, John Wiley & Sons. This book includes tips on avoiding big mistakes and determining scope, which are very helpful in the exercise of building a segmentation strategy.

- *On the Boston Consultancy Group matrix:*

  Stern, C W and Deimler, M S (2006) *The Boston Consulting Group on Strategy: Classic concepts and new perspectives*, John Wiley & Sons

References

Henderson, B (1970) [accessed 1 November 2015] The Product Portfolio [Online] https://www.bcgperspectives.com/content/classics/strategy_the_product_portfolio/

Internet World Stats (2018) [accessed 20 January 2019] World Internet Users Statistics [Online] http://www.internetworldstats.com/stats.htm

London and Partners (2014) [accessed 1 November 2015] $1.4bn of New Tech Funds Set Up in London in Last 6 Months, *London and Partners* [Online] http://www.londonandpartners.com/media-centre/press-releases/2014/140902-14bn-of-new-tech-funds-set-up-in-london-in-last-6-months

Porter, M (1985) *Competitive Advantage*, Free Press, New York

PART ONE
Knowing your business objectives and your customer

Understanding the digital ecosystem 02

What we will cover in this chapter

This chapter will provide you with a view of how the digital marketing ecosystem fits together and how the individual elements interact. Every element affects at least one other and understanding this from the start is crucial so that your strategy takes this into account when building the plans for each of the constituent parts. We will touch on just some of these areas briefly in the context of the ecosystem but you can find more on each topic later in the book. The key considerations here are:

- Paid and organic search interaction
- Social signals for SEO
- The broad reach of content strategy
- Display advertising and data strategy
- Brand and proposition effect
- The halo effect
- Attribution and omni-channel
- The full ecosystem

> **Chapter goals**
>
> By the end of this chapter you should understand how the digital marketing channels interact and therefore how to build a strategy that is truly integrated and highly effective.

Paid and organic search interaction

Paid search and organic search can be made to work together. Although the channels are very different in many ways, there is much you can learn from one and apply to the other. Let's start by looking at how each can benefit the other.

Using SEO data to shape PPC strategy

Many companies will start with SEO if they need to prove the search model or have limited budgets. As you move on to building your PPC strategy you can see which keywords are likely to be expensive due to competition and volume. In that scenario it can be worth focusing your SEO here. It will take longer to achieve results but for a significantly smaller investment.

You should also review your SEO analytics at least monthly to understand whether there are any learnings you can apply to your PPC accounts. This could be trends in topics, time of day, day of week, device type, location or many other factors.

Using PPC data to shape SEO strategy

One of the most frustrating factors with SEO in recent years has been the move by Google to delivering 'not provided' as the keyword giving us limited data to work with. One of the most widely known interactions therefore between PPC and SEO is to use PPC keyword data to inform SEO strategy.

The other key learning is that you can quickly learn effective copy trends for ads in PPC and then apply those to your site and other marketing activities to increase click-through and conversion rates.

Social signals for SEO

There has been much debate about this area for many years but we can assume that social media plays a part in SEO. There has been confirmation that Google uses social links for social media and it is possible that social engagement is another factor. The number of followers is less likely to have any significant impact – as it should be because follower numbers are purely a vanity metric. We will talk about this more in Chapter 11.

At the moment social signals are still a relatively small ranking factor but the likelihood is that they will grow as social media continues to expand and be integrated into every digital experience.

We should consider how regularly and broadly we post, how much engagement we achieve, the links we gain and sentiment we achieve. Locality, speed of response and user behaviours on our site for those that arrive from social should all be considered. Even if the effects on SEO performance are small today, we should be preparing for tomorrow.

The broad reach of content strategy

Your content strategy, as we will see in Chapter 15, should be very sophisticated. You should be building proactive plans for what you know is a future content opportunity, reviewing historic performance to improve and develop your strategy and ensuring you have robust reactive processes in place to be able to produce content quickly when an opportunity arises.

Your content is then distributed across various channels according to relevance. Perhaps the same content in different formats (infographics, video, quotes, facts, pure advertising messages). For this you may use Facebook, Twitter, Snapchat, your own website, PPC, display advertising, e-mail. The list is long. From that you must be reviewing your data and the impact of this content by channel as well as by type and topic.

For example, SEO content writing skills should be fused into your content and this can in turn not only affect SEO but also your PPC Quality Score as your conversion and engagement rates improve. Content strategy, as we will discuss later in the book, is central to any marketing strategy now.

Display advertising and data strategy

Display advertising has moved a long way from the simplistic banner ads of the early 21st century. Display in the form of programmatic and real-time buying is now a sophisticated and highly targeted channel utilizing complex data platforms. We will explain this in more detail in Chapter 10 but we can for now appreciate that, without a clear data strategy that ensures your customer and enquiry data is as complete, accurate and current as possible, it risks targeting the wrong people with the wrong message at the right time.

Your data strategy also affects your digital communications. For example, if we consider e-mail marketing, holding data that is incorrect, does not have accurate marketing permissions or is incomplete could mean not only sending out poor performing communications but could even result in a regulatory breach.

Brand and proposition effect

Your brand and proposition(s) should of course be reflected in everything you do. No area of marketing is doing its job effectively if it doesn't reinforce or strengthen the brand and key messaging in its external communications. It should also be acknowledged therefore that this will have an impact on your performance. We will talk more about branding in the next chapter but as part of the ecosystem it should be considered as a key influencing factor.

This is not, however, under the direct influence of the digital marketer. Your brand can be affected by company performance, positive or negative PR, growth or downsizing decisions, customer service performance, pricing and many more factors, some of which we have already touched on in the previous chapter.

The halo effect

The halo effect is a term often used to describe the uplift you see across your channels as a result of above the line advertising. For example, if your marketing department runs a broad campaign across TV, radio, outdoor and press reaching many millions of consumers you are likely to see this reflected in numerous metrics across your strategy.

You would likely see an increase in brand searches on SEO and PPC, increased click-through rate on your brand terms on PPC, improved performance of display, higher conversion rates, more app downloads, stronger e-mail open rates and higher social media engagement.

Attribution and omni-channel

Finally, we need to understand that we can track all of these channels together and how they interact through attribution modelling and omni-channel management. We will look at this more later but, in the meantime, it is vital that we appreciate that understanding the picture of the data set together rather than in silos is what will really enable us to gain full oversight and therefore to apply the optimal improvements to our strategy.

The full ecosystem

Figure 2.1 The digital marketing ecosystem

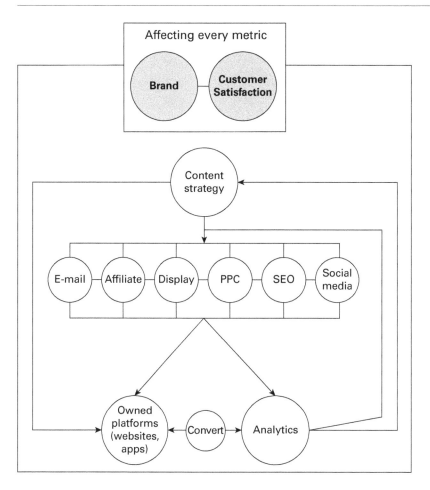

Summary

No marketing channel has ever worked truly independently of the others, but now the effect is highly scientific. We will look at attribution modelling in Chapter 19 to understand this further, but for the most impact we cannot simply understand the interaction, we must also plan for it. This means using the channels to effectively amplify each other. The most effective digital marketing strategies use this technique.

Chapter checklist

- Paid and organic search interaction ☐
- Social signals for SEO ☐
- The broad reach of content strategy ☐
- Display advertising and data strategy ☐
- Brand and proposition effect ☐
- The halo effect ☐
- Attribution and omni-channel ☐
- The full ecosystem ☐

Integrating digital into wider organization strategy

03

What we will cover in this chapter

We have already examined the key business and marketing models you need to bring into your strategy. Alongside this you need to develop your strategy within the framework of your business. This will include your industry and any regulatory challenges that may bring, your company structure and culture, your brand and goals. Only by working within this context can your strategy succeed. We will consider the following:

- Business model
- Global strategy
- Brand
- Vision
- Culture
- Innovation
- Research and insight
- KPIs

> ## Chapter goals
>
> By the end of this chapter you should understand what the key factors in your business are that need to be pulled into your digital marketing strategy to make it effective and as easy as possible to implement.

If there is one message to take away from this book it is that your digital strategy must not and cannot be built independently of your business strategy if it is to truly succeed. We are in the technology age and this brings new opportunities for the digital marketer every month. This means that every digital strategy evolves at pace (we will examine real-time planning in Chapter 7) and so the temptation to move your digital strategy forward independently of the restrictions that your wider organization brings can be too much to resist. In this chapter we look at how aligning to your broader business strategy is important and so this temptation must be resisted. We examine some of the areas to consider when ensuring that your strategy is aligned with your business.

Business model

Your business model could be one of many and ensuring your digital strategy fits into this is crucial. Creating an aggressive e-commerce strategy for a relationship-based B2B business would not be a good fit. Likewise, leading with a pure content and social media strategy for a sales-focused retailer is highly unlikely to deliver the sales volumes you need to achieve. It is vital that you therefore fit your strategy to your business model. There are many different definitions of business model and within those there are many models. Below is a list of three common business models, some of their qualities and how they apply to your digital marketing strategy.

Mass market B2C

This model includes organizations that sell products that appeal to a broad range of consumers at an affordable price. An example of this type of business is fast-moving consumer goods (FMCG) companies. Selling a large number of products such as food, clothing or toys involves being able to attract a high volume of customers to your website and stores. This means creating awareness through above-the-line advertising, acquiring visitors and converting them into customers. This would also require a robust customer service process. Therefore all digital channels are relevant here.

Niche B2C

This model is a direct-to-consumer business that has a highly targeted offering. This could include selling products to people living with a specific disability, in financial difficulty or to ultra-high-net-worth individuals. Using broadcast media is not relevant in most of these scenarios as the majority of the viewers will not be potential customers. Creating trust and advocacy is essential, however, so a deep content strategy and first-class experience are crucial to success as are precision targeting techniques and a comprehensive data strategy.

B2B

The B2B model includes organizations such as wholesalers or technology resellers that are selling directly to other businesses. Here you are dealing with other business people rather than end consumers. These business people are of course still individuals and it is important not to forget that human psychology still applies. They do, however, have very different expectations. You may be seen less as a brand and more as a supplier, which creates a very different relationship. Your customers may be more cynical or aggressive than B2C customers as they have specific objectives and goals to achieve. You may find that traditional marketing messages and sales techniques are less well received. Therefore the focus should be more on relationships through CRM, content and direct value-added discussions rather than through advertising. It is still important, however, for these customers to be able to find your site and the information they need to get to.

Within these broader business models there are of course many specific models. A B2B IT company may be a hardware product provider or a service support provider. The service model would require more of a focus on screen sharing and CRM whilst the product model would require more of an acquisition and conversion focus.

Freemium

One interesting trend in business models in the 2010s is the freemium model. This model has grown in popularity and is essentially the method of attracting users by giving a percentage of your product or service for free and offering a more interesting, deeper experience for a price. A good example of this is the music-streaming industry with businesses such as Spotify and Deezer employing this technique.

Whilst we have reviewed some of the more common business models here it is important to appreciate that business models can also adapt over time to the changing needs of the customer, society, regulators or other external factors.

Changing business models

Facebook

Facebook is a great example of a business model that has had to adapt quickly. I would imagine that even Mark Zuckerberg was surprised by the speed at which Facebook grew from being one of many college social networks to the leading global hub for a significant percentage of the world to share their lives on. The initial model of providing a network for college students had to develop a broader appeal once the growth became inevitable. As this growth took hold it was clear that costs would also accelerate and, with no obvious income, something had to be done and so the business pages and advertising models had to be developed in order to monetize the site. These shifts in the way that the business had to change to deal with its own growth have been both significant and impressive in their speed and success. This is an excellent example of how adapting your strategy to meet the changing needs of your consumers and the evolution of your business is vital. Facebook has had to do this through the above changes to their website and user experience. We will look at this area in more detail in Chapter 16.

Google

It is hard to believe that Google spent a long time with no real income channel. The initial business model was successful by creating the best search engine in terms of accuracy and simplicity. Google became a verb as people realized that Googling something would give better results than using another engine. However, a source of income needed to be developed. This is why Adwords (now Google Ads) was introduced in 2003 and that has gone on to become the foundation of the growth of every other arm of the Google we know today – a business with an incredibly diverse and profitable range of services. This has led to Google having to closely manage its brand and how it is perceived, which it has done with significant success. Their digital marketing strategy has been a minimalist approach. They promote their service and products such as Google Ads and Chrome through display advertising and CRM but they do not broadcast as much as most organizations of a similar size. This is because much of their success is through word of mouth. This networking approach has been encouraged by supporting businesses that use their products, through strong and personalized customer service, networking and learning events and training materials. This personalized and deep-content digital marketing has ensured that people have trust, belief and understanding of their products, which further encourages word of mouth.

Global strategy

Globalization can be a very challenging process for any organization. It can also take some companies by surprise as they outgrow their initial local plans. This brings cultural, language, process and many other challenges. With the growth of digital, almost all businesses have an international presence through the internet even if their target audience is very localized and so some aspect of global strategy should be included in almost every digital strategy – even if that aspect is to ensure that global presence is minimized.

Culture

There are many cultural differences around the world, too many to count, and the relevant ones must be understood when building a global strategy. This can range from religious beliefs to manners and it is impossible to know what we don't know – so doing your research is important here.

For example, did you know that Mexicans celebrate New Year's Eve by eating 12 grapes at the stroke of midnight? That the colour red is lucky in China? That Suriname's land is 91 per cent jungle whereas there are virtually no trees left in Haiti? These facts can affect your copy, conversations, brand and many other factors.

From a digital perspective there are several cultural considerations. You should look at whether each region you are targeting responds well to buying online and, if not, whether your strategy should focus on thought leadership, brand awareness and directing people to your offline conversion channels. Understanding the penetration of smartphones and tablets alongside mobile coverage will also influence your strategy. For example, at the time of writing, Google's Consumer Barometer tells us that more people use five or more connected devices in Japan than use a single device, and in Morocco only just over half of those surveyed used the internet for personal use (Google, 2018). This could mean that ensuring your business uses and understands multichannel analytics and attribution is more or less of a priority for your business and you may not require the app that you have budgeted for. You will also need to understand broadband speeds and coverage as this will dictate how fast your website and off-site content will download and, therefore, the design of your assets.

Lifestyle points such as working hours and average commute times will influence your targeting and customer support programmes. Even weather, which is not cultural itself but does influence culture, is an important factor to consider as it will affect the amount of time spent indoors (near computers) and outdoors (on mobile or offline). It is also important to understand that the digital landscape may be very different in territories away from your local country. In Europe and the United States you would most likely consider Twitter at the core of your micro-blogging strategy whereas in China you would be more likely to need to look at Sina Weibo. Thoroughly researching cultural points and ensuring you are working with, or at least speaking to, local people with strong knowledge are important considerations – getting this right can be incredibly powerful and getting this wrong can be extremely damaging.

Language

Language is perhaps the most obvious consideration but one that must be considered very carefully. To give a potent example of how important this is, some organizations have been guilty of not considering language when creating their global brand and identity – leading to a name that, when translated, has been found to mean something rude in other countries. There are many examples of this and it leaves your business with four very difficult options: don't trade in that country, create a separate brand just for that country, change your brand name entirely, or carry on and work to minimize the damage and criticism. The prouder leaders often go for the last option, whereas option two is perhaps the most sensible. Some interesting examples of this are that Galaxy chocolate in the UK is known as Dove in many other countries; Burger King in Australia is Hungry Jack's; and T. K.

Maxx is the international name for the company that is known as T. J. Maxx in the United States.

For digital marketing, language is clearly important when considering digital presence. This is not only in ensuring that our call to actions are correct and powerful but also in dealing with languages with different characters to our own. For example, English, Russian, Mandarin and Arabic are all widely spoken languages but all use different characters that need to be accounted for. This can create tricky design challenges when building your platforms and communications.

Payments

This is a very specific category but one that is worth highlighting as it can dramatically affect the result of your digital strategy. Payment methods are often overlooked when constructing a global strategy but it is very dangerous to assume that the world uses the same methods. Even countries that you would assume are very similar to your own may in fact be very different. For example, people in Eastern Europe are far more likely to use a debit card or cash on delivery and far less likely to use a credit card than any other region of the world, whereas gift cards are three times more popular in North America than other regions (Statista, 2016). This behaviour is of course vitally important to appreciate when developing an e-commerce strategy.

Brand

Your brand is, of course, one of the key parts of your business and one that every element of your strategy must align. This is understood by most people and so I am sure there is no need to spend too much time convincing you that this is the case. There are, however, some vital reasons for this that are worth examining. I often talk about how imagining your company's brand as a person can be a powerful framework. The values of your company are like the values that you hold yourself. You may try to be polite to everyone you meet, you may be someone who wants to achieve a lot in life and you may be always looking to learn more and grow your knowledge. These values in a business could be translated as service, sales and innovation and they create the personality of your business.

Further, your brand has the fact that non-marketers often consider a brand to be – a visual identity. What is your logo and how does it look in different scenarios? What is your colour palette? How do you design your materials? Again, this could translate into what do you look like, do you keep fit, how do you dress and what are your favourite colours? By combining your values and visual identity you create your personality and look, and therefore your brand. By using this method it becomes easy to assess whether something strays from your brand values, visuals or any other element.

Values

As we have just discussed, the brand values of your organization are its personality, and having a consistent personality is important to enable consumers to understand you and therefore believe in you. Your digital strategy must therefore stay true to these values and to how they are expressed elsewhere.

You cannot and must not express any values differently through digital channels than you would offline. Some brands do try to be more edgy or innovative online than they might offline. This must be resisted or your brand can look like it is trying too hard to be digital and may well be considered inauthentic.

Visual identity

Your visual identity can be difficult to control and easy to compromise online and so discipline is important. There are many opportunities to stretch your logo or tweak your colour palette to fit in with another website, app store or digital opportunity, and staying true to your guidelines is vital here wherever possible. Compromising your visual identity can create a lack of trust as you can appear less like an organization that is in control. To that point it is key to remember that your guidelines must work for digital. It is certainly less true now than it was 10 years ago, but some guidelines are still not built with digital in mind. An understanding of accessibility rules for colours, challenges around using your logo on other sites such as affiliates, and creation of logos or icons that work in limited spaces, must be built into your guidelines. Your identity may already be in use in newspapers, on television, in direct mail and on stationery. Your consumers will be seeing these in their day-to-day lives and so ensuring consistency with these is vital. In Chapter 9 we look at how consistent messaging at every step on your digital channels, such as paid search, creates a far more powerful result – and the same is true of your brand.

Innovation and pushing the boundaries is important, especially in digital, but not at the expense of a consistent face of your business as this will be detrimental to your organization as a whole.

Vision

In Chapter 7 we look at your mission and how you build your goals and objectives from this to effectively plan the delivery of your strategy. Sitting above all of this, however, is your vision. This is the statement that must embody everything your business is striving to achieve and everything it represents. Your company is likely to have a vision in place and if not you should consider whether it is appropriate for you to review this with your leadership team. This summary of what you stand for can be powerful when talking to investors, shareholders and customers alike. Whatever your company vision, it is important that every strategy within your organization fits within this vision, otherwise you run the risk of delivering something that does not align with the direction of your business.

A vision would read something like this:

'To be Earth's most customer-centric company; to build a place where people can come to find and discover anything they might want to buy online.' (Amazon)

'We work hard every day to make American Express the world's most respected service brand.' (American Express)

You can ensure that your strategy aligns with your vision by adjusting some of your goals, channels and messaging. Using the above examples your strategy could be adjusted as follows. If you were building a digital strategy for Amazon you should consider everything we discussed above on customer centricity. You should also be focused on creating a deep level of personalization to be able to deliver the latter part of the vision.

For American Express on the other hand, you would want to ensure you have a robust and integrated service response process in place across all channels including social media. You should invest in a leading CRM system and ensure your service offering is reliable and your digital channels minimize downtime and errors.

So we can see from this that the focus for Amazon would be on personalization and service whilst for American Express it would be on service. This is of course oversimplifying the facts, but it is clear that aligning to these visions will have an impact on your strategy.

Culture

The culture of your business will likely be unique. Every business builds its own culture from the day it launches. This culture stems primarily from the decisions and behaviours of the leadership team. It also, in turn, stems from HR policy, office layout, growth plans, recruitment, location and many more factors. This culture has an effect on everything you do as an organization. Your culture may encourage your staff to be hungry for career success and willing to take risks to show they have what it takes to be the next leaders of the business. It may on the other hand simply encourage staff to be careful and try not to cause any issues and risk being fired. You may have a culture that drives towards growth and therefore a high percentage of sales-focused employees, or you may be comfortable with your market position and therefore have staff who are excellent at service and the softer skills of customer relations.

The culture of your organization will have a direct effect on your digital strategy for many reasons but some specific ones should be considered. If your business is a results-focused business then this suits channels such as paid search very well, as it is performance focused and relies on data to accurately track performance. If your culture is not performance focused then you may find that this allows more flexibility for your content strategy but this may frustrate your paid search team. If your business is highly focused on service then ensuring that social media is fully set up for customer service, has robust procedures in place, is aligned with your business processes and is fully resourced are all vital considerations. We will look at this in more detail in Chapter 18.

Whichever culture your business has it should be positive and energizing. If it is not then you should at least be trying to create that within your area. There are many books on building an effective company culture and there is a wide range of models to review. I am a big proponent of the importance of building a positive culture and I would recommend: *The Power of Company Culture: How any business can build a culture that improves productivity, performance and profits* by Chris Dyer; *The Character of a Corporation: How your company's culture can make or break your business* by Gareth Jones and Rob Goffee; and *FUSION: How integrating brand and culture powers the world's greatest companies* by Denise Lee Yohn.

Innovation

In any leading business there must be at least one eye on innovation. The world is a fast-paced and ever-changing place now and no longer can any company simply rely on the successes of the last 10 or even 100 years to guarantee future success. Defining innovation is important and so we will look at this now and how you can effectively embed it into your business both quickly and meaningfully.

Before we discuss what innovation is, let's be clear on what it is not. When we think about innovation now we often lean towards technology but innovation is not about technology. Tech can play a big part in innovation, of course, and there are many examples of fantastic achievements through technological innovation but innovation is, in its truest sense, the development of new ideas and the application of those ideas to the progress of your company. That may be improvements in process, structure, pricing, product or any other area.

To embed this change in the business there are some key areas to focus on. Consider the following checklist to get the sparks of innovation to take hold within your organization.

Define innovation within your business

It is vital for your business to understand what innovation means. As we have discussed above it is the generation of new ideas to drive change within the organization. This can happen in any role, department or function.

Empower champions

By assigning individuals within your organization who already show themselves to have the passion and creativity to Innovation Champion roles you can spread the message continuously throughout every area. Consider how you reach the depths of every team and use personalities that are likely to be effective at spreading the message to a broad range of colleagues.

Build flexible processes to enable innovation and implementation

You must ensure that any processes you create from this point forwards are flexible. If things need to change in the future are you able to change people, tools, filing, timings etc? You should also revisit existing processes to achieve the same goal. Through this you will find your journey much easier in the future.

Innovation cannot come from one person or even from one small group

You cannot simply set up an innovation team and think of that as your innovation requirement being complete. You must embed throughout the organization. Oversight from a board or forum is helpful but they should review, steer and provide energy – perhaps even budget – but not be the sole driving force.

Create innovation spaces

Innovation spaces are a great way to encourage fresh thinking. Spaces that don't look or feel like your standard office. Spaces that perhaps have pleasant views or a relaxing feel. The spaces should enable free thinking and no one should be able to interrupt you here. It is a haven where the mind can run free. If you are not disciplined about this and compromise it in any way then it will fail and ultimately be pointless.

You must innovate with direction

If I were to ask you to innovate right now you would probably struggle. Innovation is not something you just do randomly. It involves free thinking, but it also requires direction. You must be innovating to solve a problem or create an opportunity. What is it that you are trying to achieve? This is where aligning with your business strategy is so important. Always ensure there is an end goal.

Innovation must deliver results

Innovation also has the danger of being a buzzword. For the more cynical employees you will struggle to gain buy-in unless you achieve results. Aim to deliver on your ideas. Having a really funky innovation space and a list of great ideas with nothing being delivered will quickly kill your innovation culture.

Innovation is a tap that is always on

Finally, don't forget that innovation doesn't stop. You cannot innovate for this year and then stop next year. This is a long-term commitment to embed innovative thinking in everything and everyone. Your leadership team must support this and thankfully there are few who would not, after so much evidence for the benefit it can bring.

Research and insight

Research is a driving force behind any strategy and so understanding what your data is telling you is vital to the success of your strategy. You may have a specific research function and separate insight team, both together or neither. Whatever the capabilities within your organization it is important to bring broader research into your digital strategy. Figure 3.1 is an interesting piece of digital research that clearly demonstrates that the percentage of consumers buying online is, in most countries, far beyond the percentage of businesses selling online. Understanding this data for your specific market will allow you to understand where the gaps are for your business to exploit.

The data you gain from your activity will inform future plans and tactics and even the shape of your strategy. This data, however, has one main restriction that takes two forms. This restriction is simply that it can never tell you what it doesn't know. That may sound obvious but when we look at the two forms we can begin to understand why the broader picture is vital.

First, your data cannot tell you what has not happened yet. But how can you build a strategy without understanding what is going to happen? By gaining insights into your customers' and consumers' behaviours, understanding what motivates them and how they respond to other materials, you will be able to gain an advantage that will set your strategy on a positive path from day one. Second, your data is digital and so is not tracking anything outside of your digital marketing. You may be able to use search volumes to give an indication of the success of a television advert but you cannot see directly what people thought about your creative. You may be able to see a peak in response rates when you send an e-mail about a specific product but you cannot see whether people think your competitors' products are better. By using both qualitative and quantitative research from across the organization you can understand buying patterns, interests, competitive analysis, creative feedback, customer behaviours, primary areas of dissatisfaction and many other data sets that would otherwise be unavailable to you at the start of your strategy or even when it is very mature.

Quantitative research is usually used when trying to gather data to validate a hypothesis or support a business case. This is the type of research that some would consider more 'real' in terms of there being a clear story backed up by undisputable facts. The limitation of quantitative research is that whilst it can give you a clear view of the 'what' it does not always tell you the 'why'. So if 100 people were to visit your website from a competitor and 300 from a news website then you will be able to make some decisions

Figure 3.1   European online shopping

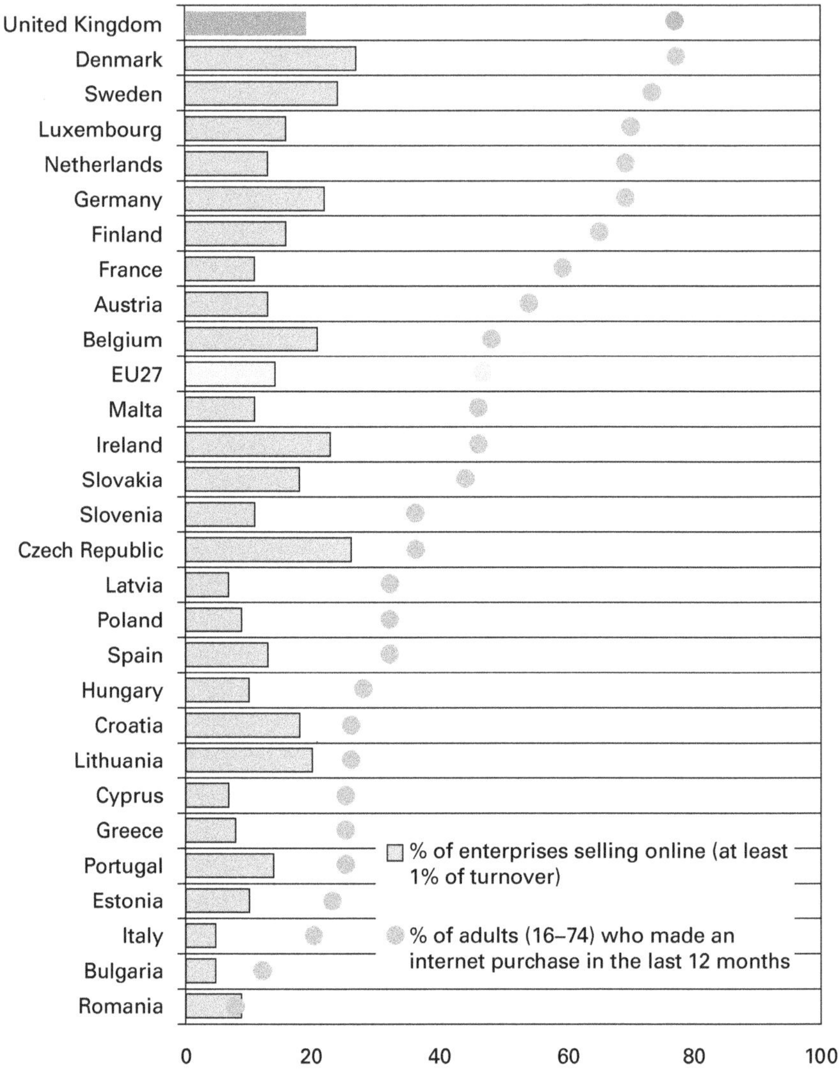

SOURCE UK Office for National Statistics

about media buying such as whether to continue your display advertising on the news website and expand to other news sites or whether to put more resource into competing with your competitors more effectively on the search channel. Without understanding why this happened, however, you cannot get to the bottom of the issue and therefore cannot understand if this will be an ongoing trend or a single peak.

Qualitative research has quite the opposite challenge. With this research method you can gain a deep understanding of the motivations and thoughts of customers and consumers. You can understand what they like and do not like about you or your marketing materials. You can understand what excites them and what really gets them down. You cannot, however, directly apply this to sales. If someone says they don't like your advertising then this does not necessarily mean that they will not buy your product.

The common approach is therefore to use both qualitative and quantitative together. An example of this is to circulate a data collection method such as an online questionnaire in order to gain quantitative data from which to construct a qualitative piece of research. That research would then be gathered from the same participants and the data could tell a more compelling story.

KPIs

Key performance indicators (KPIs) are an essential method of measuring the success of your campaign. We will look specifically at this in Chapter 19. The reason for taking a quick look at this now is to ensure that, when building your reporting and dashboards for your campaign, you align the measures of success with those of the business. We have discussed that there are different business models with different objectives, visions and cultures. These will ultimately dictate what the business KPIs are – and if you are going to ensure that your strategy is accepted by your decision makers and is perceived to be a success then you will need to be shown to be delivering what the company needs to deliver. As well as this consideration you will also need to be agile enough to align with any changes to the company's KPIs that you may not be expecting. It is entirely possible, and in fact quite common, for a business to change its primary goal, for example, from acquiring a large volume of customers to maximizing profit. This could be due to market conditions, shareholder demands or activity by the competition, amongst many other factors.

Business KPIs could come in hundreds of different forms such as customer numbers, customer satisfaction, profit, sales, retention and share price – the more top-level metrics that determine the success of a business in a given period.

Summary

In this chapter we have looked at your business and how your strategy must align with it. It is crucial to understand this in detail to ensure your strategy is working with, and not against, the existing business model and therefore to give it the best possible chance of success. Even with digital transformation, where the goal is to change the organization, you must still appreciate this detail and align with it. We will discuss digital transformation in Chapter 6.

Chapter checklist

- Business model   ☐
- Global strategy   ☐
- Brand   ☐
- Vision   ☐
- Culture   ☐
- Innovation   ☐
- Research and insight   ☐
- KPIs   ☐

Further reading

- *On customer centricity*:

  Richardson, N, James, J and Kelley, N (2015) *Customer-Centric Marketing: Supporting sustainability in the digital age*, Kogan Page, London. A very relevant and interesting book on the subject of customer centricity, which examines disciplines such as knowing your company research and why companies fail through the lens of sustainability.

- *On business models*:

  Osterwalder, A and Pigneur, Y (2010) *Business Model Generation: A handbook for visionaries, game changers, and challengers*, John Wiley & Son. This handbook is not only visually pleasing but contains helpful advice on how to take many business models and implement them within your organization.

- *On brand identity*:

  Lerman, S (2014) *Building Better Brands: A comprehensive guide to brand strategy and identity development*, How Design Books. This is a great book for further reading on how to create and evolve brands. It includes positioning, as we discussed in the last chapter, experience and identity, as well as some helpful guides and powerful statements.

- *On business culture*:

  Cavanaugh, A (2015) *Contagious Culture: Show up, set the tone, and intentionally create an organization that thrives*, McGraw-Hill Professional. A great book to read for inspiration on how to do business culture. It includes step-by-step techniques on how to lead from the top to create a performance culture; something that is vital to deliver your strategy in the most effective way possible.

- *On research methods*:

  Walker, I (2010) *Research Methods and Statistics*, Macmillan Education. This covers research methods, testing hypotheses and normal distribution, amongst other more detailed research techniques, and is worth reading if you are seeking a deeper understanding in this field.

References

Google (2018) [accessed 19 November 2018] Consumer Barometer [Online] https://www.consumerbarometer.com/en/

Statista (2016) [accessed 20 November 2018] Most Popular Payment Methods of Online Shoppers Worldwide as of 2016, by Region [Online] https://www. statista.com/statistics/676385/preferred-payment-methods-of-online-shoppers-worldwide-by-region/

Understanding the evolving digital consumer 04

What we will cover in this chapter

This chapter examines the modern digital consumer. To understand how to market to people through digital channels we need to understand our audience. This includes how behaviours are changing technology and vice versa. To understand this we will look at:

- Who is the digital consumer?
- Digital consumer behaviour
- How technology affects the digital consumer

Chapter goals

By the end of this chapter you should understand the digital consumer in more detail. You should have an understanding of who they are and who they are not, how they behave and how you can build your strategy around those behaviours. Finally, you should appreciate how technology advances are changing the consumer and how to stay attuned to this as you build and deliver your strategy.

Let's acknowledge from the start that people are unique and, whilst segments can be valuable tools, personalization is really the key (we will talk about this point in more detail in Chapter 15). It is no longer acceptable, with the tools we have at our disposal, not to appreciate this principle, understand this information and deliver personalized experiences and highly targeted strategies. Let's take some time here to look at what we need to consider when thinking about digital consumers.

Who is the digital consumer?

No consumer is fully digital or vice versa

One important consideration when thinking of your consumers, and your employees for that matter, is to remove the idea of digital customers and non-digital customers. Everyone is somewhere on the digital scale.

I am an excellent example of this. Most people would consider me highly digital. I work in digital marketing, I write books and speak on the subject, my house is automated and I use smart phones, watches, tablets, TVs etc. I do not, however, read books on screen; I cannot stand that experience: I only read books in paper form. I don't read newspapers – I get my news digitally, but books are always a physical thing for me. It is an experience that currently cannot be replicated digitally. Call it a quirk, but the fact is that everyone has these unique qualities that stop them from fitting neatly into the boxes, no matter how much human nature wants us to cleanly categorize them.

It is vitally important to appreciate the unique nature of every individual and not to assume the over-simplified view of 'digital or not'. This is where accurate and complete data sets become key to your strategy. Consider, when you collect data, not just demographics but also desires, interests and behaviours.

The digital consumer can be anywhere

It is vital to remember that the digital consumer can be anywhere and at any time. You must ensure this factors into all of your decision making. The obvious place is with your digital platforms – the website, apps etc, but you must think more broadly as well. Does your app need to be connected on start-up? If not then consider handling this a different way as you will stop those with no connectivity from accessing your platform. Do your videos require sound? If so how will users in busy places or private locations access your content? You must build this 'Anywhere Factor' into your strategy.

Also, looking at this both globally and regionally, the average consumer has changed. Asia Pacific, for example, accounted for 60 per cent of new users coming online between 2013 and 2018 and is now home to more than half the world's internet users (Evans, 2017). It is vital, therefore, to keep abreast of how these changing trends affect your behaviour. There is still a great deal more growth potential, especially in Asia Pacific, Latin America and Africa. Even when close to 100 per cent internet penetration is reached there will still be fast-changing trends in technology adoption and behaviours that should be reviewed at least annually to keep your strategy relevant.

They're not all young

Assuming digital consumers are young is a fundamental mistake. As we mention above, digital users can be anyone, and everyone is somewhere on the scale. Even the oldest consumers and biggest digital cynics have some interaction with digital tools through their bank, clock, television or via their grandchildren.

The internet has been around for a long time now and people who are 70 today were only in their forties when this channel started to open up, and people in their forties are more than capable of adopting new technology. Do not fall into the trap of assuming digital consumers are young:

> Recent internet use among women aged 75 and over trebles from 2011 to 2017.
>
> (Office for National Statistics, UK, 2017)

Digital native versus experience

Digital natives, those who have grown up with digital surrounding them (born after 1985) have a view different from the more experienced users, but again we must not fall into the trap of thinking digital natives have a more valid opinion. Often they will have their finger on the pulse of digital trends but they will also lack the insight that the older generations have where they have witnessed technology come and go, and understand more about how and why that has happened. Understanding this difference enables you to adapt your messaging and channel strategy appropriately.

Digital consumer behaviour

Digital consumer behaviour is constantly changing. This change is both push and pull in that the consumer is pulling the changes towards them by desiring faster, simpler, safer shopping across multiple channels and is being pushed by changes in technology such as voice-controlled home hubs and improved targeting techniques.

These consumers can shop at any time, on any device, in any location. They are more savvy than they have ever been and they expect control over their data. There are even regular conversations between consumers about whether they should be selling their data to companies and this is a trend we in digital marketing should watch carefully. The expectation is also for quick results and minimal effort. Here, we highlight how some of these changing behaviours are exhibiting themselves and what you need to do to consider them within your strategy.

In 2018, 51 per cent of Americans preferred to shop online, 80 per cent bought something online in the last month and 96 per cent had bought something online at some time in their life. This data (BigCommerce.com, 2018) reflects a significant growth in trust of online shopping. Statista (2018) tells us that global retail e-commerce sales will have doubled in just the four years to 2018. This is reassuring for our digital marketing strategies, of course, but we must also take into account that this growth may be more or less mature in our industry and territories, and adjust our strategy accordingly.

For millennials the 51 per cent figure from above becomes 67 per cent, and even for Baby Boomers this number is still at a strong 41 per cent. What else can we learn about these shoppers? This is where understanding your audience becomes essential. Through knowing your customer and consumer you can understand their specific needs and begin to predict their behaviours – a powerful tool when analysing performance data.

According to the same report by BigCommerce, parents spend more time online and more money online than non-parents: nearly half said they could not live without online shopping (an exaggeration, of course, but a powerful insight into their psychology). Men spend 28 per cent more time online and city dwellers, although living nearer to a wealth of physical stores, spend more money online than those in rural areas.

Nearly half of online purchasers use a mass online marketplace rather than a niche site. This is a key factor in considering your brand and distribution strategies. If your brand is strong and selling directly is more profitable then you may only see a small loss of volume, which is compensated by the increase in profit. If, however, your brand is weak or niche then using a mass marketplace may be the only route to achieve significant volume until you can grow your brand.

Going back to location briefly, we can be even more precise than region, country or city. The survey found that 43 per cent of online shoppers had made a purchase in their bed and 23 per cent at the office.

The key factors in the decision-making process were price, shipping cost, discounts/offers and speed. Ultimately, three of these are the same – price. The fourth is in line with the shift towards ease and speed that we mentioned above.

I have used this survey as it is representative of many similar research papers and surveys that we see today. These trends give us some insight into consumer behaviour but also make it clear that there are significant differences between consumer segments. It is vital not to bundle large groups of consumers together and make assumptions. We will look at personalization later in the book, and segmentation also has a useful role in tailoring messages, but these principles must be remembered and should feature in your strategy and your tactical delivery.

How technology affects the digital consumer

Above we mentioned that there is a push factor from technology that drives consumer behaviour. This is very true. Some things are beyond the reach or influence of the consumer and can only happen when the technology enables it. Technological advances such as the smartphone and tablet have significantly shifted consumer behaviour even though the consumer was not crying out for either of these devices; at least, not consciously.

Coverage is the first area to consider here. Internet access penetration is now at 54.4 per cent of the world's population (Internet World Stats, 2018) with the highest penetration in North America (95 per cent) and Europe (85.2 per cent). Networks with 4G mobile coverage are now available in three-quarters of the world with only a few countries in Africa and Asia either on 3G or GSM coverage (WorldTimeZone, 2018). The world is moving towards 5G, which will cause a significant change in consumer behaviour as, for example, movies become available to download on mobile devices in just a few seconds. This extensive coverage has led to enormous leaps in usage of the internet in recent years and will continue to impact shopping behaviours as we mentioned above.

This access also enables over 4 billion people to get access to the other new technology trends that are impacting our world right now. These include voice-led devices, augmented and virtual reality, fingerprint recognition, chatbots and automation. We will look at these throughout the book, especially with a view to how they can impact our content strategy (see Chapter 14).

What does this mean for digital marketing?

As a leader of a digital marketing strategy it is vital that you keep your finger on the pulse and use data appropriately to make well-judged decisions. I do not say right decisions, as there are no guarantees of how your plans will roll out, but the best chances of success lie in understanding your audience and delivering experiences, journeys and propositions to them that meet their needs. This is not possible, especially in such a fast-changing environment, without regular reviews of consumer behaviours.

Summary

The world is changing. You must change with it because your consumers will. In the next chapter we will look at some of the barriers that you might experience in building your strategy. Remember to keep these consumer behaviours in mind when assessing the potential barriers you face, as technology and consumer data are both key factors that you need to consider.

Chapter checklist

- Who is the digital consumer? ☐
- Digital consumer behaviour ☐
- How technology affects the digital consumer ☐

Further reading

- *On digital consumer psychology*:
  Nahai, N (2017) *Webs of Influence: The psychology of online persuasion*, 2nd edition, Pearson Business

References

BigCommerce.com (2018) [accessed 20 November 2018] 147 Online Shopping Statistics Behind Why These Ecommerce Trends Matter Most, *Ecommerce Trends in 2018* [Online] https://www.bigcommerce.com/blog/ecommerce-trends/#147-online-shopping-statistics-behind-why-these-ecommerce-trends-matter-most

Evans, M (2017) [accessed 20 November 2018] 5 Key Stats That Will Define the Digital Consumer in 2018, *Forbes* [Online] https://www.forbes.com/sites/michelleevans1/2017/12/18/5-key-stats-that-will-define-the-digital-consumer-in-2018/#7a7a9d7d32a4

Internet World Stats (2018) [accessed 20 November 2018] Internet Users in the World by Regions [Online] https://internetworldstats.com/stats.htm

Office for National Statistics (2017) [accessed 20 November 2018] Internet Users in the UK: 2017 [Online] https://www.ons.gov.uk/businessindustryandtrade/itandinternetindustry/bulletins/internetusers/2017

Statista (2018) [accessed 20 November 2018] Retail E-commerce Sales Worldwide from 2014 to 2021 (in billion U.S. dollars) [Online] https://www.statista.com/statistics/379046/worldwide-retail-e-commerce-sales/

WorldTimeZone (2018) [accessed 20 November 2018] 4G World Coverage [Online] https://www.worldtimezone.com/4g.htmli

Barriers, considerations and data protection in digital marketing strategy

05

What we will cover in this chapter

Now that we have a view of some useful business models, the context of our business and how the ecosystem and consumer behaviours are changing, we need to understand what challenges we may face and how to tackle them. The key areas covered in this chapter are:

- Technology
- Skills
- Budget and resources
- Business priorities
- Regulation

Chapter goals

By the end of this chapter you should have an understanding of some of the most common challenges you will face and how to overcome them in the development of your strategy.

Despite what we have already said about how long digital marketing has been amongst us, it is ever evolving and this creates challenges for businesses of all shapes and sizes. One of the issues is that consumers are adapting to the digital age very quickly, but most businesses simply cannot keep up. In this chapter we examine some of the difficulties in embedding your digital strategy and the approaches that can be taken to tackle them.

When you consider that in the late 20th century consumers generally bought their products either face to face or on the phone, it is clear to understand how the digital revolution has significantly affected several areas of an established business. For example:

- New technology such as social media, marketing automation platforms and smart devices has led to radical changes to established processes.
- Regulations around privacy such as GDPR in Europe and the right to be forgotten have resulted in changes to sales techniques, cookie policies, data storage, communications strategy and data collection.

Long-established business cultures have had to change or suffer the consequences, including those that have been successful despite poor service and those that have led with inauthentic messaging. As completely new opportunities arrive there is inevitably a skills gap as no one has yet developed a strong skill set in the new scenario. A good example of this is social media. As the channel has become increasingly important it has become apparent to many businesses that a specific skill set is needed. Rearranging budgets to take advantage of new opportunities often means that something else has to suffer. If, for example, your strategy looks to quickly take advantage of a new technology such as the launch of a new wearable, but this launch was unexpected and arrived in the middle of a budget year, then what do you cut to ensure that you maximize on the opportunity? Your business may have established priorities that are difficult to change in order to pursue unproven opportunities. For example, your company may see press advertising as a crucial channel due to a history of success in the channel many years ago. This channel may not be measured for success, but convincing the company to depart from a stalwart to delve into something that is not understood can be challenging. Ensuring you leave room in your budget for the unexpected is good practice but even more so in the digital world.

In the 21st century, consumers expect sites that are available on any device with cross-device functionality and personalized experiences and they expect to be able to directly contact businesses and get a response within minutes. As I write this, many businesses are still only some of the way to achieving this, and with Google now prioritizing the indexing of mobile sites over desktop this is critical to get right. Many of the challenges that you will face will effectively be risks to the delivery of your strategy and so an understanding of risk is useful.

Technology

Digital marketing is of course very closely linked to technology, although it is not quite as heavily reliant on it as some may have you believe. It is often common that people outside of digital perceive it to be hand in hand with technology and, whilst that is true to an extent, it is not true that your business needs to make significant technology advances in order to take advantage of the opportunity. For example, paid search, SEO and display advertising require almost no technology internally to launch. E-mail marketing and social media require some technology but this can be bought rather than built. In order to effectively manage offline marketing channels you would also want to use technology and so the digital world from a practitioner's perspective is not always as reliant as some may think. We discuss technology, innovation, specific tools and the future throughout the book but here we look at technology from a broader perspective and view it as a challenge rather than an opportunity – in order to understand the barriers it can present.

Whenever new technology arrives it brings with it excitement and nervousness. According to the Technology Adoption Lifecycle model, by Everett Rogers, innovators will quickly take up new technology, whereas laggards will be slow (Figure 5.1). This model can also be applied to businesses with the added complexity that intention and ability to adopt do not necessarily go as hand in hand as they do for consumers. As with most models it is understanding how to interpret the model in its finer detail that really makes the difference. Here we understand that innovators take up new technology early but we need to understand that few individuals are always innovators and few always laggards. Someone may be an innovator when it comes to mobile phones but an early majority for smart TVs. You must avoid the simple interpretation of assuming if someone is an innovator then he or she is always at the front of the curve. It is useful to appreciate this level of complexity in all models. Individuals are truly that – individual – and you putting them into simple segments never quite tells the whole story. This is why personalization is so important and we will look at that later in the book.

Technology developments are inevitable and have been since animals started to use tools. Never more so than in this technology age where disruption is seen by many as a positive word. Technology has always been a part of the human progress story but sometimes the mind moves faster than the hand,

Figure 5.1   Technology adoption curve

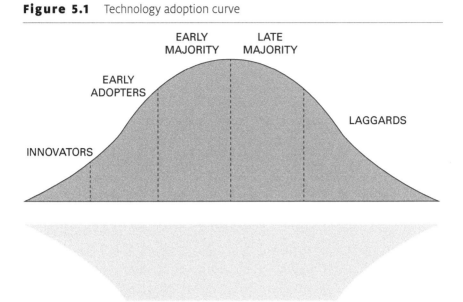

so inevitably we cannot always deliver the inventions and innovations that are dreamt up. One of the many concerns that stops businesses from adopting new technology is a lack of historic performance. History is strewn with failed technology and it is not always the innovators who win. There are many cases of the early adopters or even the early majority winning the battle. Apple's entry into the mobile phone market is an excellent example of a business that was not first, learnt from those that were and was able to make significant gains due to this. Closer to digital marketing we have seen many examples of businesses that have leapt into new channels and had to make the mistakes for others to learn. Social media is a fantastic example of this.

British Gas

In the UK, British Gas opted to run a live Q&A on Twitter with the hashtag #AskBG. However, they did this on the same day that they increased their prices. This led to British Gas being bombarded with insults and aggression from unhappy customers. This is one of many similar examples and one that businesses the world over have learnt from.

One of the main challenges within technology adoption is gaining support for the adoption. This can be a challenge as it is rare that senior leaders in a business are hungry to take significant risks, for obvious reasons although this is gradually becoming less rare as leaders see the advantage their competitors are achieving. Specifically for technology, one of the main routes forward is proof of concept. Reviewing competitor adoption or creating a business case is often not enough. Testing and trialling new technology in controlled, minimal risk conditions allows for a gradual implementation and roll-out programme and this could be by feature, customer segment, country or another factor that is strategically sensible for your business. Of course every roll-out programme needs a roll-back plan to cover the eventuality that things may go wrong. This may not be possible for all technology but is a valuable method where possible. A roll-back plan is a process of ensuring that, should something unforeseen happen upon launch, you can quickly reset the programme back to the previous state. We have seen this in software for many years via the use of a backup and restore process. A roll-back plan is similar to this but a little broader. It is not purely technology based. You need to consider what to do not only if your technology fails but also if the market changes or there are many unfavourable reviews. This plan should be a part of the ongoing programme management agenda.

Many of the reasons that businesses do not adopt new technology are skills, budget and resources or business priorities related. We look at each of these below.

Skills

When new technology arrives and new consumer behaviours take hold there is inevitably a lack of experience around them. There is no data to enable planning and forecasting, no one who has an understanding of the limitations or potential of the opportunity and no case studies of best practice.

If you were launching your company's first paid-search activity you might find an experienced agency or internal candidate who could bring in excess of 10 years' experience. Someone who understands what ads work, what keyword targeting techniques to use, how to optimize and rotate the adverts, how to use location and time of day to best effect, how to use analytics tied to the ad management platform, what tagging needs to be in place to enable remarketing opportunities and so on. Were you to bring in someone who has never worked on paid search they may understand the concept of bidding on keywords in an auction style and writing ads that get a strong click-through rate but almost everything else would have to be learnt on the job or through training, which would slow your progress and give you a considerable competitive disadvantage. Advances in digital marketing also create this situation. The only difference is that you do not initially have a competitive disadvantage as everyone is in the same boat. However, the slower you are to react, the more this disadvantage becomes very real.

There are ultimately two methods for tackling skills gaps within organizations: 1) upskill the people you have – training; 2) bring in people who have the skills – recruitment.

Training

This would always be the preferred route for most companies where a team already exists. Making staff redundant and bringing in new employees is an unpleasant and costly exercise for everyone involved. Training often comes with its own costs both in terms of paying the training supplier and lost productivity, but the value that can be gained from a full day of training can often easily justify itself versus spending a considerable time learning through trial and error. The latter approach is not only time-consuming but is also fraught with risk to your brand and commercial goals.

There are now many courses specifically for digital marketing at universities and through organizations such as the Chartered Institute of Marketing, but also from organizations such as Google. These differ in their balance of theory and practice but whatever the goal there are many options available. As well as the official training route there are low-cost opportunities for training. For example, you may well be working with one or more agencies who have expertise in the area in which you have a skills gap. You may not be working with that agency on that specific service but more often than not your partners will be willing to help you. Leaning on established relationships can therefore achieve the same as an official course – at little or no cost.

The other key consideration for training is whether you have the skills in-house already but located somewhere else within the company. Many large organizations are guilty of assuming that people within their roles are specialists at those roles and have no experience anywhere else. Because someone is running press advertising or PR does not mean they have not run SEO in the past. It is worth doing an exercise to understand whether there are people in your organization who may have good knowledge to share.

Recruitment

Recruitment can be a slow and expensive process dependent on a number of factors but it certainly has one guarantee – and that is that you will bring a new individual with new experience and new points of view into your business. If you get your recruitment process right then, in the vast majority of situations, this will be a very positive thing. Where new technology has arrived it is often worth seeking someone who has worked in a similar field, as there will be no existing experts. For example, as the web becomes more and more of a community we find that digital marketing techniques are increasingly moving towards a content focus. We do not try to build links – we create great content that people want to link to. We do not try to buy followers on social – we create compelling content that people find of value and want to engage with. There is therefore an increasing need for people with strong editorial skills such as those from a PR background with a digital passion. If you therefore need to build out your SEO and social channels perhaps someone from a PR or journalism background could be more appropriate than a technical expert or digital guru.

Budget and resources

Most organizations face a restricted budget in one area or another, so you are probably familiar with this barrier already. There are regularly challenges around investing in new technology or running multiple, expensive IT projects. There are also often challenges around demonstrating the value of marketing against the bottom line. In digital marketing this can be achieved a little easier than with offline channels or pure brand activity but it is still rarely a simple exercise. It is also very common for businesses to have headcount restrictions in place or departmental salary budgets. These are often tightly controlled, especially during difficult economic conditions or when trying to invest elsewhere. It can be very difficult to grow your digital footprint without being able either to bring in the people you need or to lean on a large number of people across your organization.

The final resource we usually find ourselves short on (and this is certainly not restricted to digital marketing) is time. Integrating technology or new methods of working can be time-consuming to say the least, not least due to having to ensure that it fits with your business goals and processes. The 21st century's biggest challenge is finding time. The meteoric success of Amazon, Google, smart phones and the internet itself are largely down to the need to do more in less time – and the workplace is certainly no different.

Budget and resource constraints can often be the most frustrating of all barriers as they often seem so difficult to solve unless you have the context. There is one key to success here, one simple method to achieving your goals within these constraints – and that is to create a path to success. This combines prioritization and project management to build a process to get from A to B within the budget and resource challenges you have. To do this you can use project management techniques such as PRINCE2, Agile, Critical Path and Lean as well as the most relevant to a resource-constrained environment – Critical Chain Project Management. We will talk more about these techniques when we look at pulling our strategy together in Chapter 20. In the meantime let's have a quick look at the standard planning document developed by Henry Gantt around 100 years ago.

In simple terms, a Gantt chart shows the distinct elements of a project, their individual timelines and how they fit together to reach the project goal. There are many packages that can be used to manage your Gantt chart easily such as Microsoft Project (MSP) Hansoft or Celoxis.

The Gantt chart in Figure 5.2 shows a sample project, Project Morris, being run by Lulu Kennedy. This project has just three tasks and each has tasks underneath it that ensure the above level can be completed. Each task can then have a clear start and end date so that it can be tracked. You can also add dependencies to the chart to show where one task cannot be completed until another has been completed first. It is also quite common now to include a RAG (red, amber, green) status to give an immediate indication of the status of the task. In Figure 5.2 we can see that today is 12 January and everything is on track. The dashed line indicates where we are on the chart.

Gantt charts are of course not exclusively for projects and are useful tools when pulling together any timeline-based piece of work such as marketing campaigns, or even your overarching marketing strategy. For example, you may be launching a paid search campaign and so the tasks could be as follows:

- Task 1 – create a landing page, including sub-level tasks such as create imagery, write copy, gain sign off.

- Task 2 – ads, including writing the ads, gaining approval, uploading to the campaign.

Figure 5.2   A Gantt chart

| PROJECT MORRIS | | | | | | | Today's Date | | 12/01/2019 | | | | | |

Project Manager	Lulu Kennedy
Project Start Date	02/01/2019
Project End Date	17/02/2019

ID	Tasks	Owner	Start	End	Duration	% Complete	02/01/2019	09/01/2019	16/01/2019	23/01/2019	30/01/2019	06/02/2019	13/02/2019	20/02/2019	27/02/2019
1	Task 1	Nick	2/1/19	13/1/19	14	90%									
1.1	Sub-level 1		2/1/19	6/1/19	7	100%									
1.2	Sub-level 1		9/1/19	13/1/19	7	80%									
2	Task 2	James	16/1/19	10/2/19	28	0%									
2.1	Sub-level 1		16/1/19	27/1/19	14	0%									
2.1.1	Sub-level 2		16/1/19	20/1/19	7	0%									
2.1.2	Sub-level 2		23/1/19	27/1/19	7	0%									
2.2	Sub-level 1		30/1/19	10/2/19	14	0%									
3	Task 3	Ali	6/2/19	17/2/19	10	0%									
3.1	Sub-level 1		6/2/19	17/2/19	10	0%									

- Task 3 – measuring success, including ensuring that tags are in place, reviewing relevant internal reporting.
- ... and so on.

Business priorities

One issue that often rears its head is the need for immediate returns and a focus on the short term. You can spend months constructing an intricate strategy with solid long-term goals, quick wins and key milestones. You can achieve full buy-in to this strategy from the business and begin to put it into action. But then...

- a new competitor enters the market;
- unexpected regulation is put in place;
- the economy takes a downward turn;
- a new CEO with very different ideas is appointed.

Or a thousand other things can happen. Each of these can remove funding for a key strategic pillar, stop you from recruiting the team you need to deliver your strategy or remove the support for your strategy altogether. There are, however, a few things you can do to mitigate the impact, albeit you can never fully remove this risk.

It is vital that your strategy is delivered in a structured way with clear, demonstrable progress milestones. If something is delivering results and showing a very visible positive impact on your business then the chance of it being stopped or impacted by change reduces significantly. As with many other areas of business this can be as much about the presentation as the content, so ensure that you are able to tell the story.

Storytelling

Today's world is run by storytellers. Perhaps this has always been the case. Storytelling is an important skill to master. It is not about manipulation and certainly not about lying. You must be able to create an emotionally and rationally strong case for your proposal or review of your results. You must understand your audience and paint a picture that they will buy into. This skill is one of the softer skills I would strongly recommend everyone to develop.

It is also vital to understand fully where your business is headed and any potential challenges along that road. We have already discussed aligning with your broader business strategy (Chapter 3), and understanding it fully gives you the opportunity to have a back-up plan ready at every potential hitch. For example, if your business goal is to grow customer numbers and the business is failing to achieve its targets then how would you stop money being diverted from your web development project into direct sales and acquisition activity? How can you demonstrate that your web development project will deliver increased sales immediately? Being able to show any impact your milestones have had to date is key to success in this argument. And if your goal is gaining market share, but a big-spending competitor is making you suffer, then are you able to demonstrate the improved digital branding that your strategy is delivering and how your site is now more visible on organic search and therefore gaining digital share of voice?

There are other techniques worth using to ensure you fit with the broader business priorities, such as having a continuous improvement programme in place, including test and learn plans. You may also be able to receive anecdotal feedback from visitors and customers through research to support your strategy. No strategy will ever be 100 per cent correct first time and so evolving your strategy is vital. It is impossible to evolve it in a structured manner without a plan – and so this should be part of your story.

Highlighting changing consumer behaviours

If we stop the long-term activity we may make some savings for a few months but then we will be even further behind our competition. It may also be impossible to catch up as consumers have already decided to shop where they can receive the digital experience they are looking for. Reducing digital activity or marketing in general is a dangerous path. You could trial reducing activity in specific areas if necessary and display the impact of this on the business in order to tell your story.

Quick wins

As mentioned above, these appeal much more to those interested in the short term or those you just need to convince quickly. If the business buys into your long-term strategy then that is great, but it is the short-term wins that will excite many of your decision makers and mitigate risks from priority changes. You should ensure that a key part of your strategy, and one that is highlighted when proposing your strategy, is quick wins. What are the immediate gains we will make from this?

Regulation

There are many regulatory bodies in the world of marketing, from the FCC in the United States to the ASA in the UK and also many that are specific to industries, such as the APRA in Australia and CFDA in China. We cannot review each of these now and nor is it relevant to, but there are some issues of regulation that are worthwhile interrogating. Regulation is a complex area and one that has received a great deal of attention in the 21st century.

Data protection – examples of getting it wrong

- In the United Kingdom, a county council faxed details of a child sex-abuse case to a member of the public and as a result was fined £100,000 for breaching the Data Protection Act.

- In the same year a business was fined £60,000 for losing a laptop filled with personal details and unencrypted.

- In the United States Google was fined $22.5 million by the Federal Trade Commission for monitoring internet users who had selected 'do not track' from their Safari settings.

- In Australia a telecoms company was fined $10,200 and warned over privacy breaches after exposing the data of over 15,000 customers online.

Privacy and data protection

Two of the most important regulations to look at, and seemingly the most popular to discuss, are privacy and data protection. They are two sides of the same coin, so let us look at them together.

Regulations differ from country to country and sometimes from state to state. Understanding these for your global strategy is important, but more important is understanding good principles of data usage, consumer protection and security. If you build your strategy to fit consumer behaviour and demand, whilst ensuring they are safe to trade with you, then you are most likely to be aligned with any of the laws and regulations that exist around the world.

In 2018, GDPR came into effect in Europe. This regulation ensures that users have more control of their data, which is done through ensuring explicit opt-in to any form of personal data collection. This affects the way marketing permissions are collected and held and also affects cookie policies across your platforms.

If you are not already familiar with this regulation then you should make this a priority as it is a key focus for many regulators and customers alike and can result in significant fines and brand damage.

An increasingly common use of data is for location purposes. There are regulations here around anonymity that are vital to understand. There are many apps now that collect location data and need to do so to function. These include apps for local weather, finding lost phones, satnav and other services, and it is not appropriate – and therefore in many cases legal – to collect data unless it is essential to provide a service. As well as being relevant and 'anonymized' you must also have permission to do this. We are all familiar with accepting these conditions when using a mobile app and I expect you will agree that you would not want it any other way. GDPR plays a part here again as your location is considered personal information and so should not be collected without explicit consent.

It is worth saying at this point that whilst GDPR is Europe-focused it is likely that other regions will follow suit and so it is perhaps worth considering taking your approach global as it makes for simpler integration, management and is customer focused.

Cloud storage is another area of concern as personal data is kept outside of the physical control of the individual. By this I mean that, whilst the individual does have a great deal of control over what is shared to the cloud, that data is not held on their device but in another location. This involves the transmission of that data and the storage in a location or locations that are unknown to the user. This therefore has a number of associated risks such as damage as the data is in multiple locations, or theft as multiple individuals are involved in the handling of the data. There is also the risk that the supplier may go out of business and then your data has a risk of not being returned or of being disposed of via an insecure method. This is important to consider when using any cloud-based services such as marketing automation or e-mail software, as well as in the broader context around your customer data.

Social media is also a concern for privacy and there have been many controversies around the policies of various social media sites as they have been trying to establish best practice in this new channel. A great deal of information can be captured as users share deep levels of information about their lives on social networks. This includes not only their interests and friends but also their locations and media such as photos and videos. Some of these items, when shared on a network, will give the rights to that network to use them, yet not every user will be aware of this. You will be able to view this information through your social insights and use it to develop highly targeted campaigns. To maintain trust it is important to ensure that your campaigns do not overtly demonstrate that you have collected more data than necessary.

There is also the right to be forgotten, which has been a significant talking point in recent years and a concept that has been agreed by the EU and other parts of the world since 2006. The cases have become more common as people have begun to share more information online, and especially as some employers have begun to research potential employees online. Many of us share things on social media that we would not want a potential employer to find, and we may also have had life events that in our past have been reported online but which no longer represent who we are. One of the challenges here is that the controlling of information in this manner may restrict freedom of speech and may start to affect the neutrality of search results.

E-mail regulation

E-mail is probably the most established digital channel and there is even discussion that it has had its day, although I do not believe this to be the case and think it is likely to be used when relevant rather than as a catch-all digital communications channel. As it is a mature channel, the regulation is fairly well established. Having permissions from your recipients is vital and most companies have databases with clear marketing permission flags. Collection of this permission is also fairly standardized with the opt-in and opt-out routes. How these can be implemented differs regionally and, again, I would recommend you understand the implications fully if e-mail (or data collection as a whole) is a part of your strategy. Including unsubscribe options, implementing preference centres and automating your content strategy are all routes to ensure that your recipients receive and continue to receive what is truly relevant to them. There is no benefit in sending e-mails to consumers who are not interested, simply because you can. GDPR as discussed above focuses on explicit opt-in and, as well as ensuring data regulations are met, this gives you the highest data quality and therefore best chance of a successful communications strategy.

Viral marketing and regulation

Finally a quick look at viral marketing. This is the ultimate goal of many social campaigns and has been a buzzword in digital marketing for many years now. It is a bit of a dark art, although there are of course themes that we can extract from successful viral campaigns. The key point to remember here is that regulation, or at least guidance, exists in many regions that dictates that companies should ensure any encouragement of promotion is clearly positioned as such when asking individuals to pass on messages. This is to stop companies from using their customers to get around marketing regulations by asking them to pass on your messages for you without the necessary regulatory wording. It is important therefore that anyone passing on a message should be asked to ensure that the person they are passing it on to would be interested in the message. This in turn ensures that they are not just spamming their friends in exchange for some benefit from the company.

That is all for now on the topic of regulation, but it is a deep and complex area – of which it is worth having a good understanding, so I encourage you to speak to your company's legal and compliance departments and read up about this yourself.

Successful viral marketing campaigns

The Ice Bucket Challenge (2014)

This concept swept across the world with a huge number of people taking part, or at least refusing and therefore donating, including many A-list celebrities and even the president of the United States. It raised US$98.2 million in a single month for Amyotrophic Lateral Sclerosis Association, also known as motor neurone disease and Lou Gehrig's disease, compared with $2.7 million in the same period of the previous year (Townsend, 2014). This was clearly a phenomenon, but why was it such a success?

#nomakeupselfie (2014)

This phenomenon happened as women posted photos of their faces without make-up on social media sites in order to encourage donations to female-focused charities and to charities such as Cancer Research UK. This raised £8 million for the organization in just six days, even though the charity itself had not started the campaign. A fantastically successful campaign, but why?

Both of these campaigns are interesting as neither was actively designed by the respective organizations. They happened as the concepts caught on and evolved quickly on social media. As celebrities got involved and people challenged their friends, the fun nature of the ice bucket challenge and the challenge to the norm that the #nomakeupselfie represented took hold. The speed and depth of the success made it newsworthy, which then meant it reached people who were not active social media users but wanted to get involved.

So why did these work?

Ultimately the common themes here are charity, selflessness, simplicity, vanity, uniqueness and the use of social media. These in themselves are not a formula for success with viral marketing, but let's look at each one:

- *Charity*
  Charity is something that many people like to be involved in but it can be difficult to know which charity to give to and to actually go about starting the process. Simply being asked is not enough. You need a reason to get involved. The story of the charity itself is not enough. The story, combined with an easy route to take action, is the real goal. This is why other campaigns such as Live Aid and Red Nose Day have been successful for so many years.

- *Selflessness*
  In today's society we all do a lot to look after ourselves. There is a good feeling that comes with helping others and most of us would freely admit that we do not do as much as we could. The opportunity to do something for others is often well received.

- *Simplicity*
  If it is difficult to understand or to take action on then it will fail no matter how strong the idea. If the message is easy to understand, the action is simple to undertake, the donations easy to make and the sharing simple to do then you have a potential viral campaign.

- *Vanity*
  This may seem odd, especially as the no make-up selfie seems to be about the exact opposite, but actually both of the above have an essence of vanity about them. Showing others how generous you are and wanting to push your activity in front of other people could be seen as a form of vanity.

- *Uniqueness*
  This is important. If your campaign is too similar to another it may gain some momentum but ultimately will never become a global phenomenon. A good example of this is the 'Rice Bucket Challenge', which quickly followed the ice bucket challenge. The concept was to donate a bucket of rice to someone in need. It didn't make any serious progress.

- *Social media*
  All of the above are of course significantly escalated by social media. The channel makes it incredibly easy to understand, watch, share and click straight through to a destination to donate online. Without social media it is likely that the above campaigns would have failed, even with a great deal more investment.

CASE STUDY   Airbnb

Background

Airbnb is a highly successful business that continues to see rapid growth and is operating in over 190 countries. Its model of allowing people to rent out their property and therefore earn an income when they are not there seems like a no-brainer to many and is an excellent example of the opportunities presented to us by using the internet as a community. According to Craig Smith of DMR, as of March 2018 Airbnb had 150 million users, half a million stays per night and was operating in 65,000 cities, which is phenomenal growth in just 10 years (Smith, 2018).

Strategy

When you stop to think about the complexities of this global model, the barriers that the team at Airbnb have overcome are clear to see and they deserve a great deal of credit for it. One of these is the huge variations in laws and regulations around uses of property. Some locations do not allow people to have paying guests without licences or similar arrangements, which can result in fines or other consequences. It would not be possible to cater for all of these different scenarios, but not mentioning these issues at all could be damaging to their customers and could also create negative PR, damaging the brand significantly. Airbnb have therefore decided to include some wording within their Terms and Conditions to cover this information, thus tackling the issue globally and simply without causing any alarm.

Results

This low-key approach keeps their model working and ensures that consumers understand the regulatory concerns.

Key lessons

- When producing your digital marketing strategy it is important to understand potential barriers by researching your market thoroughly, including regulations in your territories.
- Working to employ the simplest possible solution ensures that your business, the consumers and the regulators can all have the best possible relationship.

Summary

In this chapter we discussed some of the more common challenges with implementing your digital strategy. There are of course many more, and so remaining flexible with your strategy and ensuring you plan for as many of these eventualities as possible is important. In risk management many people have adopted the terminology used by Donald Rumsfeld (the two-times United States Secretary of Defence, who is interestingly both the oldest and youngest man to serve in that position). Mr Rumsfeld spoke in a 2002 news briefing about three states of information:

> There are known knowns; there are things we know we know. We also know there are known unknowns; that is to say we know there are some things we do not know. But there are also unknown unknowns – the ones we don't know we don't know.

To give this some perspective, technology would be a known unknown – we know that technology will develop and change society and our behaviours but we do not know how. Skills would be a known known – we know the challenges that we have and that we need to train our staff to overcome these. Unknown unknowns are not listed in this chapter, for the simple reason that we cannot predict them. It is this latter category that can only be tackled by remaining as flexible and agile as possible with our strategy and delivery plans.

Chapter checklist

- Technology ☐
- Skills ☐
- Budget and resources ☐
- Business priorities ☐
- Regulation ☐

Further reading

- *On risk*:

  Waring, A E (1998) *Managing Risk: Critical issues for survival and success into the 21st century*, Cengage Learning EMEA. Alan Waring explores risk assessment and management alongside specific concerns such as organizational environment, change and culture.

- *On managing budgets*:

  Sleight, S (2000) *Managing Budgets*, DK. This offers some excellent guides on managing a budget, including managing the process, identifying potential problems, tailored budgeting, writing the budget itself and ongoing monitoring. It is a useful handbook if you will be building and managing budgets for the first time or on a regular basis.

- *On regulation*:

  Lodge, M and Wegrich, K (2012) *Managing Regulation: Regulatory analysis, politics and policy*, Palgrave Macmillan. This goes into great detail on the theories, standards and enforcement of regulation as well as looking at what good looks like. If you work in a regulated environment, this is a worthwhile read.

References

Smith, C (2018) [accessed 19 November 2018] By the Numbers: 23 Amazing Airbnb Statistics, *DMR* [Online] http://expandedramblings.com/index.php/airbnb-statistics/

Townsend, L (2014) [accessed 1 February 2016] How Much Has the Ice Bucket Challenge Achieved? *BBC News* [Online] http://www.bbc.co.uk/news/magazine-29013707

PART TWO
Integrating digital change into your wider organization

Enabling technologies for online marketing and digital transformation

06

What we will cover in this chapter

This chapter will give you an understanding of what digital transformation is and is not. It will also give you an overview of how to work with Technology functions to ensure your strategy is implemented fully, effectively and in a timely fashion with no surprises. We will also look at some relevant techniques and technologies. The key areas covered in this chapter are:

- What is digital transformation?
- Technology development techniques

Chapter goals

By the end of this chapter you should understand digital transformation and some of the key considerations and techniques that should be understood when beginning or reshaping a transformation programme. You will also understand specific technology development techniques and how to apply these to your plans.

What is digital transformation?

Digital transformation is probably the biggest topic of conversation in the digital arena today. If a company is not already doing it, it is almost certainly planning it. Google shows exponential growth in searches for 'digital transformation' as a set of keywords since 2011 (Figure 6.1) and many of the larger management consultancies have moved into this space, but this does not shed much light on exactly what it is.

What it does tell us is that digital transformation is increasingly important. The difficulty in defining it is that most experts have their own subtly different definition. This urgent drive towards digital transformation evokes memories of the social media frenzy of the late 2000s and early 2010s, the website frenzy of the late 1990s and in more recent years the urge for every business to have its own app without having any real purpose in mind. Everyone wanted a new website, many people were not sure why and most didn't know how to create one.

In some ways, digital transformation is in danger of being seen in the same way as any of these – a confusing mishmash of themes, trends, buzzwords and 'next big things'. Examples of significant digital transformations that have occurred in the early 21st century include the rapid growth of the smartphone, Web 2.0, social media and contactless payments. Each has forced companies, sometimes in a specific sector and sometimes universally, to change their practices or even their business models. Each has meant new measurement, operations, technology, people, marketing and process changes.

It is also important at this stage to understand the difference between digitization and digitalization. Digitization is simply the transfer of something analogue to something digital. For example, taking paper documents and turning them into PDFs. Digitalization, however, is the transformation

Figure 6.1 Growth of 'digital transformation'

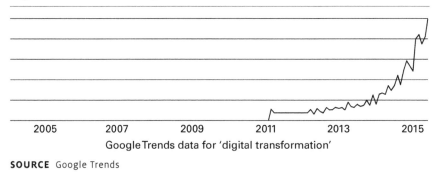

Google Trends data for 'digital transformation'

SOURCE Google Trends

of a culture into more of a digital focus. For example, consumers beginning to rely more heavily on mobile phones or using What's App as a primary form of communication. Both ultimately lead to digital transformation, which reaches far beyond technology. This means business change, internal behavioural change, consumption behaviours, legal changes and much more.

Many organizations embarking on digital transformation are spending significant amounts on technology; yet while these solutions are clearly enablers, they should not be thought of as transformative in their own right. Digital transformation is not purely a technology journey but, more importantly, a mindset. It consists of these hallmark traits:

- A relentless, all-consuming focus on the end consumer and their needs, including actively co-creating solutions with those customers.
- An organization that does its best to go out of its way to pursue that customer focus (ie historical, cultural and structural standards).
- A can do, collaborative and flexible attitude to the customer and the work of serving customers (ie never accepting no for an answer).
- Agile and adaptable ways of working.
- A focus on value creation and breakthroughs, rather than the incrementalism of efficiencies (though this is not to say that efficiency is not important).
- A greater focus on getting to outcomes, rather than process, quickly (ie the company is more interested in customers and their needs than in itself).
- People and their ingenuity are prized.
- Technology is a smart enabler of the above.

The business case and bottom line

Before embarking on a transformation journey the strategic drivers need to be understood, because the road ahead can be long, difficult and potentially costly. This means that a business case laying out how those drivers will be addressed is essential and fundamental for getting the necessary senior management's buy-in for the change journey – not to mention the investment. One of the other difficulties faced in embarking on transformation is generation differences. Boards are often made up of older, more experienced professionals who do not see the day-to-day impact of digital on their business, nor the role it will play in the future. They are also less likely to be impacted by new trends in their personal lives. These are, of course, generalist statements and not true of every board or decision maker. Mary Meeker, of venture capital firm KPCB, delivers an in-depth report every year about internet trends and their accompanying behaviour shifts. In her 2015 report she detailed US statistics that, in 2015, millennials became the dominant generation in the workforce, ahead of baby boomers and Generation X.

This is significant because millennials have grown up with the internet and will not have experienced a workplace without digital technologies. Their expectations and behaviours will therefore be quite different in many regards. According to Meeker, millennials expect different things from their work lives, and fully embracing technology is not considered a perk, but a hygiene factor. This means that robust cases for digital transformation must consider three areas: the customers; the employees; and the business itself. Entering into a transformational process on the premise that 'our customers are online' is unlikely to be a sufficiently robust starting point (Meeker, 2015).

CASE STUDY   The Met Office (UK)

Background

For the UK Met Office, the digital transformation has had to span the entire organization impacting everything from research to content marketing and internal culture. One of the biggest challenges for the Met Office has been differentiating itself in a competitive market. New technology in the form of apps and IoT has resulted in weather data becoming much more accessible. It was clear that the Met Office needed to find a point of differentiation through digital transformation. As the Met Office put it, to find the 'what, the why, the where, the when' of the data.

Strategy

The strategy was to bring the weather content to life. Not just temperatures but information that helps decision making and event planning, for example. Drawing on the huge knowledge of expert scientists working within the organization, the Met Office has separated itself by creating and distributing this kind of content. Through this relevancy it has been able to build on its social strategy, growing to a combined audience of around 1.75 million by mid 2017. This strategy has included contextual content, video, infographics, blogs, interactive tools such as a rainfall map and pollen push notifications. This has then been targeted to audience demographics: a smart and broad content strategy.

Alongside this, the company has worked on improving its collaboration and culture to move marketing and the business experts (scientists for this organization) close together to help bring data stories to life. For example, if the core digital team is able to determine that a specific area of content works well on social – let's say satellite imagery, for instance – it is able to feed this back to the satellite team to help them better understand the type of information they should be sharing.

The organization also works with business partners including a number of companies in the retail space, with this market particularly interested in how weather data can be used to better understand and optimize product sales. One example is an affiliate network that worked with the Met Office to optimize product feeds, enabling them to recognize what products to promote and when, in accordance with the weather.

The Met Office has also been involved in voice technology – weather being the second-most popular search activity enabled through voice devices. The Met Office's Informatics Lab designed an Amazon Alexa Skill, which helps users to make decisions by talking to the device. Instead of merely responding to a request for the weather, the technology also recommends recreational activity based on the forecast, including contextual detail.

Results

This strategy has delivered superb results. The culture of the business has changed, the data is more freely available across the organization, people are working closer together, their content is growing across multiple channels and the Met Office has managed to stay highly relevant when, without this transformative work, it could have quickly become irrelevant.

Key lessons

Innovating and working together within an organization, not in silos, optimizes your opportunity to deliver interesting content across multiple channels. Through different distribution plans you can maximize your reach and through constant innovation and culture change you can transform a business from being in a high-risk scenario to leading the field in a relatively short space of time. This is the power of effective digital transformation.

It is vitally important when developing your business case that you set out the goals to your leaders, colleagues and staff. Transformation can take many forms and it is important to appreciate which of these are the key drivers. For example, is the goal simplification (ie improving the efficiency of internal or customer-focused processes) or sophistication (ie improving your product or service offering)?

Here is an example of how these could play out:

1 **Simplification.** Your new customer on-boarding process includes excessive paperwork, telephone calls and some online interaction. Your systems don't keep accurate records of this process as it moves forward. You need to transform to make this easier and faster for customers whilst improving your internal tracking.

2 **Sophistication.** You offer travel booking services to customers around the world. At the moment they can search and find holidays; a simple service that works effectively. However, you want to understand your customers better so each gets a personalized offering and your service develops more of a tailored nature. This means more data and perhaps some artificial intelligence to learn behaviours and predict the best offerings for each individual.

These examples are transformative but on a small scale so as not to overcomplicate the example. A business transformation would be on a much larger scale, of course.

A transformation must be exactly that – a transformation. There is a danger that companies will spend large sums trying to fit existing business models into a digital delivery. This is not a transformation but an evolution and will not, in most cases, deliver the desired result. For those companies that are prepared to accept digital into the core of their DNA and undergo a transformation, there are potentially big rewards to reap. Data from the UK Design Council's report entitled 'Designing Demand' in 2007 revealed that every £1 invested in design returns £20 in increased turnover, £4 in increased profits and £5 in increased exports (UK Design Council, 2007).

The US Design Management Institute reported that '2014 results show that over the last 10 years, design-led companies have maintained significant stock market advantage, outperforming the S&P by an extraordinary 219 per cent' (US Design Management Institute, 2015).

Evidently the effort and investment is worthwhile for the companies prepared to act. At the other end of the spectrum will be organizations that essentially try to preserve the core of what they have always done, perhaps trying to find ways to make it more palatable for end consumers.

What this means is that, as well as the brand, the actual business model of any company must be reviewed as it goes through the process of digital transformation. Take car manufacturers, for example – not only are they competing with other car makers but now also with new digitally enabled services such as Zipcar and Uber, which are challenging the core ownership model for cars. It is not correct to infer from this that every company with an established business model needs a complete overhaul. However, it is important that companies embody a core element of digitally native behaviour where possible and relevant.

Escaping the legacy of the past

As we discussed in Chapter 3, many of the companies currently considering embarking on digital transformation will point to legacy systems as one of the key hurdles to be overcome. One of the ways to accelerate digital transformation is through the application of middleware – software to bypass older, problematic software.

CASE STUDY   British Friendly

Background

Pancentric Digital, a British service design agency, worked with niche insurance company British Friendly to help it begin its journey of digital transformation.

British Friendly was looking to develop a more customer-centric business. The business had been running on a patchwork of legacy systems that broadly corresponded to the different silos around which the operation of the business had traditionally been arranged. This created a challenge for the business strategy as it was very restricted about what it could deliver. For example, its legacy systems did not have an API, and when the system providers were asked to quote for developing an API, the costs were going to be too high to fit within the available budget.

Strategy

To prevent the project being derailed or delayed, Pancentric developed a layer of 'middleware' that interfaced with the legacy back end and allowed the front end of the website to be delivered in line with a new customer journey, thereby enabling the business to begin its customer-centric approach.

Results

The application of middleware has allowed British Friendly to revolutionize its digital presence and start leaning into a meaningful process of customer-centric transformation. It can renew its back-end stack, whilst still progressing in a digital transformation.

Key lessons

- Transformation can be a challenge.
- The key point for your strategy here is to ensure you explore all avenues.
- Budgets and legacy systems are common constraints within the area of digital transformation, but by seeking out experts and creating innovative solutions you can overcome most of these issues.

The state of digital transformation

Whilst digital transformation has been underway in many organizations for many years the maturity of it is very different by country and industry. Many retail businesses are a long way along the path, whereas others in industries such as manufacturing and financial services are many years behind. This is not to say that all retail businesses are mature and all financial services firms behind the curve, that is absolutely not the case, but broadly speaking there are sectors of those industries that are a long way behind the curve.

The World Economic Forum and Accenture launched the Digital Transformation Initiative (DTI) in 2015. According to the World Economic Forum website the DTI 'supports collaboration between the public and private sectors focused on ensuring that digitalization unlocks new levels of prosperity for both industry and society'. Their 2017 report looks at digital maturity in a range of industries giving an excellent insight into the progress businesses are making with the digitalization journey.

Also in 2017, a study by McKinsey & Company argued that 'On average, industries are less than 40 per cent digitized, despite the relatively deep penetration of these technologies in media, retail and high tech' (Bughin, LaBerge and Mellbye, 2017).

It is clear from these and many other studies on digital transformation that, whilst the journey is well underway there are certainly leaders and laggards, and there is little consistency in how businesses are approaching the solution.

Technology development techniques

Whilst, as we have established, digital transformation is not a technology project but a business transformation, there is certainly a heavy reliance on technology to deliver many of the key elements. We will therefore now look at some key technology development techniques, as it is vital to understand these to be able to deliver your transformation.

There are many models for technology development but it is perhaps most important to appreciate the differences between Agile and Waterfall development.

Waterfall

Waterfall development is a long-established technique that ensures methodical delivery of projects. The structure is quite simply linear like a waterfall. It is often heavily criticized and has been for many decades due to its rigid nature. It was Winston W Royce who first described it in any clear sense and even then it was only to give a negative view. He expressed it as having six stages:

1 Requirements
Captured in a requirements document. Referred to in many businesses now as a BRD (business requirements document).

2 Analysis
Building the requirements into a model and rules system that expresses a structural design.

3 Design
Designing the architecture. This involves making high-level decisions about the key building blocks. Code languages, for example, and other elements that would be difficult to change at a later date.

4 Coding
The development phase where the product is built and integrated into whatever other system it has been designed for.

5 Test
Thorough testing of the new development to ensure it is robust and to remove any bugs or defects found.

6 Operation
Finally, the installation or implementation of the development including any future maintenance.

The above is just the earliest view of this model and many variations exist. Another common interpretation of these stages, for example, is Plan, Design, Develop, Test, Release, Feedback. The key part of this model, however, is that one stage should only begin when the previous phase is complete. This ensures each is thoroughly delivered, there is no confusion on priorities and the timeline is very clear. It also enables and indeed encourages a great deal of documentation to be produced, which creates stability even if the team delivering the development changes mid-project.

Agile

Agile was developed as an almost entirely opposing approach and was first popularized by the Manifesto for Agile Development (2001) although iterative development techniques have been around since at least the 1950s and much of what is now regarded as Agile is pulling together techniques that already existed at the time the Manifesto was published. Where the Waterfall model ensures methodical discipline, the Agile approach ensures far more fluidity and the ability to react to changes in requirements that are regular occurrences in practical delivery of development projects.

In Agile development the work is broken into small incremental developments called Sprints which last just a few weeks and includes a cross-functional team working on all elements at once from build to test.

There are many methodologies that are categorized under the term Agile. These include Scrum, Kanban, Adaptive software development and Lean software development. There are many more but these are perhaps the most commonly discussed in the non-technology disciplines. Having an understanding of these is useful for the digital marketer. There are many books worth reading on these subjects for deeper detail including *Brilliant Agile Project Management: A practical guide to using Agile, Scrum and Kanban* by Rob Cole and *Learning Agile: Understanding Scrum, XP, Lean and Kanban* by Andrew Stellman.

As well as these two very different development models it is also useful to have an understanding of some of the other key technology concepts so we will look at each of these briefly now.

Proof of concept (PoC)

A proof of concept is, as the name suggests, producing something that delivers a success or failure of an idea. This is not unique to technology development, and is in fact a widely used phrase, but in development it is key to be able to develop and produce simple deliverables to test a concept for the business. In marketing, for example, we may wish to test whether a landing page delivers a better conversion rate if it contains dynamic data. We may need our technology team to implement an A/B test to establish this, as it is not possible through our Content Management System. Whatever the result, we will understand whether this development work delivered the hoped-for increase in conversions or not.

Minimum viable product (MVP)

A minimum viable product is a development that does enough to be able to test the concept. This is effectively the actual item that is delivered to prove the above concept. In start-ups this is often what early investors are looking to see to prove that the concept and team have potential. This MVP does just enough to prove the model and no more. Other features can be added later, but there is no need to waste investment on those at this early stage, as the MVP may not prove successful.

What does this mean for digital marketing?

Digital marketing is only one small part of the digital transformation of an organization, but all elements of that transformation need to be understood by you as every element affects you. Digital marketing should feed into the project requirements and remain key stakeholders throughout. Transformation must be appreciated as transformative. That seems clear but transformation and iteration are often confused and it is vital that the digital marketer does not make this mistake.

Summary

Digital transformation remains a key area of focus for many organizations whether they are mature on this journey or at an early stage. Appreciating the key differences between digitization and digitalization is vital and understanding technology development techniques improves your communications with one of your most important stakeholders, technology.

Chapter checklist

- What is digital transformation? ☐
- Technology development techniques ☐

Further reading

- *On digital transformation*:

  Herbert, L (2017) *Digital Transformation*, Bloomsbury Business

  Perkin, N and Abraham, P (2017) *Building the Agile Business Through Digital Transformation*, Kogan Page

  Rogers, D (2016) *The Digital Transformation Playbook: Rethink your business for the digital age*, Columbia University Press

References

Bughin, J, LaBerge, L and Mellbye, A (2017) [accessed 20 November 2018] The Case for Digital Reinvention, McKinsey Quarterly, February [Online] https://www.mckinsey.com/business-functions/digital-mckinsey/our-insights/the-case-for-digital-reinvention

Meeker, M (2015) 2015 Internet Trends Report, *KPCB* [Online] http://www.kpcb.com/blog/2015-internet-trends

UK Design Council (2007) [accessed 1 November 2015] Designing Demand [Online] https://www.designcouncil.org.uk/sites/default/files/asset/document/Designing%20Demand_Executive_Sumary_Final.pdf

US Design Management Institute (2015) [accessed 1 November 2015] Design-Driven Companies Outperform S&P by 228% Over Ten Years [Online] http://www.dmi.org/blogpost/1093220/182956/Design-Driven-Companies-Outperform-S-P-by-228-Over-Ten-Years--The-DMI-Design-Value-Index

Planning your digital marketing strategy – Objectives, teams and budgeting

07

What we will cover in this chapter

This chapter covers effective planning processes and how to apply them to your digital strategy. The key areas covered in this chapter are:

- The planning process
- The phased approach
- Goals
- Objectives and strategies
- Action plans
- Controls
- People
- Budgeting and forecasting

Chapter goals

By the end of this chapter you should understand different planning models and how to use these to create a robust plan for the delivery of your strategy. You should understand the differences between goals, objectives and action plans and be able to build resource plans. You should also understand how to manage budgeting and forecasting (Figure 7.1).

Figure 7.1 The planning process

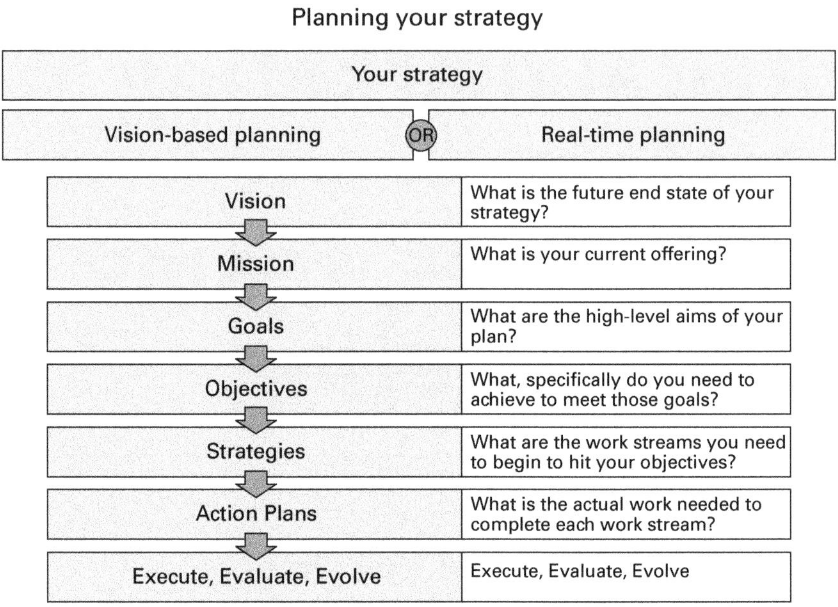

Planning your strategy

Your strategy	
Vision-based planning OR Real-time planning	
Vision	What is the future end state of your strategy?
Mission	What is your current offering?
Goals	What are the high-level aims of your plan?
Objectives	What, specifically do you need to achieve to meet those goals?
Strategies	What are the work streams you need to begin to hit your objectives?
Action Plans	What is the actual work needed to complete each work stream?
Execute, Evaluate, Evolve	Execute, Evaluate, Evolve

A strategic approach to digital marketing is impossible without having strong planning techniques in place. Building a plan involves similar techniques to building a house. We need to understand what we are trying to build, we need solid foundations, we need to know the intricate measurements and details of the brickwork and walls, the costs, timelines and skills of our builders. Having a plan is essential if we want our house to meet our requirements and to stand strong for a long time to come. A strategy without a plan is no more than an idea. Putting a plan in place for the build and delivery of your digital marketing strategy is no different and so this chapter looks at how we build a plan that clearly lays out the delivery of our strategy.

In order to deliver our digital marketing strategy we need to understand three things:

1 Where are we now (A)?

2 Where do we want to get to (B)?

3 How do we get there?

The first of these is answered through research, data analysis and insight, which we looked at in Chapter 3. The second is designed through the construction of a vision and mission, which we also looked at in Chapter 3. This chapter therefore focuses on the third question: How do we get from A to B?

Digital marketing has created its own challenges here. Many digital channels can be switched on and off in real time and at a low cost and so are sometimes added into marketing campaigns and plans at the last minute. The power of effective planning, however, is in the early thinking, co-ordination and integration of the key elements of your strategy – without planning, your strategy is at serious risk of failing. Without effective planning you can spend twice as much time, money and resource trying to fix problems and find solutions, you can demotivate your people and even find yourself having to pay suppliers to help you when that should not have been needed. In extreme cases this can even lead to budgets being used up too quickly, staff resignations and your overall strategy being seriously compromised. A good planning process is essential. Planning is not the most glamorous part of your strategy and it probably won't win you any awards, but often the least glamorous parts of any project are the key success factors – that is certainly true here.

In this chapter we examine some of the processes and approaches to planning that can help guide the implementation of your strategy.

The planning process

Pablo Picasso once said, 'Our goals can only be reached through a vehicle of a plan, in which we must fervently believe, and upon which we must vigorously act. There is no other route to success.' Whilst it is fairly unlikely that he was talking about digital marketing, it is certainly a point that applies here. The starting point and the key to success with planning is to have a process in place and to stick to that process. We look at the discipline of that later in this chapter, but let's start by looking at the process itself.

There are several planning models that can be used for effective planning and in this section we look at two core methods: vision-based planning and real-time planning.

Vision-based planning

Definition: the process of creating a vision and following a clear six-stage process of delivering against it.

This method is probably the most common form of strategic planning. There are six phases to this model, beginning with creating a vision and ending with analysis and evolution where needed. This method takes you from a starting point through to a final result which may remain fluid. It is an excellent way of organizing the delivery of your strategy and helps to guide your thinking during the strategy development process. It is, however, more structured than some organizations would be willing or able to implement and more rigid than the real-time planning model we look at below. It also works on a future to present time frame, ie there are specific goals to be achieved by a specific point in time and this may not be relevant to every plan.

Let's look at the six stages:

1 Identify your vision statement.

2 Produce your mission statement.

3 Establish your primary goals.

4 Create specific objectives and strategies to reach each goal.

5 Implement action plans to fulfil each strategy.

6 Put the action plans into effect, evaluate and evolve.

The six stages of vision-based planning

Example A – an FMCG retailer

1 To be everyone's favourite place to buy doughnuts.

2 We provide the tastiest doughnuts in the United States to anyone, anywhere, at any time.

3 Improve brand awareness.

4 Create a social media strategy.

5 Build a viral video marketing campaign.

6 Build the campaign, select target audience, budget, launch, test and measure.

Example B – a B2B service provider

1 To be Europe's number one IT support services supplier.

2 We offer the fastest and most reliable competitive IT support across Europe.

3 Gain word-of-mouth promotion.

4 Create a member-get-member scheme.

5 Build a personalized e-mail contact and content strategy.

6 Build the campaign, select target audience, budget, launch, test and measure.

As mentioned above, at this point you should be clear on your vision, as we have already in Chapter 3 reviewed the creation of this and how to align it with your company vision. Below we look at the mission statement and then go on to review steps three to five. Step six, the execution of your strategy, is considered throughout the book.

Mission statement

There is often confusion between vision and mission statements. The easiest way to remember the difference is that your vision statement is an expression of your desired future state, whereas the mission statement expresses your current state. With this differentiation in mind we can look at the two examples above and begin to see a clear difference. Creating this mission is important for your business but just as important for your digital strategy. Knowing what you are trying to achieve now alongside the future vision begins to clearly lay out a path that the rest of your planning process can follow.

Real-time planning

Definition: a plan that retains fluidity to your planning process to ensure your plans are malleable to the circumstances.

The real-time model is effectively a 'casual' version of the vision-based model. This model is notable for its lack of structure and, some may even argue, its lack of a model, which may seem a fairly odd way to start an explanation of a planning model when we have already discussed the importance of structure. The reason this was developed, however, is because the modern world changes at pace and so building a formalized five-year plan is considered by some to be an outdated concept. The world in five years' time is likely to be very different from now, so how can such a long-term plan still be as relevant as when it was finalized? Indeed, the world has changed a great deal since the publication of the first edition of this book with AI, AR, VR and IoT developing significantly and major changes in every digital channel in this short time frame. The real-time model therefore keeps the planning process 'alive' as an ongoing piece of work. It is never formally documented and so evolves continuously. It is reviewed at regular intervals, for example monthly board meetings, and therefore develops alongside real-time issues and developments within and external to the company.

The advantage is therefore that your strategy stays highly relevant and can change quickly to meet current insights. There are, however, two primary disadvantages to this approach and both ultimately come back to the lack of documentation. The first is that there is no document to share with your business. It can be extremely difficult to articulate your strategy to the wider business in this situation and so can create confusion and lack of synergy if your communication is not excellent. One way to address this is to ensure that the project lead or equivalent for the delivery of your strategy develops and manages an internal communications plan. This could involve e-mails to key stakeholders, steering group meetings, regular update seminars, internal desk drops or even launch events. The extent of this is down to the size and culture of your organization but you should never assume that people will know how the project is progressing – great communication is essential.

Second, there is no fully formed document to share externally. Should investors or other external stakeholders wish to understand your strategy it would not look very professional only to be able to articulate this verbally from what was discussed at the last meeting. This can be tackled by ensuring that the core principles and stages of the plan are documented and the flexible elements are regularly updated and version controlled.

That is not to say that there is no structure here at all. A process of planning the goals and how the business aims to achieve them is still followed in a similar style to the vision-based approach we mentioned above, but you do not need to stick so rigidly to these goals for a set period of time and so are more able to retain the flexibility that this process demands. For example, the doughnut company we mentioned above would still go through the same six steps to create their plan but this may not then be documented and may evolve just a few weeks later. Should your competition launch a viral video campaign, you would change your social media plans to adapt to this challenge and perhaps create a video-based advertising campaign for YouTube that will both reach a different audience and reduce the gains your competitor makes from their video campaign.

Vision-based versus real-time example

A company decides that it wants to grow its digital footprint.

Vision-based approach

The company in question would conduct research into consumer needs and behaviours, competitor offerings and technology. An audit of the current capability would be completed and a strategy would begin to be formed. This would involve committing resources in terms of people, time and money into the work streams necessary to deliver the strategy. This would then be laid out for the following three to five years in order to ensure that those resources were ring-fenced. Perhaps the front end and back end of a website need development and so do a number of apps, so this is all planned together and committed together. Agencies and contractors may be hired to deliver this over the next 24 to 36 months. Deviating from this plan in the first two to three years would therefore involve significant loss of investment and complexity. It may also cause confusion. The end result is likely to be as per the plan and this would be a success. If, however, technology has significantly changed in that period, as we have seen many times in the past over a short period of time (the launches of the iPhone or social media, for example), then this end result may no longer be relevant.

Real-time planning approach

The company would again research and audit to establish the beginning state and desired result. Steps would then be put into place to begin moving towards this end result. This may include appointing an agency, but keeping their brief fluid and ensuring that their contract is not a long-term commitment. The goals would be based on working towards delivering the next step in the journey but perhaps not laying down any significant commitments at the early stages for what may or may not happen in year three. Decisions are made at the points that action is needed rather than a long time in advance. Should a new technology launch, or behaviours change, this plan is able to adapt to those. Therefore the back end of the website may be developed first, as it is less susceptible to consumer behavioural needs. The front end may not be scoped until the back-end work is nearing release. The apps may be the last element, as the mobile market continues to change at significant pace. This means a great deal more focus on the project from the senior leadership team, perhaps less ability to plan ahead for cost savings and a greater need for excellent communication, but it does mean that the end result is likely to be highly relevant when launched rather than risking seeming outdated.

Here is a useful comparison of the above two scenarios:

- *Stage 1*: goal – establish opportunity:
  - Vision-based: research consumers and market, internal audit, resource commitment.
  - Real-time: research consumers and market, internal audit, resource commitment.

- The difference: no difference here. Both methods begin by understanding the current position, challenge and opportunity.
- *Stage 2*: begin development of strategy:
  - Vision-based: structure the strategy and prepare the formal document.
  - Real-time: begin test and learn.
  - The difference: the vision-based approach now spends several months beginning to structure the proposal, add supporting data, creating pillars, gaining commitment from stakeholders and producing detailed financial forecasts. The real-time approach creates a loose plan and begins to test some of the assumptions in a scientific manner to shape the development on the plan.
- *Stage 3*: finalize strategy:
  - Vision-based: commit budget and finalize full five-year plan.
  - Real-time: plan for one to three years.
  - The difference: the vision-based approach would result in the above planning process being committed and bought into by all senior stakeholders. This would then become part of the business strategy. The real-time process would also need buy-in from the senior team but would be more fluid and have less of a time commitment.
- *Stage 4*: delivery:
  - Vision-based: work to plan with very limited deviation.
  - Real-time: continue to evolve and change direction as needed.
  - The difference: as the work begins there is a very clear path for the vision-based strategy to follow. The milestones must all be met and this allows full visibility of progress and clear resource management. The real-time approach has a clear beginning but must now be managed closely to create a path and direction as the strategy evolves based on the learnings, internal and external factors.
- *Stage 5*: result:
  - Vision-based: delivered as per plan but possibly now out of date and a new strategy is needed.
  - Real-time: delivered in an evolved state, which can continue with minimal work but at a higher cost.
  - The difference: the vision-based approach should accomplish its end goal and if not then the project has failed. However, if the environment has changed then the result may not be as strong as

first expected and changing course can be expensive and difficult.
The real-time approach should result in a more contemporary result
but the path may have been more expensive and resource intensive
due to the continuous reviewing and evolution of the plan.

The phased approach

Before we get on to steps three to five of the vision-based planning process it is
worth quickly discussing phased planning. This refers to splitting your strategy
into key development phases. These phases can be categorized into calendar-
based, theme-based and business-based phasing, dependent on your strategy.
There are other phasing approaches but these are some of the most common.

Calendar-based phasing

This approach is as simple as it sounds. Phasing your plan to match your
calendar is one method. You could start in January, aim to have your vision
completed by February, establish your goals in March etc. This type of approach is common when there is no specific delivery date in mind, no essential milestone dates or your strategy is not integrated with any other pieces
of work. That does not mean that the deadlines are any less important, but
you can be a little more flexible with setting those deadlines at the start of
the planning process.

Theme-based phasing

Theme-based phasing is used when your strategy has specific themes that
would be logical to deliver together. For example, there may be specific customer experience elements that would be powerful to be delivered together
such as a new training programme and online chat technology. There could
be complementary marketing channel strategies that would be far more
powerful if released together, such as direct mail and e-mail.

Business-based phasing

This phasing method is focused on aligning your strategic plan with the
overall business goals. Your company's strategic plan is likely to be made of

key strategic pillars, which may in turn be delivering projects and change programmes. This may be less formalized in a smaller business but there will still be key areas of focus, and funding will be directed towards those. The business-based phasing approach means aligning the key parts of your plan with these pillars. This is a path of least resistance and will resonate with many senior stakeholders, but it can compromise the ideal timeline for your strategy.

Now we can come back to look at stages three to five mentioned in the vision-based planning process above. These are goals, objectives and strategies, and action plans.

Goals

Goals are high-level statements about what you need to achieve in order to deliver against your vision. Goals tend to be long term and therefore set out the underlying elements of your vision. They bring your vision statement to life by moving it towards a practical reality.

Goals need to be structured to meet a set of criteria. The model that I developed to give a memorable structure to this goal setting is the 4 Rs:

- **Relevant**: does it fit with your vision?
- **Resonating**: does it fit with your business's values and goals?
- **Responsive**: is it adaptable and flexible so that it can change if needed?
- **Recognizable**: is it easily understandable?

Some example goals are:

- increase sales;
- improve profitability;
- provide best-in-class customer service;
- deliver a world-class digital experience;
- hire the best talent;
- become the thought leader;
- gain market share.

You should aim to set a limited number of goals that focus on the key aims of your strategy and fit with the strategic pillars of your business. They also need to be integrated so that they fit together without any conflicting elements. Your business strategy will have goals and each goal will have objectives, strategies and action plans below it. Some of these strategies may in turn have goals that have their own objectives and so through a waterfall effect the goals of your organization are delivered.

For example, if we take the first goal above we could create a waterfall of goals and strategies that looks something like the process shown in Figure 7.2.

Your goals are unique in the planning process in that they require the least detail but the most thought. If your goals are not thought through then the river will be flowing in the wrong direction and the waterfall doesn't work. How you go about meeting your goal of 'increase sales' is not something that the goal itself is concerned with. You do not need to focus on the 'how' at this stage, simply the 'what'. Your objectives and strategies will deal with how these goals are met, as we will see below. Whilst goals should be grounded in reality they do not need to be specific or be the result of thorough research. They therefore do not need to be entirely realistic. It may sound counter-intuitive to have a goal that cannot be met, but an aspirational goal can drive your business forward faster than a realistic one.

That said, there is a careful balance between being aspirational and being so unrealistic that you demotivate your people, which can compromise the delivery of your goal, especially if unrealistic goals are set regularly. If, for example, your sales goal for the year is 20 per cent above the previous year and the company has never achieved more than 10–15 per cent then this is aspirational. It feels achievable if everyone works hard and you have some luck on your side. This may stretch the team to work towards this, especially if they are incentivized to do this. If you miss the 20 per cent target but still

Figure 7.2   The planning flow of an organization

achieve 17.5 per cent then this is still the best result your business has ever seen and a good outcome. If, however, you set the target at 40 per cent the following year and 60 per cent the year after, whilst reducing investment in the business, cancelling bonuses and reducing the workforce, then your people will begin to believe that the targets are unrealistic and this will seriously demotivate and have a negative impact on productivity. They may also openly criticize the management, which can lead to severe cultural issues and even resignations – all of which will in turn affect the delivery of your goal.

Objectives and strategies

Your objectives and strategies are where you start to build specific plans that create a journey for your overall strategy. Once these are in place we can create action plans that demonstrate the detail of how we deliver them.

Objectives

Your objectives are specific, quantifiable and time-based. They are the steps or milestones that you need to take towards meeting your ultimate goal. Many businesses use a SMART approach to creating objectives. SMART is simply a mnemonic that helps us to ensure that the objectives are well thought through and ultimately will serve their purpose. The SMART method has a number of interpretations but the 'SMART' box below outlines one of the more common ones.

SMART

- **S**pecific: no matter who were to look at your action plan it should be absolutely clear what needs to be achieved for the action plan to be met. There must be no ambiguity. Using the five 'W' questions can help here – again, there are differing interpretations of the five (or sometimes six) 'W' questions but below are those that I find the most useful:
  - Who: who will be involved in achieving the action plan?
  - Where: is a specific location involved?
  - What: what exactly needs to be achieved?
  - Why: what is this action plan going to achieve?
  - When: what is the deadline and any milestones along the way?

- **M**easurable: how will you know when you have met your action plan? It is vital that there is a clear measure so that everyone involved knows when the action plan has been hit and there is no confusion. This also allows you to understand how much progress you are making towards meeting your action plan.

- **A**ttainable: setting action plans that are realistic is crucially important. If your action plans are not attainable then you can never meet them, which ultimately means you can never reach your goals. There is no harm in setting a stretching action plan – and indeed getting the balance between too stretching and too easy is important here. Setting an action plan that does not have this balance right can also cause demotivation amongst the team working on it.

- **R**elevant: the action plan needs to be relevant to your goal. Having an action plan that does not tie in with the wider work is not only irrelevant but also a distraction from achieving your goal. Think back to the five Ws above and consider whether each of these are relevant.

- **T**ime-based: this is where the fifth 'W' comes in: 'When'. Your action plan needs a time frame and also specific milestones. As with any piece of work, having a deadline gives the action plan a much greater chance of being delivered.

If we were to take our goal of increasing sales we might create one of the following objectives: 1) increase sales of batteries through the online channel by 10 per cent to 100,000 units by the end of the sales year; 2) increase room bookings by 55 per cent to achieve 55 per cent capacity by this time next year.

These give us a target to hit and a deadline to hit it by. There is no ambiguity and it could even be more specific by breaking down into a series of objectives around the different products being sold.

If we were to take the example of the doughnut company mentioned above, their SMART objectives could be:

1 *To be everyone's favourite place to buy doughnuts*: increase footfall by 25 per cent by end of year.

2 *We provide the tastiest doughnuts in the United States to anyone, anywhere, at any time*: customer satisfaction levels on food quality at least 98 per cent for full year.

3 *Improve brand awareness*: brand search queries up 20 per cent within six months.

4 *Create a social media strategy*: improve engagement on Facebook by 100 per cent by December.

5 *Build a viral video marketing campaign*: 1 million views in a three-month campaign period.

So now we know exactly what we have to do and by when – we have a simple flow. Meeting our action plans means that our strategies will deliver. If all of our strategies deliver then we will hit our goal. If all of our goals deliver then we will deliver against our mission, which means our overall strategy is working.

Strategies

The word 'strategy' in this sense refers to the specific things that we will do to meet our objective. Do not confuse this with the broader meaning of strategy that the title of this book refers to. Your strategies are the plans that spell out how you will achieve your objectives. When goals are fairly broad, strategies must be much more focused. This is where we demonstrate what we are going to do and from this we create our action plans. Without strategies your work so far will have been for nothing. Going back to our sales goal we know that we need to increase sales. In itself that does not help us a lot. Our objectives have given us something specific that we need to achieve but we still do not fully understand what we need to do to achieve that. Our strategy needs to look at the key work streams we need to implement to achieve our 100,000 sales.

What we need to do at this stage is start to look at the levers we can pull to achieve the desired outcome. For this strategy the outcome is increased sales, so what levers can we pull to achieve this? Well, let's break down the full sales funnel:

- Awareness: are consumers aware of us and our products?
- Consideration: do consumers find our brand and products appealing?
- Findable: can consumers find us either deliberately or through generic searches or channels?
- Informative: do consumers get the information they need from us to make a decision?
- Ease of use: is it easy for consumers to buy from us?

We should have a strong understanding of all of these factors from the research and insight work that we reviewed in Chapter 3. Each of these areas has its own internal levers, for example:

- awareness: above-the-line marketing spend, PR;
- consideration: proposition, brand values;
- findable: SEO, PPC, social media;
- informative: content;
- ease of use: user experience, customer service, conversion funnels.

These specific areas are direct contributors to the sales objective that we are trying to build our strategies for, but there are also indirect contributors. For example, customer service. Whilst providing great service to existing customers does not directly create sales it does create higher retention rates, greater repeat business, more cross-sell opportunity and word-of-mouth promotion. Each of these will directly result in increased sales and so the indirect levers are also vitally important to consider and can often be the difference between exceeding and missing objectives.

From these areas we can now build strategies such as:

- increase display advertising across highly targeted sites (awareness);
- develop a market-leading proposition (consideration);
- make significant SEO improvements (findable);
- broaden our content strategy (informative);
- improve our funnel signposting (ease of use).

Each of these strategies will need a level of detail below it to dictate how it is delivered. These are called our action plans.

Action plans

Action plans clearly define the specific pieces of work that will be done within each of the above strategies. These must not be confused with the planning processes mentioned above, or the wider use of the word 'plan' in this chapter. Ultimately this is where your strategy will succeed or fail. Action plans are where your goals, objectives and strategies come together into the hard work. At this stage, more so than any other, the detail is crucial. Planning how the work will be done, ensuring nothing is missed, working with key stakeholders, checking the legal and regulatory frameworks are in place, ensuring budgets are planned and managed accurately, selecting and managing your agencies and many more factors will be crucial to success here.

We focus on these elements throughout the book, so rather than cover all of this here we instead look at tactical delivery of the strategy. In order to create the action plan we need to review what specific tactical actions we are going to take to meet the strategy. To bring this to life we can focus on one of the strategies above that are contributing to our 'increase sales' goal. Let's look at 'Make significant SEO improvements'.

SEO can be broken down into three core areas: technical, content and links – the SEO triangle. We will look at this in Chapter 8. When looking at how you build your action plan for this strategy you would need to consider all three areas:

- *Technical implementation*
  - URL structure: is it optimized for the products we are looking to sell?
  - Code: does it need cleaning, are there any errors?
  - Experience: is our site responsive? Will it be a great experience for all of our visitors?
  - Speed: does our site load quickly?
  - Responsive: is our site optimized to all devices?
- *Content*
  - Topic: are we producing content that covers the key areas that consumers care about?
  - Social: is our content proving to be engaging socially?
  - Fresh: is our content of the moment?
- *Links*
  - Profile: is our link profile clean?
  - Baiting: do we have an ethically sound link strategy such as link baiting rather than link buying?

In Chapter 8 you can find more detail on how SEO contributes to your strategy; Chapter 14 covers content strategy.

---

10 steps to an effective action plan

1 Know your strategy.

2 Understand the bigger picture – your goals.

3 Be specific.

4 Create a written plan.

5 Create deadlines and milestones.

6 Ensure it is measurable.

7 Don't compromise.

8 Build in known factors.

9 Be clear.

10 Be thorough.

Controls

The above processes are very effective ways to ensure that you meet your overall business mission, but all of these are ineffective if they are not implemented and run correctly. I have seen many businesses that are excellent at this from top to bottom, but also some that are very good at the theory but fail to hit their action plans due to lack of clarity, poor communication or a fall down in the process. There are some clear disciplines and controls to have in place when building and delivering a plan that are crucial to success and they are no less important than any of the other parts of the planning process.

The most important of these controls is to implement a documented, management approach, assuming of course that you are not operating a real-time planning process (as mentioned above). This is where the Gantt chart comes in (as mentioned in Chapter 5). Using a Gantt chart to clearly illustrate the progress of each of the action plans, and therefore the strategies, gives a clear reference point at any moment for how progress is being made towards meeting the objectives and therefore goals of the business. This covers the deadline and milestone elements of the strategies. Also, implementing reporting and measurement is vital to allow monthly, weekly or even daily progress reports against the objectives. These are discussed in detail in Chapter 19 and cover the target elements of the strategies.

Reviews

Reviews are also crucial to success. A standard approach here is to implement a quarterly review, but this should be structured to fit with your strategy and business and so quarterly may not always be the appropriate time frame. These reviews should cover how each action plan is progressing against the milestones and whether targets are being met. From these reviews the strategies should be evolved. This could be the implementation of new action plans to replace failing ones, the restructure of strategies or teams or even the increase in targets due to unexpected success to date.

Risk management

Risk management is another important control. Your business and your industry will have its own risk positioning, which will be dependent on a number of factors such as regulation (we looked at this in Chapter 5). A full understanding of this dictates the plans that you produce and how you take action on them throughout their delivery. Constructing a risk matrix is a useful method of visualizing the risks that your strategies will encounter (Figure 7.3). You should familiarize yourself with the risk management techniques relevant to your company and industry.

Contingency planning

Contingency planning is an important control to have in place. With all the best strategists, planners and best practice methods in place there will still be

Figure 7.3   A risk matrix

5	10	15	20	25	Major	
4	8	12	16	20	Significant	
3	6	9	12	15	Moderate	IMPACT
2	4	6	8	10	Low	
1	2	3	4	5	Negligible	
Remote	Unlikely	Occasional	Likely	Frequent		
		LIKELIHOOD				

unforeseen factors. Macro-economic factors such as recessions are a good example of this. You cannot fully predict what will happen, so having plans in place to allow you to be flexible and implement plan B when something goes wrong is crucial. In order to build contingency plans effectively you should think through what the top 10 most likely impacts could be and how your plan might need to evolve to deal with them. This does not involve the creation of 10 new plans but simply a realistic alternative that can be built on if the situation occurs. Some examples of this are:

- A new competitor enters the market with significant impact.
- New technology is launched that our consumers would prefer to use.
- The global economy enters recession.
- There is a serious negative PR story about our business.
- New regulation is brought into force that restricts our operations.

People

A business is nothing without its people. A crucial part of planning is getting the right people working on delivering your plan. There are two key areas to consider here: skill set and resource. Do we have enough people and who should look after which part of the process?

Skill set

This really starts at the top. It is not a simple matter of ensuring that your social media experts are implanting social media correctly, it is more important to ensure that your strategists and planners are experienced and have the right mindset for the role. If this early part of the process is not conducted correctly then the rest of the strategies and action plans will be heading in the wrong direction no matter how well they are executed. For the implementation you need experts who understand their own channels but who also have an understanding of the other channels and the wider strategy. Whilst it is possible to implement a marketing strategy with individuals working in silos, this creates a long list of issues that can be seriously detrimental to your strategy, so having people who are good communicators and leading them to behave as one team is crucial.

This brings us to the leaders themselves. For this role you must have an individual who understands each and every area of the strategy. They do not need to be a paid search expert, a research guru or a PR genius, but they absolutely have to understand what each channel and element of the strategy does, how it works and how they should fit together. Without this, the guidance will not be there for the experts who are delivering the action plans. Without guidance there is nowhere to turn for direction and that will lead your action plans off the path to success. It will also lead to decisions being made on personal preference rather than experience or data, to guesswork and to a HIPPO culture prevailing (Highest Paid Person's Opinion) which is the biggest danger to the success of your strategy.

An interesting method of discovering the types of personality you have in your business is the Myers–Briggs Type Indicator (MBTI), developed by Katharine Cook Briggs and her daughter Isabel Briggs Myers. This family team developed a set of four cognitive-behavioural dichotomies, which are widely used to assess the personalities and attributes of employees.

The four dichotomies or scales are:

- thinking and feeling (T/F);
- extroversion and introversion (E/I);
- sensing and intuition (S/N);
- judgement and perception (J/P).

The theory is that these will dictate whether an individual will make decisions on an analytical or an emotional basis: there is some debate over its predictive accuracy but it remains a useful perspective, and it is worth reading up on the model to help you frame your thinking on the decision-making style of your decision makers, stakeholders and leaders.

Resource

Quite simply, this refers to the number of hours available for delivery of the action plans. This can be quite complex and it is crucial here that the strategists have a solid understanding of what resource is available to deliver the plans. Many plans fall down due to an unrealistic expectation of the number of hours available in a team.

A good process here is to begin by allocating time to existing processes or 'business as usual' (BAU) work. For example, a team of 20 marketers may consist of one director, three senior managers, six managers and 10 executives. They work 40 hours a week. Everyone in that team has some admin to do every week such as expenses, invoicing, time management etc. The managers also have people management responsibilities such as signing off holidays, running reviews, recruiting etc. Senior managers will also have strategic plans to write, business projects to be involved with, budgets to plan, contracts to negotiate etc. The director will also have the overall department strategy, board meetings, pay reviews and other strategic projects. If we were to allocate this time at the start we would see that where we had 40 hours per week × 20 staff = 800 hours a week, we now have 35 hours a week × 20 staff = 700 hour a week. Simply through the standard BAU we have lost 100 hours a week.

We then have to look at the work that goes on within marketing that forms the foundation of keeping the department running. This may include website updates, paid search optimization, sending weekly e-mails, copywriting and uploading to the content management system (CMS) to keep our content fresh and much more. This may well take another 300 hours per week for our team, leaving us with 400 hours. We need to factor in that individuals in the team will have holiday and some sick leave, which will lose us 25 days per person on holiday and 5 days per person on sick leave during the year. This is 30 × 20 days per year = 600 days. That results in 11.5 days a week or 92 hours. So now we have just 308 hours left.

This is all hypothetical of course, but you can see how we could plan for 800 hours a week when we actually have around 300 hours a week of available resource. This kind of detailed planning is essential if you are to create realistic action plans that are deliverable.

Budgeting and forecasting

Last, but certainly not least, is the budgeting and forecasting process. This is a crucial area of planning, for obvious reasons, and there are some important techniques that can be used to ensure this process is as smooth and accurate as possible. This section deals specifically with media budgeting rather than departmental budgeting. We will therefore not be considering the running of our department, including items such as salaries, expenses, IT costs etc. We are purely concerning ourselves with budgeting our marketing spend, including items such as media costs and agency fees. Digital marketing is an area that is very transparent. Where some marketing channels may not be able to directly attribute sales or revenue, digital channels generally can. As such budgeting and forecasting accuracy expectations are high, so using solid techniques to enable you to establish this accuracy is key.

Master budget

This is a document that is often used within business to establish a budget for the coming period based on previous results. This is a static document and it would never be adjusted, no matter what results are actually seen. You therefore report against this as your master budget and, ultimately, you will be judged at the end of the year on performance against it. To produce this you will need to review historic performance of all of the key metrics such as conversion rates, engagement rates and response rates. Understanding how they have performed historically, and the trend you have seen over the previous period, will inform your view as to what to expect over the coming period. You also need to consider known macro factors such as seasonal changes, competition and regulation.

It should be noted that you can create your master budget based purely on aspirational goals if you choose, but this is likely to be inaccurate, difficult to measure against and not given credence by external parties such as analysts and investors.

Forecasting

Your forecast is a more fluid version of your budget and should be reassessed regularly. Monthly forecasts are fairly standard, especially within digital marketing where updated market and business performance can be considered in close to real time. There are several different techniques that can be used for forecasting but the most common, and the one we look at here, is the trend-based model. This technique looks at your budget alongside a 13-month rolling performance. This provides a view of your month-on-month performance and your year-on-year performance whilst showing any trends within the data and your goals from your budget. This is a robust technique as it builds on solid data to make predictions. What this model does not cover, however, is any known future events.

For example, if we were to forecast our sales from paid search for August 2019 we would look back at the period from August 2018 to July 2019. We could see from this how we performed last year and see any trends since that date right up until the previous month. We can build into this our own knowledge of what has happened and we can make some predictions about August this year. But what if we know that we are repricing our products mid-month or there will be a new competitor product launching? The model does not take account for that. We therefore need to add a second element to this model.

This second element is to review the known future. If we know that a competitor is launching a new product then we need to model the effect we think that will have on our paid search channel. Have they done this before? Has someone else done something similar before? Will they promote it on paid search? Are they well known to our consumers? Are they direct competition or will we actually be less affected than we first thought? Looking at our data and making assumptions is key to being able to model this into our forecast and therefore have an accurate view of the future.

Summary

There are several planning processes that can be used to ensure that your strategy is delivered – without effective planning your strategy is unlikely to be a success. Vision-based planning enables you to have a clear, documented flow from your vision through to each individual tactical action. The real-time planning process is far less formalized and so has more flexibility. The phased approach allows you to adopt a calendar, theme or business-based structure to your timelines to ensure that you meet the integrated objectives of the business. Goals give you high-level aims that are made specific by objectives. Strategies are then formed to meet the objectives, and action plans are developed to deliver the strategies. These stages allow complete clarity at every stage of the planning process. Controls are vital to delivering your plan. Regular review, risk management and contingency planning ensure that your plans are robust. Ensuring your people have the right skill set and the correct people are put into the correct roles is essential, as is understanding in detail the resource that is available. Finally, budgeting and forecasting accuracy ensures that your strategy can be delivered within the financial resources available, so using appropriate models for these helps to ensure that this happens.

Chapter checklist

- The planning process ☐
- The phased approach ☐
- Goals ☐
- Objectives and strategies ☐
- Action plans ☐
- Controls ☐
- People ☐
- Budgeting and forecasting ☐

Further reading

- *On mission and vision:*

  Bowhill, B (2008) *Business Planning and Control*, JW. To understand more about mission and vision and how they apply to your organizational structure, it is worth consulting this guide by Bowhill, which has some useful insight into this area.

PART THREE
Using channel strategy to reach your customers

SEO strategy and organic techniques

08

What we will cover in this chapter

In this chapter we look at search engine optimization (SEO). This includes setting up and operating the channels but with a primary focus on how to integrate it appropriately into your strategy. The key areas covered in this chapter are:

- The SEO triangle
- Researching your SEO strategy
- Technical SEO
- Content and SEO
- Links and penalties
- The changing landscape
- Organizational structure

Chapter goals

By the end of this chapter you should understand SEO in terms of technical concerns, content, and link techniques. You should understand how to research your SEO strategy and how best to structure your team. You should also have an understanding of SEO penalties.

Key terms

Some of the key terms used in this chapter are:

SEO: optimizing your site for the search engine's natural results.

Natural / organic links: links that are not paid for.

Algorithm: the search engine's code used to decide how sites are ranked.

On-page: SEO factors on your website.

Off-page: SEO factors away from your site such as backlinks.

Metadata: code that tells robots about your site.

Robots: the crawlers that work their way across the internet checking content.

Keyword density: the number of repeat keywords on a page.

Tags: pieces of code attached to parts of the page to give signs to robots.

Hierarchy: the structure of your pages on your site.

Site map: a simple display of the entirety of your site.

Alt text: text associated with images to tell robots what the image is about.

Crawl: what robots / crawlers do to index sites.

Index: each search engine has an index of websites that the robots update.

Backlink: a link pointing back to your site from elsewhere.

Anchor text: the text that is visible when clicking on a link.

The SEO triangle

A simple way to remember the key considerations of SEO is to picture a triangle. All activity you focus on and all of the key ranking factors can be driven by the three corners of the triangle. They are Content, Technical SEO

Figure 8.1   The SEO triangle

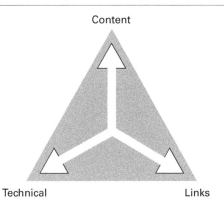

and Links. If your site has compelling, broad, relevant and timely content that is fast to download, easy to navigate, works across all platforms with no errors and a large number of reputable sites link to you because they also think your site is valuable, then your SEO strategy is likely to be on the path to success.

If we consider just a few of the key ranking factors we can see how they fall into these three categories rather neatly:

1	Domain name	Technical
2	Domain history and future purchase status	Technical
3	Title tags and Heading tags on your page	Technical, Content
4	Content length	Content
5	Keyword density	Content
6	Page load speed	Technical
7	Image optimization	Technical
8	Alt tags	Technical, Content
9	Frequency of updates	Content
10	Internal link volume	Links, Technical
11	Main content is visible	Content
12	Quality of incoming links	Links
13	Time spent on site (Dwell time)	Content
14	Local information	Content
15	Appropriate use of meta tags	Content, Technical

There are many more ranking factors and when we look at the categories we find that the value of each seems to be fairly equal, and this is why the triangle is so relevant. Not only are these factors each important individually, but also they often affect each other. The Alt tags we use for our images are technical implementations but are dictated by our content strategy, keeping the technical elements of accessibility in mind. Whilst very few people in the world fully understand the complexity of the search engine algorithms at any one time, there is a great deal of work that is always ongoing to give some known factors and some best guesses. It is important to keep one eye on this changing landscape as your SEO strategy will need to evolve every year.

It is vital to understand a lot of detail in the complex world of SEO. Simply creating a lot of content, building a responsive site and gaining a lot of links is not enough – in fact, if you go about this the wrong way you could move backwards or even be removed from the search engines altogether. We will look at each corner of the triangle in this chapter, and how to ensure you get this right and have a fruitful SEO strategy.

SEO is a digital marketing discipline that divides marketers. It is also arguably the discipline where a little knowledge really is truly dangerous, whilst a lot of knowledge is essential if you want to be able to deliver your digital strategy. This is because as soon as you have a website you are using the SEO channel whether you like it or not. If your knowledge is minimal then you might try to rank number one on a specific key term and this could cost a significant amount of money and time to achieve. However, developing a strategy that improves performance more broadly would be far more efficient and would also reduce the risk of a penalty.

It is worth noting that throughout this chapter, we focus on one search engine: Google. In most markets Google dominates by some margin but of course this is not the case in all. If Google is not your average customer's search engine of choice then please do consider further research. That said, if you focus on the three corners of the SEO triangle your strategy will work across most if not all search engines.

Researching your SEO strategy

One of the biggest mistakes that marketers make when creating an SEO strategy is to start with the following question: 'What keywords should we be focusing on?'

This is not a bad question. In fact it is a very good question, but it should never be the first question asked. The starting point for good SEO, as we have discussed more generally, should be creating the goals and objectives for the SEO channel (for example, will SEO be your primary channel?). Once you have covered those basics the next crucial step is a thorough understanding of your customers.

Persona development

The best way to do this is to create audience personas. Consider the audience types you have and try to create no more than five distinct personas. This approach will help you considerably when you move to the next step of keyword research. Personas and segmentation are discussed in Chapter 1 but it is worth taking a quick look here at how personas apply to SEO. As we have already discussed, personas are a useful way of understanding the personality and potential behaviours of your customers. This becomes useful in SEO (and paid search) in predicting what the user may search for. As we move into the next phase of keyword research (below) this is extremely useful to understand.

If, for example, our persona is a woman in her early thirties with a young family who lives in a large city (let's pick New York for this example), we can start to understand some of her daily needs. We can be fairly certain that she is time poor and will want things now, so she may use words such as 'now' and 'fast'. She is likely to want something in New York as it is often harder to travel any significant distance in cities than in rural areas, so she may do a lot of searching for 'in New York' and other local terms. She will probably search for children's products and may also search for helpful tips on parenthood such as 'how much milk should I give my baby' or 'best things to do with kids at the weekend in New York'. She is still young herself though, and so it is likely she will search for babysitters, restaurants and perhaps bars and clubs. She may well buy her groceries online as it is easier than dragging the children around the local store. All of this insight that we can gain from the persona can steer our initial keyword research and we can then use the below process and evolve the campaign over time.

Keyword research

Having created personas the next job is to start to build your focus keyword list. This might seem daunting, especially as some companies have target keyword lists that run in the thousands. However, if you break down the process into the following steps the process is relatively painless:

- Step 1: create logical segments.
- Step 2: mine your data.
- Step 3: mine secondary data sources.
- Step 4: sense check.

Note that within this section we will use the term 'keyword' as a catch-all for search terms. While some searches are just one keyword, increasingly people use natural language and therefore longer phrases as we will discuss later in the chapter.

Step 1: create logical segments

Most businesses sell a multitude of products or services, some of which might well be quite diverse. So a good starting point is to split your products/services into logical segments. The good news is that if your site hierarchy is logical you have probably already done this.

Then consider each segment in detail. Which are the most valuable to you? How do customer types vary? Which should you prioritize?

Step 2: mine your data

An obvious step is to mine the data you already have. However, even in the digital world we sometimes go backwards and, sadly, in October 2011 Google implemented changes that mean it is now extremely difficult to work out the keywords or phrases that site visitors used to find a particular site. What used to be simple to understand simply by checking your Analytics platform is now very difficult. This is due to Google removing the keywords returned within Google Analytics and instead simply labelling all SEO traffic as 'keyword not provided'. This has been a frustration for many digital marketers as knowledge is a crucial part of building any strategy.

However, this SEO cloud may have a silver lining, as ripping keywords directly from analytics could be a self-fulfilling prophecy, ie your strategy would be too focused on what you currently rank for rather than what you could rank for. That said, it is worth looking at the data you do have. A good starting point is considering the most visited landing pages as a proxy for user intent. In addition, you may have some data from other search engines, or even historic analytics data, which can help add to the keyword set.

But do not just rely on data that is stored in hardware – brainstorming is a great way to quickly start a keyword list. To do this, review each persona and write down the keywords you think they might use. Spend no more than five minutes for each and focus on the simple/more obvious terms. Once completed, remove any duplicates and you will likely have a fairly short list. This is a good thing – these are most likely your 'halo' terms, or in other words the terms that are most commonly used and therefore have the potential to drive a lot of traffic. At this stage though you don't need to worry whether you have all your halo terms – as long as you have a few, the others will come out of the woodwork during the following phases.

Step 3: mine secondary data sources

By this stage you should have established some keywords. The next step is to expand that keyword set. Thankfully there are many third-party tools that can help do this. Rather than offer up a list, simply search 'keyword research tool' or similar for the latest and greatest. Naturally, one of the best is provided by Google itself (as of course it has more data than most), the Google Keyword Planner. To access this, you will need a Google Ads (Google's paid-search advertising platform) account, but you don't need to actually advertise or spend anything to use the tool.

Using the tool is fairly self-explanatory, it acts somewhat like a thesaurus offering similar and related terms and, importantly, gives you an idea of the search volume. You will very quickly find that your keyword list has grown substantially. However, the quality of the data you get out is completely dependent on what you put in, so don't be tempted to skip the previous steps. There are of course other tools: both SEMRush and KeywordTool.io are well-respected alternatives.

Step 4: sense check

So now you have a big list. The temptation at this stage is to begin, but a sense check is needed. A very common mistake is to focus too heavily on the search volume: while it is important (as you don't want to pin your business hopes on a term that gets only 10 searches a month) it is only one factor. It is also important to consider the following:

1 What commercial value might this keyword have? For example 'pound/ euro exchange rate' has large search volume, but if a bank were to rank number one for the term how many current accounts would get opened on the back of it? Not many. The bank might sell some currency but this term is probably not the most commercially critical.

2 What right do I have to compete for this keyword? There are very few examples of David beating Goliath in the more mature online industries.

For example, the keyword 'casino' drives well over 50 per cent of natural search traffic in the online casino market and therefore trying to gain traffic in this industry is difficult without competing for this specific keyword, which is of course very competitive. If you built your site yesterday and have a small marketing budget you are best to point that resource elsewhere. Find a battle you can win and focus your attention there, at least initially.

3 Ask others. Sense check your list with others in the business. Remember: this is the foundation of your SEO strategy so it is worth spending some quality time getting it right. As with any research, the more minds and voices, the more robust the data so don't feel that this is for you and your team only. Use the knowledge you have in the wider business.

Technical SEO

Whilst we will not delve deep into technical SEO, in order to understand it fully you at least need to know what the main technical elements are. This section provides a high-level overview of the main technical considerations; however, it is important to know where your strengths are and to appoint an agency to assist you if you do not have deep knowledge or resource in this area.

The tags that matter

The two most significant 'tags' that warrant attention are title tags and meta description (Figure 8.2). Neither are as scary or inaccessible as they might sound.

Title tags

The title tag is a brief description of the page content and is contained within the HTML. It is visible in search results and used by search engines to interpret site pages. Title tags should be unique, ideally less than 75 characters and have important keywords close to the front. In addition, it is generally good usability practice to include your brand at the front. As the title tag is highly visible to potential site visitors it is of course crucial to make sure it is as compelling as possible.

Figure 8.2 Tags

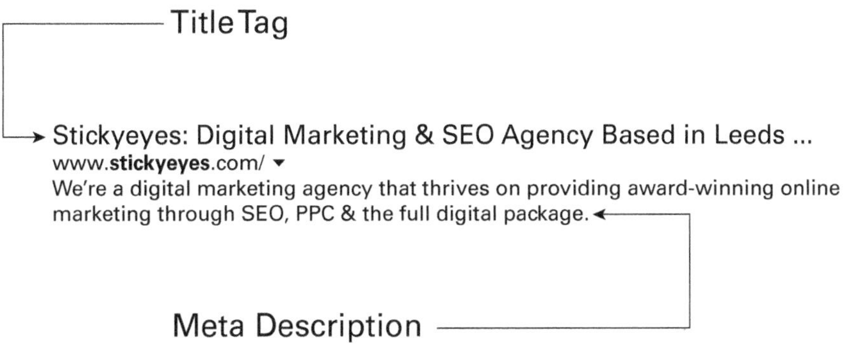

Title Tag

Stickyeyes: Digital Marketing & SEO Agency Based in Leeds ...
www.**stickyeyes**.com/ ▼
We're a digital marketing agency that thrives on providing award-winning online
marketing through SEO, PPC & the full digital package. ◄

Meta Description

Meta description

The meta description is a longer description of the page content and is also displayed within the search engine results if Google feels it is relevant. No more than 160 characters are recommended – and make sure they are unique, relevant (and therefore hopefully include some of your focus keywords) and, most importantly, readable. While the meta description does not appear to influence rankings directly, a well-written one can improve click-through rate, which in turn might help drive a ranking improvement.

Other tags

You should also consider heading tags (H1, H2 etc) in the correct structure to give clear signals to the search engines on the page layout. Tags for content (eg blog topics) can help give further signals on the content. The relative strength of these tags has changed over the years and the increase of natural language search will shift this further but these tags remain important signals for the search engines and users alike.

Site structure

As we are in danger of getting too technical we will not spend too long on this section, but hopefully we can provide enough ammunition to ask some questions of your chosen SEO expert:

- Hierarchy: your navigation flow should be logical. By this we mean that each level of your structure should sit logically below the previous level. For example, a page on your website that promotes ballpoint pens should sit underneath a page on pens, which should in turn sit under a page on stationery so that there is a logical path for a user to follow to effectively filter their way down to their destination. In other words, make sure your hierarchy uses some common sense.

- URL structure: search engines use 'robots' to interpret sites. If your URL looks something like this – **www.mysite.com/categorypage. asp?prodId=1274234** – then you are not helping the robot to work out what your site offers. The ideal is: **www.mysite.com/Stationery/Paper/ A3_Paper/Economy_A3_paper.html**.

- Site maps: create two – one for users and one for search engines. The search-engine-friendly one should be an XML site map file, which can also be submitted through Google's Webmaster Tools (see below).

- Provide alt text for images. In the HTML you can assign 'alt attributes' to help search engines interpret visual content.

- Avoid overusing Flash as it cannot always be read and therefore hinders the discovery process.

- Avoid duplicate content. Note that this means not reusing copy on other pages of your site, as well as 'borrowing' others' content. Google will penalize a site that uses a lot of duplicate content, so it is best avoided. If you cannot avoid duplicate content, do some research on '301 redirects' and the 'rel='canonical' attribute'.

- Search Console: make sure someone in your organization knows how to navigate Search Console (a Google-provided platform). Search Console helps in a number of areas and is quite powerful. It is therefore also quite dangerous in the wrong hands, so proceed with caution. A summary of the main functionality available within Search Console is as follows:

  - Shows crawl errors: this is useful as a site with a lot of errors is unlikely to rank highly.
  - Allows submission of an XML site map.
  - Allows for modification of the robots.txt files (which can be used to remove URLs already crawled by Googlebot).
  - Identifies issues with title and description meta tags.
  - Provides a high-level view of the top searches used to reach your site.
  - Removes unwanted site links that Google may use in results.
  - You receive notifications of quality guideline violations.
  - You can request a site reconsideration following a penalty.

The danger mentioned above arises from the fact that these functions could enable someone to cause serious SEO issues to your site such as deleting your robots.txt file, uploading an incorrect site map or simply not being aware of serious SEO issues with the site.

Content and SEO

SEO is now much more reliant on a good content strategy. The good news is that there is no real need for a 'Content for SEO' section in this book. Chapter 14, looking at content marketing, works for SEO – as good SEO content is intrinsically linked to good content generally. It is, however, worth taking a quick look here at some specifics.

The content you need

Google uses 'robots' to try to interpret your site. It therefore stands to reason that informative content helps. The content that sits on your site that describes your services/products and so on is commonly referred to as functional content. It will never win any awards but it really is a crucial requirement.

A technically sound site with great functional content will go a long way, but to get real traction the site needs a degree of popularity. To help make it you will need a very different type of content: engaging content. This is content that gets attention from your target audience wherever they may be online. It can be fun (but doesn't have to be), it must be relevant and it must be on brand (for a full definition see Chapter 14). Engaging content done well will get published elsewhere and some will cite or link to your site. Each citation/ link acts as a signpost to Google that you are producing something of value that others like and, as such, you might warrant a higher position in the search engines for related terms.

SEO rules for content

The secret to SEO is not to optimize for the search engines but for your audience and this applies to content as much as any other area. If you have done your research right, you should find that you are naturally using very relevant keywords and the content you create should fly. Second, it is important to keep producing. Whilst online content will not disappear unless you delete it, Google does like to see fresh content, so ensuring an ongoing production of content is important. Finally, but perhaps most critically, you should make sure your site has a home for content. The great engaging content you produce should live on your site so that Google knows the origin and so that other sites have a reason to link back to you. This may seem obvious but, with the growth of social media, many companies have concentrated on producing content for YouTube and Twitter at the expense of the content on their own site and this can harm SEO performance. Having said that, Google does like YouTube content so consider this in your social media strategy.

Links and penalties

A link strategy is the third corner of the SEO triangle. This is the one where you need to be very careful. Google does not like websites that have a deliberate goal of acquiring links. Google firmly believes, and rightly so, that if your site is good it will attract links and this is why Google offers this value.

Therefore, a link strategy is not about buying links (this is Black Hat SEO and must be avoided), nor is it about link swaps or any other means of unnaturally trying to obtain links into your site. It is also not about obtaining as many links as possible as quickly as possible. A significant volume of links from poor sources actually moves you backwards not forwards. A fast growth in links is a definite sign to Google that something unnatural is happening that warrants investigation.

Instead, your link strategy should be about creating great content on- and off-site that encourages links. This can be through PR, Outreach or simply through your content strategy. It can include great advice or tools. We will cover this in Chapter 14 but there are considerations you need to understand to ensure you get this right, monitor it and avoid the dreaded penalty.

Very few marketers have not heard about Google penalties. However, very few actually understand what they really are.

There are two types of Google penalty: 1) algorithmic; 2) manual. But rather than explain the intricacies of each it is perhaps better to briefly cover how to avoid a penalty in the first place. While not exhaustive, the list below will go a long way to keeping you on the right side of Google:

- Check your backlink profile. You will need some SEO expertise to do this, but in short you need to look for the quantity of low-quality/spammy links you have. If the ratio is high then remedial action may be needed (see below).

- Take remedial action, if needed. If you have a high proportion of links that are clearly low quality then you are advised to remove them. Of course this is not easy as it involves trying to contact webmasters who are unlikely to be that responsive. However, this is the preferred route. A last resort is to use Google's 'Disavow' process. Available through Webmaster Tools the disavow tool allows you to inform Google that you no longer want association with the site links uploaded. However, this is a very powerful and therefore dangerous tool and it would be remiss of me to try to advise on how to use it in one paragraph. In short, get expert help if you think you may need remedial action.

- Do not buy links. The significant majority of your links should be earned. Of course business is business and there may be a place for some high-quality paid placements but they should be the exception rather than the rule. There is a history of a high volume of poor-quality links being bought, when it was volume that counted. This is no longer the case and so paying someone to attain thousands of links for you will be quickly visible to Google, will add almost no value to your SEO and will give you a very high risk of a penalty.

- Check for duplicate content. If you reuse your own content or, worst case, reuse others' content, you may trigger a penalty.

- Ensure that your site is largely original content (not a mash-up of auto-generated content or adverts).

- Ensure that you do not have too many pages with thin or no content (ie few words that add little value).

- When you actively seek out links (ie coverage for the great compelling content you have crafted) make sure you are seeking them from related/relevant sites.

- Avoid unnatural anchor text (anchor text is visible text in a link, for example: cheapest sun tan lotion) – although if you are not buying links this really should not be a problem as most naturally created links will be your brand name.

- If you accept user-generated content, for example reviews, ensure that you are not vulnerable to exploitation by using the nofollow attribute. This ensures that Google will not use your link for SEO purposes and therefore will not punish you.

The changing landscape

SEO is an ever-changing landscape. Techniques that would have been the core focus in the early 21st century could now result in penalties. There are some vitally important changes in the landscape that you need to be aware of as you build your strategy.

The SEO world has increasingly moved away from a focus on keywords in recent years. Keywords still have relevance as you need to be findable on the relevant topics, but focusing on this very narrow view is no longer relevant. There are many reasons for this but one key change in society is the move from typed words to spoken phrases. This is driven by a significant increase in technology such as Siri from Apple, Alexa from Amazon and Google's Assistant. It is becoming more common, especially amongst younger generations, to ask questions rather than type keywords.

Where in 2005 we might have searched for 'cheap flights London Paris', natural language such as 'What is the cheapest flight from London to Paris next week' is now growing in use at quite some pace. This means that our content, which may have historically been optimized for keyword search, may become less effective. Natural language recognition is becoming increasingly important including areas such as artificial intelligence. One reason this is so vital is that the keyword approach is basic and struggles, for example, to differentiate between words that are spelled the same but have different meanings. For example, if we consider the verb to lead someone and the metal, lead. 'Please can you lead me home' and 'Is there lead in my home' are very different queries but could both be searched for through the keywords 'lead home'. How would the search engine know what to deliver as your results? It wouldn't.

Alongside this change there has also been a growth in search that requires AI due to improved focus and investment in AI technology. Image search technology has made very real progress in recent years and so considering a development of an image SEO strategy or at least considering SEO when choosing images for your site will become increasingly important. There will be a greater focus on intent as AI begins to use behavioural data to understand what users are doing and make intelligent assumptions about their intent. Consider your content strategy here.

Another consideration for SEO is taking advantage of the SERP (search engine results pages) real estate. Using structured data to answer queries directly, provide recipes or other elements that Google can display directly at the top of its results gives you an advantage right at the point of search, not having to rely on the visitor clicking through to your site. Understanding more about structured data is something you should ensure you and your technical team do to fully take advantage of this.

Finally, we should discuss mobile. There has been a considerable shift towards mobile internet use in recent years and in fact 2017 was the first year that mobile searches overtook desktop searches. Google has moved its algorithms in line with this by first penalizing sites that are not mobile optimized and more recently beginning to use the mobile sites as the primary source of data over the desktop sites. It is crucial now more than ever that you embrace this focus. You must, however, keep your audience in mind. A small number of industries, especially those in the B2B space, will primarily have visitors who are using desktop machines during office hours and so you cannot neglect the desktop in favour of the mobile. The key is to ensure all channels are optimized rather than seeing mobile as secondary.

Organizational structure and SEO

One of the surprisingly important areas of SEO and one that is often overlooked or not implemented, due to its complexity, is organizational structure. To ensure that your SEO strategy can be fully implemented it needs buy-in and ownership from the top down. If your board of directors have the level of understanding that this section offers then you will likely be in a good place – the reason being that to do everything discussed requires multiple departments working very closely together.

CASE STUDY   MoneySupermarket

Background

The UK financial services comparison site MoneySupermarket.com (MSM) is a company that dominates most of the high-volume terms in their market. Very early on, they understood that organizational structure was key to successful SEO.

Strategy

Extracts from an interview with Ben McKay, who was then Head of Organic Performance, explains how they achieved this success:

We have dissolved the SEO and social media teams in their traditional form, and remoulded them to be more consumer value and campaign centric – the team is now called Organic Performance. This means that the energy and talent of a wide variety of digital marketing professionals is integrated under shared KPIs... Where MSM has been most successful (from its core employees to its board) is by being very ambitious and progressive in removing organizational barriers, and thus helping consumers save money. (McKay in Devenish, 2012)

By developing a strategy that brought content, social media and SEO into one organic team the channels have been able to work much better together.

Results

This organizational change has resulted in MSM becoming perhaps the major player in the financial services space on SEO. As a result, MSM are now returned in results across an extremely wide range of topics and questions as well as having this content distributed through their social channels to a wider audience. For example, if I google 'car insurance quotes' and 'cheap car insurance' in the UK today – two high-volume terms – MSM are top on both. If I search for 'MoneySupermarket' I see 693,000 results, which is 200,000 and 300,000 ahead of their nearest competitors respectively. The numbers speak for themselves.

This has led to their dominance and is one of the major contributing factors to their success whilst their competitors have struggled in the SEO space. This is particularly important in an industry where the above-the-line marketing costs are very high amongst the major four players and a point of marketing differentiation such as this can bring overall acquisition costs down and volumes up.

Key lessons

The key learning for your strategy here is that:

- It is not just good techniques that are important, but also enabling these techniques to strengthen through better integration.

- By pulling together the teams that directly influence the result you can significantly improve performance.

- SEO, social and content are great examples of where you must align your goals and communicate highly effectively.

So, in short, SEO is perhaps the most wide-reaching digital channel and, as such, to get it right you need to consider the structure of your entire organization.

Summary

In this chapter we have examined SEO and how it applies to your digital marketing strategy. We have looked at how to research your strategy and build an effective and relevant plan keeping the SEO triangle in mind. We have also touched briefly on some technical elements, although we avoided going into detail here as this is not a technical manual (please see 'Further reading' for recommendations for additional study). We considered how content affects SEO and we will look at this again in Chapter 14. Finally we looked at link strategy and the danger that penalties represent before looking at the changing landscape and reviewing your organizational structure in relation to SEO.

One key take-away from this chapter is a point I have made time and time again throughout my time in digital marketing. When we think of our SEO strategy we do not optimize for Google, Bing or any other search engine. We optimize for the consumer. The search engines are ultimately trying to do the same thing and so if we set our focus here we can worry less about changing algorithms and user behaviours as we will already be one step ahead of both.

In this next chapter we look at paid search – the sister of SEO.

Chapter checklist

- The SEO triangle ☐
- Researching your SEO strategy ☐
- Technical SEO ☐
- Content and SEO ☐
- Links and penalties ☐
- The changing landscape ☐
- Organizational structure ☐

Further reading

- *On SEO techniques*:

  Williams, A (2015) *SEO 2016 & Beyond*, CreateSpace. This includes detailed analysis on current techniques and an SEO checklist as a tool for preparing your SEO strategy as part of your broader digital strategy.

- *On SEO tips*:

  Cameron-Kitchen, T and Exposure Ninja (2018) *How to Get to the Top of Google*, independently published

  Coombe, W (2017) *3 Months to No 1*, independently published

  McDonald, J (2018) *SEO Fitness Workbook*, CreateSpace Independent Publishing Platform

  O'Dwyer, S (2015) *500 SEO Tips*, CreateSpace. This offers a practical look at some simple actions that can be taken to maximize your strategy.

- *On technical SEO*:

  Adodra, S (2014) *SEO Expert Strategies*, CreateSpace. To gain a deeper understanding I would recommend reading this, which looks at SEO in a broader sense than purely technical SEO but it does give clear guidance for beginners and intermediates alike, which you may find helpful alongside this book.

References

Devenish, A (2012) [accessed 1 November 2015] #exclusive MoneySupermarket: We Expect to Save Consumers £1bn in 2012 [Online] https://anthonydevenish. wordpress.com/2012/10/02/exclusive-moneysupermarket-we-expect-to-save-consumers-1bn-in-2012/

An implementation guide is available at:
www.koganpage.com/DigitalMarketingStrategy/2

Building and optimizing a winning paid search strategy

09

What we will cover in this chapter

In this chapter we look at paid search, including a background on the channel and how to refer to it, how to set up campaigns and measure and optimize your results, as well as advanced techniques and ongoing management. The key areas covered in this chapter are:

- An introduction to paid search
- Setting up a campaign
- Measurement and optimization
- Advanced paid search
- Managing paid search campaigns – humans versus robots

Chapter goals

By the end of this chapter you should understand why and when to use paid search, how to set up a campaign that is relevant to your business, how to optimize and manage the campaign and have a perspective on the advanced techniques used in order to differentiate your organization.

Key terms

Some of the key terms used in this chapter are:

PPC: 'pay per click', a term often used instead of paid search.

SEM: 'search engine marketing' – usually refers to paid search.

Bid: an auction-style bid price for your advert's ranking.

Keyword: the word people use to search.

CPC: 'cost per click' – the amount paid for every click on your ad.

Ad copy: the words that make up your ad.

Match type: the way that your keyword is matched to the phrase searched for.

Quality score: a formula that Google uses to determine your ad quality.

Publisher: a site on a network that shows ads from other organizations.

Search network: a network of sites that provide the search results.

Metrics: a measurement (see below for specific metrics).

Day parting: tailoring your campaign to days and times.

Site link: a link to a part of your website; this is one of the extension options.

Ad extension: these are extra functions you can add to your campaign.

An introduction to paid search

Paid search is a deceptively complex channel and one that, like many other marketing channels on and offline, takes many years to understand in detail. There are two primary reasons for this. First, paid search has more jargon and acronyms than any other form of digital marketing and so the above key terms may be useful to refer to throughout this chapter. This is ironic, considering that good marketing copywriting involves avoiding exactly this type of situation but, irony aside, it is essential to understand the language of the channel to be able to communicate your strategy effectively. Second, it is remarkably easy to begin paid search activity and to gain an understanding of the very basics but, unfortunately, very difficult to get it right and to understand the tremendous number of options and variables.

As a result, it is important that within this section we start by providing an overview of the basics of paid search (and at the same time tackle the jargon) then quickly move to measurement (as good measurement criteria reduces the risk of getting it wrong). We will of course look at measurement more generally later in the book, but as measurement in paid search is unique and crucial to success it is key that we address it here also. We then cover some of the more advanced paid search techniques and discuss whether humans or robots are best suited to managing paid search. Finally we cover how paid search can work in harmony with SEO, how the boundaries between paid search and display are blurring, and demonstrate how paid search can bring substantial rewards if done correctly.

The main paid search platform is of course Google and therefore this section focuses on the functionality provided by them. However, the others (Microsoft Bing, Yahoo, etc) follow a very similar approach.

The basics of paid search

Paid search can be quite simply defined: it is the process of bidding for potential clicks on an advert you create that is displayed within the search results pages of most search engines. However, given that this is the land of jargon, let's get to the point: it is the ads you see at the top, bottom and side of the search results page. Unlike traditional advertising, paid search is 'bought' via an auction model. For a given keyword or phrase an advertiser can place a maximum bid; the higher the bid, the higher the likelihood that the advert will be displayed in the top positions. However, one of the big attractions of paid search advertising is that the advertiser only pays each time the advert is clicked, not displayed.

This is obviously highly compelling and is perhaps the main reason why paid search has been adopted by one-man bands, multinationals and every company in-between.

What do we call the channel?

Confusingly the industry has seen fit to use different terms to describe the same thing, so let's start by clarifying this. Paid search can also be referred to as:

- PPC, or pay per click: quite a logical name, given that it very accurately describes the basic mechanics of paid search – ie you pay every time someone clicks on your ad. However, some other channels, such as affiliate and display, can use this payment method and so it can be confusing.

- SEM, or search engine marketing: SEM was once used as an umbrella term to encompass both search engine optimization and paid search, albeit mainly in the United States. Somewhat oddly the industry, again though mainly in the United States, has adopted the SEM acronym to refer solely to paid search, therefore creating a split between SEO and SEM.

- Biddable media: a newer term that covers any media you can bid on to buy. So paid search sits under biddable media.

Of all of these terms paid search is the clearest and most accurate so that is the one we use here.

Setting up a campaign

As noted above, setting up a paid search campaign is incredibly easy. However, many businesses will see this as an easy entry to digital marketing but it is important before starting to consider this: paid search can drain marketing spend very quickly and an ill-considered campaign may very well have a negative return. So this section is designed to cover the basics of getting a strategic paid search campaign set up. As per the approaches we have been discussing so far, it starts with defining your objectives and understanding your audience. We will assume that you have looked at this as part of your initial strategic planning.

Keyword research

Having set your objective and identified your audience, the next step is keyword research. In Chapter 8 there is a suggested process for this and it applies just as well to paid search. Perhaps unsurprisingly, Google's own Keyword Planner (available as part of the Google Ads platform) is a great tool for building out keywords. However, as with SEO, you need to pick your battles. If your budget is $500 a month, then the highly popular volume-driving or 'halo' terms are not within your budget and instead you should focus on niche or longer tail keywords that you are more likely to win the battle on. To put this into context, some of the most expensive keywords have average cost per clicks well above $50 and so you can see how quickly your budget can be depleted if your keyword research and planning is not conducted thoroughly.

CASE STUDY   Watchfinder

Background

Watchfinder improved its retargeting ads with audience granularity from Google Analytics. Watchfinder is the UK's largest online watch dealer and had the focus you would expect of a major retailer: to increase sales.

Strategy

Watchfinder used its visitor data to create 20 specific audience lists that showed intent, but did not go through to a final purchase. These lists enabled the company to retarget those individuals with specific advertising.

It then defined these audiences by funnel stage, location, on-site behaviour, and internet service provider (ISP). This enabled the company to understand how mature the customers were in their purchase journey (funnel stage), what signals their behaviours indicated and local information.

The company also used the opportunity, as with any good marketing campaign, to run creative split tests to understand what was most effective in this channel.

Results

In just six months, Watchfinder achieved an ROI (return on investment) of 1,300 per cent. Average order value increased by 13 per cent and it achieved CPAs that were 34 per cent cheaper than the non-brand search campaigns. It is quite clear that this highly effective targeting through paid search platforms to specific target sets using advanced data proved very effective.

Key lessons

Inside your Google Analytics account, you can build audiences in many different ways with the data available there. You can in fact create up to 2,000 different audiences for remarketing. You can then target these audiences by importing them into Google Ads and pairing with your specific retargeting ads.

This example is indicative of where paid search continues to move as digital targeting is increasingly focused on audiences and individuals rather than keywords.

Campaigns and ad groups

Google and thousands of other sources provide plenty of guidance on how to structure a paid search account. In short, you will have one or more campaigns. A campaign defines your overall budget settings and determines where your ads appear (both in terms of geography and ad networks).

If you are setting up the paid search campaign for an auto dealership, for example, you might have one campaign for cars and a separate campaign for bikes. Within a campaign you should have a number of ad groups. Think of ad groups as logical storage buckets. You would not throw all your stock into one big bucket so don't do the same with your ads. Each ad group should contain similar keywords/phrases and therefore similar products. So you might in the cars campaign have an ad group for each individual type of car you sell.

For example:

- Campaign one – cars:
  - ad group one: Fords;
  - ad group two: Toyotas.
- Campaign two – bikes:
  - ad group one: Harley Davidsons;
  - ad group two: Triumphs.

Think strategically

The keywords are the start of the user journey. This is what your user is specifically looking for. Users are individuals and want to be treated as such, therefore try to ensure that your journey is as unique as it can be. You can best achieve this by aligning your journeys to the user needs and this means creating a very large and organized set of keywords. Spending the time building out your keywords can be the difference between success and failure.

Ad copy

Paid search ad copy is an art form as you have a limited number of characters (140 including the display URL and just 70 characters for double-width languages such as Chinese, Japanese and Korean) to create something that is highly relevant and compelling. The good news is there is no limit to the number of ads you can create, so try out a few and refine as you go.

Think strategically

Following on from the section above, at this stage it is vital that your ad copy matches to the search term as closely as possible.

Ad copy

A manufacturer of socks would have a wide range of socks available, including smart socks, sports socks, casual socks and perhaps even tights. Differentiating these is vital in your ad copy to ensure maximum relevance to the user. Imagine if a user searches for 'white sports socks' and receives the following three ads in the results from three separate companies:

- Buy white socks today.
- White sports socks.
- Get cheap socks here.

Option two is returned based on the campaign set-up and is an exact match to the keyword, as the account has been built into a logical structure with deep customization to keyword type. This option is clearly a perfect match to what the user is looking for and will receive an increased level of clicks versus other ads that are returned in the same position. This in turn means that this company can bid lower in the knowledge that being returned in position two or three is fine as the relevance of their ad will ensure that they still receive the most clicks.

Match types

Once you have created your ads and defined your keyword list you need to consider match types for each keyword. In short, you can tell Google whether you want your ads to appear for just the exact keyword/phrase entered or widen it out with a number of parameters – the widest being a 'broad match', which will show your ads for the keywords/phrases requested and any related keywords. Broad matching will generate the most traffic, but by its very nature it will be less targeted and therefore performance may not be as good. In addition, broad match can very quickly get expensive. Typically most paid search experts only use broad match for an initial period of exploration to help find the keywords/phrases that convert the best.

Table 9.1   Match types

Match Type	s=Symbol	Keywords for this Match Type	Your Ads Will Show on the Following Searches	Example Searches
Broad match		white socks	These words, similar words and misspelt words	buy socks
Broad match modifier	+	+white +socks	Containing these words in other orders	socks that are white
Phrase match	" "	"white socks"	This phrase and very similar ones	cheap white socks
Exact match	[ ]	[white socks]	The exact phrase and ones that are very close	white socks
Negative match	-	-white	Anything that excludes this word	black socks

A description of the various match types, courtesy of Google, has been included in Table 9.1. The final modifier in Table 9.1, 'negative match', is worthy of more detailed discussion as it can be very powerful. A detailed review of your ad campaign will likely show some keywords/phrases that are not a good match to the products/services you sell. If this is the case you will potentially be displaying irrelevant ads, which will affect your click-through rate (and in turn your cost per click as quality score (see below) may be affected). Removing these erroneous keywords/phrases using negative keywords is therefore highly recommended.

Quality score

Quality score is a Google metric and is a measure of the quality of the ad. The higher the quality score, the higher your position potential. If, for example, two advertisers both have a maximum bid of $10 but one has a higher quality score, the one with the higher quality score will likely be given the higher position. Indeed, even if the maximum bid for the company with the higher quality score was $9 they may still get the higher position. Why? Because

Google wants to present ads that people will find relevant and click on. The quality score algorithm is not publicly available but some of the factors that contribute to a higher score are, including how long you have been advertising, your click-through rates (CTRs) and your ad relevancy.

Search networks

Before you push your new paid search campaign live, be wary of checking the option to 'also display ads on our search network' (or similar). Checking this allows the search engine to display your ads on third-party sites that have signed up to their ad programme as a publisher. You will have very little control of where your ads are displayed and invariably performance is much lower (albeit so is the cost). The positive is that your reach is enhanced.

When looking at paid search most of us will start with the Google product, Google Ads.

Measurement and optimization

As we discuss later in the book, before looking into measurement it is essential to revisit your objectives, as this will help shape the measurement criteria used. For example, if your goal is to maximize market share then acquisition metrics should not be your number one priority.

Traffic metrics

- Impression: each time your ad is displayed an impression is made. So 10 impressions = 10 views – or, more precisely, 10 'renders', as of course there is no guarantee that the user actually looks at it.
- Click: (a no-brainer) a click is a user interacting with the ad by clicking on it. The end result is a visit to your site.
- Click-through rate (CTR): usually abbreviated to CTR, this is the ratio of the number of clicks to the number of impressions (clicks/impressions). CTRs are influenced by ad position, ad copy and brand recognition.
- Cost per click (CPC): CPC is the average amount paid for a click. Of course this will fluctuate based on maximum bid levels and competitive pressure.
- Average position: the average position where your ad appears on the page (the very top of the page being first position). Bear in mind that ad positions do fluctuate even if you are the highest bidder. Ad position is

heavily influenced by your bid level but it is also influenced by quality score (see below).

- Impression share: a measure of how much of the available impressions you have captured, the maximum being position one for 100 per cent of the time.
- Quality score (QS): while not technically a traffic metric, quality score still needs close consideration as it has a direct relationship to ad position and therefore traffic potential.

Conversion metrics

- Revenue generated: simply the value of the sales made. While interesting, it is margin that really counts.
- Margin generated: margin, or gross profit, gives a more accurate view of the profitability of paid search campaigns.
- Orders: the raw number of orders made.
- Leads: for some, typically B2B or companies selling high-value products, leads are the ultimate goal. Leads might be, for example, e-mail sign-up, application completion or request for brochures.
- Conversion rate: conversion rate is the ratio of orders/leads to the number of clicks. It is as much a measure of your site's ability to convert traffic as the ad itself.
- Average order value (AOV): AOV speaks for itself and is an important metric to drill down on. Look for patterns over time and also differences in AOV for different ad groups. If one ad group has particularly low or high AOV, question why. It may be down to low/high product cost/margin but also may reflect particularly good or bad ad copy or bidding strategy.

Efficiency metrics

- Return on investment (ROI): the most common measure. While this can be a revenue measure (revenue derived/ad cost) it is better to consider profitability and use margin/ad cost.
- Cost per lead/order (CPL/CPO): given that a lead may not bear commercial fruit for some time (and indeed the end transaction might be difficult to tie back if it is made offline) CPL is a good measure of performance for advertisers not expecting direct sales.

- Lifetime value (LTV): lifetime value is an estimate of the potential value that each new customer driven will generate. While it takes some number crunching, this is a very worthwhile process. It is too easy to consider a paid search campaign a failure if the ROI does not stack up; LTV analysis is the only real way to assess whether paid search truly makes sense or not.

Test, learn, refine, test...

Having defined what you will measure, and how, the next step is to put in place a process of continuous improvement. Paid search is simple to get into and therefore it is not surprising that for most sectors the level of competition is high. Therefore an account that is working well today might start failing tomorrow if you do not put in place a process of continuous improvement.

Advanced paid search

Below I have outlined some of the more advanced paid search considerations.

Day parting

Day parting, or custom ad scheduling, allows you to control the days of the week and times of day that you want your ads to display, and also adjust the maximum bid levels based on these parameters.

Site link extensions

Site links allow you to present alternative links within your ad. In the example shown in Figure 9.1, the consumer review publication *Which?* uses site links on the ad that displays for the terms 'laptop reviews' in order to present other related links.

Star ratings

The eagle eyed will notice that the *Which?* ad in Figure 9.1 also has a star rating. These ratings are in fact fully automated. However, in order to show, your business needs to hit certain criteria: 1) at least 30 reviews within the last 12 months; 2) an average rating of 3.5 or higher (so you will never show a poor star rating).

Figure 9.1   Site links

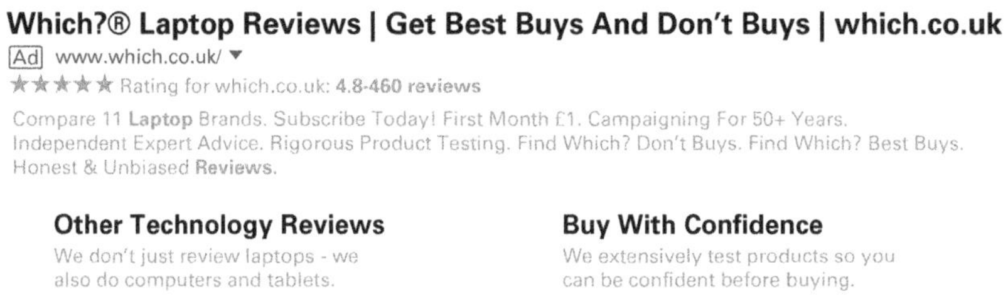

Which?® Laptop Reviews | Get Best Buys And Don't Buys | which.co.uk
[Ad] www.which.co.uk/ ▼
★★★★★ Rating for which.co.uk: 4.8-460 reviews
Compare 11 **Laptop** Brands. Subscribe Today! First Month £1. Campaigning For 50+ Years.
Independent Expert Advice. Rigorous Product Testing. Find Which? Don't Buys. Find Which? Best Buys.
Honest & Unbiased **Reviews**.

Other Technology Reviews   **Buy With Confidence**
We don't just review laptops - we   We extensively test products so you
also do computers and tablets.   can be confident before buying.

The rating received is an aggregate from a number of sources, both Google (such as Google Certified Shops) and third-party review sites (Google lists over 30 and they include Bazaarvoice, Bizrate, Feefo, Reevoo and Trustpilot).

Click to call

If you have the ability to take orders over the phone then adding your phone number to an ad is advised as it will drive up conversions. In most sophisticated mobiles a click-to-call button will be displayed.

Location extensions

Google is increasingly focused on providing hyper local results. The growth of mobile browsing has made this easier as location is straightforward to calculate. In addition, mobile browsers are more likely to be looking for a local solution. So if your business has physical stores, location extensions are very powerful as they allow the display of your business address, phone number and a map. On mobile devices, a link with directions to your business can be included. The starting point for displaying location information is the 'Google My Business' service, which will also help you to appear in Google Maps and organic listings.

CASE STUDY   Deliveroo

Background

Deliveroo were operating in the UK alone, but had big plans for international growth. They now operate in the UK, France, Germany, the Netherlands, Hong

Kong, Singapore, Australia, Ireland, Italy, Belgium, Spain and the UAE. Paid search needed to play a key part in expanding this presence.

Strategy

Deliveroo appointed Brainlabs as their paid search agency and the agency knew immediately that success relied on automation and the use of both Google Ads scripts and API. The account was therefore built in a single keyword ad group (SKAG) structure. Such a structure allows for the greatest control over ads and the agency could therefore ensure that the most relevant ads were showing for each keyword within the account, which isn't possible when ad groups contain multiple keywords. Brainlabs uses a proprietary automated campaign builder tool to reduce the time and work involved in building such a detailed account. This tool also enabled Brainlabs to quickly pull in new restaurants and locations when they were added.

Due to the local nature of the business Brainlabs also built separate campaigns for each restaurant with geographical targeting within a two-mile radius of the address. The tool also checked the restaurants against Deliveroo's coverage and automatically paused any campaigns that were no longer in Deliveroo's network.

Results

Over 17,000 campaigns were built in six languages and multiple cities in 12 countries. Growth of the search activity has been high and this supports the continued growth of Deliveroo in close to real time all around the world.

Key lessons

By innovating through proprietary platforms, working with highly experienced agencies and using smart account set-ups you can produce detailed, highly effective and low maintenance strategies for your paid search activity.

Product list ads (Google Shopping)

Product list ads (often abbreviated to PLAs) are Google's way of shortcutting customers directly to a product. They are increasingly prominent in the search results, which is a reflection of their power to convert customers (Figure 9.2).

PLAs are controlled via a shopping campaign and require your product inventory to be submitted to Google Merchant Centre. What may seem on

Figure 9.2   Product list ads

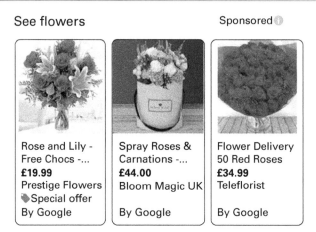

See flowers   Sponsored ⓘ

| Rose and Lily -
Free Chocs -...
£19.99
Prestige Flowers
◆Special offer
By Google | Spray Roses &
Carnations -...
£44.00
Bloom Magic UK
By Google | Flower Delivery
50 Red Roses
£34.99
Teleflorist
By Google |

the face of it to be quite complex is in fact relatively straightforward, and if you are retailing low- to mid-cost products, it is highly recommended.

Competitive intelligence

While the various enhanced options will help you to hone your campaign it is important to remember that paid search ads are an auction. In other words, it is you versus your competitors. It is therefore crucial to ensure that you are tracking what your competitors are doing in order to make sure that you can stay one step ahead. This can be as simple as simply viewing the ads that appear when you google your key terms. However, if you depend heavily on Google Ads and/or have a large budget then you will want to consider a tool that tracks ads for you. Examples are Market Defender, AdGooroo and AdThena.

These products allow you to analyse competitive data at your leisure and typically include:

- competitive ad copy;
- day parting strategy;
- split testing evidence.

As well as competitive intelligence such tools can also be used to identify brand hijacking. Brand hijacking is typically performed by an affiliate or a company selling fake goods. In short, they bid on your brand name and pass off as being your business. If you are a large advertiser, this reason alone is enough to warrant investing in an ad tracking solution.

Managing paid search campaigns – humans versus robots

All small to medium-sized enterprises (SMEs) will manage their paid search campaigns either internally or via an agency and ultimately humans will be doing all the work. However, some larger organizations use automated bidding systems. Whether this is the right route for you will depend on a number of factors but the most common reasons for considering an automated tool are:

- Tens or hundreds of thousands of products. It is unrealistic to expect humans to be able to manage a large quantity of products. Especially so when you consider stock issues and fluctuating pricing.

- Very large budget. If your monthly ad spend is measured in millions then at least some form of automation starts to make sense.

- Your main goal is hyper efficiency. If you want to drive your cost per click as low as possible then machines are generally better (however, this can result in a much smaller share of voice-over time if not managed well).

In summary, the best combination is usually one of the following: 1) humans; 2) humans who very actively manage automated systems.

Summary

In this chapter we looked at what paid search is and how it can be integrated into your strategy. We examined the complexities of setting up a campaign and the extent of the jargon and variables that need to be understood in order to be able to optimize your campaign. We looked at the methods of measuring and optimizing your results as well as ensuring that you test and learn constantly. We examined advanced techniques and how to manage your campaign on an ongoing basis. There is a great deal of complexity in this channel and so working with an expert is essential until you are capable of running the channel yourself. It should be noted that, if you are running a large digital campaign, you may never get to the level of expertise on this channel that is necessary to run it yourself and so working with the right agency, as we have discussed, is vital.

Chapter checklist

- An introduction to paid search ☐
- Setting up a campaign ☐
- Measurement and optimization ☐
- Advanced paid search ☐
- Managing paid search campaigns – humans versus robots ☐

Further reading

- *On Adwords (Google Ads)*:

  Gray, N (2018) *Mastering Google Adwords 2018: Step-by-step instructions for advertising your business*, CreateSpace Independent Publishing Platform

  Rabazinski, C (2015) *Adwords for Beginners*, CreateSpace

- *On advanced paid search*:

  Geddes, B (2014) *Advanced Google Adwords*, Sybex

- *On SEM in Asia*:

  Yamagishi, R (2013) *Digital Marketing in Asia*, Bowker

An implementation guide is available at:
www.koganpage.com/DigitalMarketingStrategy/2

Display advertising and programmatic targeting

10

What we will cover in this chapter

In this chapter we look at display advertising, with a specific focus on programmatic display, which has quickly become the de facto buying mechanism for the channel. Display was one of the first forms of online marketing and has changed significantly over time. The key areas covered in this chapter are:

- Programmatic advertising
- Types and formats of display advertising
- Key technology in ad delivery
- Types of display campaign
- Planning and targeting programmatic campaigns
- Display campaign measurement

Chapter goals

By the end of this chapter you should understand the principles and how this relates to planning, targeting and managing a campaign. You should also understand measurement and the key terms used in the channel. This will help you to understand whether the channel is appropriate for you and, if so, how to fit it into your strategy.

Key terms

Some of the key terms used in this chapter are:

CPM: a cost-per-thousand price (CPM = 'Cost Per Mille').

Impression: one instance of when an advert is shown to a user.

Creative assets: the creative files used to create the ad that users see.

Ad server: hosting tool for creative assets, with logic to control delivery to users and segment audiences. Ad servers track campaign delivery and results.

Programmatic: a more automated method of targeting and buying ad impressions. Typically buying happens in real-time and pricing is usually determined by an auction.

Direct to site: traditional bookings where the price and volume are negotiated directly with a publisher before the campaign starts.

Retargeting: targeting users based on previous actions they have performed on a site. This is most commonly used to message people who have visited a site but not completed a purchase. The creative often consists of products a user has browsed.

Demand Side Platform (DSP): a buying tool that executes programmatic media buys. Targeting, pacing, budgeting and bespoke programmatic inventory deals (aka PMPs) are handled in DSPs. This technology 'listens' to auctions of ad impressions and submits bids based on the targeting criteria, the campaign performance and goals.

Supply Side Platform (SSP): the sell-side equivalent of a DSP. Publishers use this to hold auctions for their ad impressions.

Private Market Place (PMP): a deal with a publisher, sales house, or ad network but executed through the programmatic infrastructure.

NOTE There are many more terms used in display advertising and I have tried to define these throughout the chapter.

Display advertising has many different guises. It is generally accepted that display covers ads shown on all devices, including connected TVs and streaming devices. Display ads also take many formats. These range from static imagery, animated imagery, rich media (ads that interact with the user or the environment they are shown in), native ads, video and audio. Indeed, these definitions have changed over time, as digital advertising has evolved. Virtually all paid social advertising is display, but the unique traits of the sites they are served on, and the differences in the workflow, often warrant a separate team to execute.

The effectiveness of programmatic buying can be evidenced by what percentage of display media is now transacted that way and what is predicted for the next few years as can be seen from Table 10.1.

Table 10.1 Total digital display ad spending

	2016	2017	2018	2019	2020
UK – % of total digital display ad spending	61.00%	72.90%	79.00%	82.40%	84.50%
US – % of total digital display ad spending	73.00%	79.30%	82.50%	84.80%	86.20%

SOURCE eMarketer, March 2018

Programmatic advertising

Programmatic media buying and its subset, real-time bidding (RTB), have experienced enormous growth for many reasons but the key aspects compared to buying display directly from publishers or intermediaries, such as ad networks, are:

- More targeting options across multiple sites, apps and screens.
- Easier activation or suppression of first party data. If campaigns are executed in-house there is better control of first-party data and more manageable data and privacy compliance (eg GDPR).
- More control of campaign execution and more precision.
- Control ad sequencing and frequency across sites and screens.
- Transparency into delivery and pricing when compared to buying via ad networks.
- Easier workflow for buying across multiple sites.
- Accessibility to display media is easier for smaller companies.

Programmatic allows buyers to assess every single ad impression as it becomes available (as a user's device is loading a web page or app) and make a decision as to whether this particular ad impression will make a positive contribution to the campaign as a whole. This can be decided based on factors that pertain to the environment the ad is in and the person behind the screen. The advertiser can therefore assess the following factors to determine whether the opportunity is relevant:

- the website or app;
- the specific web page and its content;
- the user's interests and intent;
- the user's demography;
- the location and language of the person looking at it;
- the time of the day, or day of the week;
- the computer or mobile operating system (OS) or type of device it is being viewed on;
- the propensity for that advert to be classed as 'in view' based on previous viewability rate of that ad's placement;
- the type of content the ad is next to (is it dangerous, defamatory or potentially scandalous for the advertiser to place an ad here?).

Or the known attributes of the user who is behind the screen:

- Is the user known to the advertiser or campaign?
- If CRM information has been synchronized with the Demand Side Platform (DSP), whether the user is a frequent customer, a high-value customer, a low-value customer or someone who it is not worth showing adverts to.
- Whether the user has started to make a purchase on the advertiser's site and qualify to be shown a retargeting message.
- The user's demographic, psychographic and behavioural qualities (see section on targeting display with data).

For example, if you are advertising televisions the following scenarios could occur:

- **Scenario A:** Your ad would appear on an iPhone but your website is not responsive.

  Decision: The experience would be poor, which may be detrimental to your brand. Do not show ad.

- **Scenario B:** Your ad would be viewed by a user who regularly visits your site but never buys.

  Decision: The user is not a serious customer, just a browser. Do not show ad or bid less.

- **Scenario C:** The user started to buy a TV last week but dropped out of the funnel.

  Decision: A hot prospect. Show a retargeting message to try to convert the user on the attempted purchase.

All of these options are available to buyers across the whole of the campaign. You should keep in mind that those scenarios are just that. The conclusions above may be incorrect for your strategy. For example, a regular site visitor could be researching with an intention to buy so you need to plan your targeting carefully.

The rapid growth of programmatic has meant that it is now the expectation for advertisers to have to buy only the ad impressions they actually want. Buying targeted inventory has always enabled this to an extent but within that targeted inventory there may be people in the wrong age range, income range or gender for the advertiser's product. Or, indeed, people who have recently become a customer. In the case of RTB impressions there is also the option for the advertiser to submit a bid for that single impression so it can be bought at a price point that is beneficial to the campaign goals as well.

The difference between programmatic and RTB is that programmatic provides the ability to assess impressions on an individual basis. Furthermore, real-time bidding, which is the basis of a lot of programmatic, adds an auction mechanic to the pricing and purchasing of ad impressions. Programmatic impressions that are not bought by RTB are often agreed media buys with publishers to access certain targeting options or preferential rates that are unique to that publisher. These arrangements are called private market places (PMPs), however, the advertiser still has the right not to buy an impression if it does not fit the immediate requirements of the campaign. The RTB element, often referred to as open exchange buying, has little restriction to entry and the targeting listed above can be applied to both. Fundamentally it is programmatic that provides this addressability that is seen in display today by combining multiple data and decision-making options across the whole of the media campaign. The result is extremely effective campaigns.

Types and formats of display advertising

The most common form of display advertising formats are banners. These have many sizes and are constantly evolving to cope with new screen sizes and resolutions, new devices and also new ways to entice and capture the attention of web users. These are displayed in-page, which is to say that they are situated within the layout of the web page itself.

- **In-page banner adverts** – these are the banner adverts that are ubiquitous around the web. They come in a variety of sizes and need to adhere to strict guidelines so that they can be delivered. These adverts can also be highly customizable to what an individual user has seen or done. In-page banners are typically animated, and are designed and built to specifications laid down by the IAB. If an advert simply and passively animates on a page it is almost certainly a standard in-page banner.

A display advert that does anything else becomes referred to as 'rich media'. This is a cover-all term used to describe any display advert that is interactive in any way (such as responding to a user hovering their cursor over the creative) or does anything more than simply existing next to content as described above.

- **In-page rich media** – these are in-page adverts that have much more functionality or content than a standard banner. The most common examples are:
  - **Video adverts** – where a full video can play inside the ad creative.
  - **Expandable adverts** – where the ad expands to take up more (or all) of the web page if the user interacts with it. These interactions can be a mouse-over (or hover) for a period of time or a click. Some formats can expand to take over all or most of the screen (especially in mobile advertising) and that space can be used for far more than graphics – a microsite could be hosted inside the ad, for example.
  - **Data-capture** – adverts where the user can submit an e-mail address to sign up for a newsletter or receive a reminder of a product launch date.
  - **Live information** – such as prices of an airline route or remaining stock levels for a heavily discounted or extremely popular product can be piped into advert creative from product feeds and POS systems.

- – **Mobile ad units** can also take control of some of the phone's features and sensors – such as the accelerator and camera, which could be used to personalize or provide an element of gamification to an advert.
- **In Stream** – this is video creative that plays before, during or after video content on the web. Depending on this positioning, these are commonly known as:
  - – pre-roll;
  - – mid-roll;
  - – post-roll.

Video advertising is extremely close to TV advertising in both the content and the form – ad slots are typically of either 15 or 30 seconds' duration and it is common for advertisers to replicate their TV adverts completely. There are, as always in digital, ways to provide interactivity.

- **Skippable video** – since 2012 YouTube has offered an additional form of video advertising called TrueView (other video providers now offer similar solutions). These adverts can be skipped by the user, which brings three big advantages over traditional in-stream placements:
  1 The skippable format results in users who truly are interested in the ad watching it.
  2 It takes away the content length restrictions. As the user gets the opportunity to skip the ad, the broadcaster (YouTube) is happy for the creative to be any length up to 10 minutes.
  3 Pricing – the advertiser only pays for adverts that have not been skipped.
- **Audio adverts** – formats and guidelines for audio, as defined by the IAB, cannot be accurately explained here and so I would recommend visiting their website for the detail.

Key technology in ad delivery

What is an ad server?

Ad servers are a core part of the display advertising ecosystem for those who buy using more than one media partner, whether that is a demand side platform (DSP), ad network, direct to publishers, or any combination thereof. Their uses include:

- storing advertising creative;
- passing correct advertising creative to publishers, networks and DSPs;
- managing sequential messaging and creative iteration testing;
- creating and maintaining control/expose groups for testing and surveying;
- recording where adverts have been shown and who they have been seen by;
- storing and creating tags for distribution to publishers;
- creating and counting cookies for exposure and conversion tracking;
- providing comprehensive reporting of media activity including attribution.

Any good, modern ad server will be able to track most digital activity using impression trackers (typically 1×1 pixels) or click trackers, and will be able to measure and attribute activity across tactics within a channel, as well as across channels. Marketers have the need to understand how their channels work together and this is where this platform fulfils that need.

Types of display campaign

Display advertising has many applications and purposes but below are three main purposes for display advertising.

Awareness

This delivers brand messages or immerses customers with interactive experiences to make them aware of a brand, product or service and its benefits. It is far less accountable for providing sales in a direct response approach than the below purposes of display. Rich media and video are common formats for this.

How this applies to your strategy

If your business is less focused on direct sales through digital channels, such as car manufacturers or estate agents, then brand awareness plays a major part in your conversion journey. Even if you are focused on high volumes of sales online you may play in a highly competitive market that therefore creates a need for awareness advertising.

Direct response prospecting

This is used to find users for a particular product or service and aid consumers on the path to conversion. This activity seeks to find users in highly relevant areas of the web and is really the most versatile use of display. Any direct response advertiser should be using this to gain new customers. Prospecting can actually be used as a proxy for awareness as it is showing adverts to new users; however, as there is often a CPA goal it is done in a more subtle way using more cost effective formats – mainly banner creative.

How this applies to your strategy

If your business is focused on sales then ensuring you are targeting the right customers at the right time with the right message and therefore achieving the maximum sales volume at the lowest cost per acquisition will be a key goal. This is where direct response display fits in. This is the area where people are most sceptical about display due to its history, as discussed above, but this history is no longer relevant.

Retargeting

This is exactly like RLSA activity in search but far more powerful as adverts can be shown to non-converting customers across the whole internet, as opposed to simply when performing searches on a search engine. Because this uses first-party data from users' actions on an advertiser's website, more segmentation can be applied to weed out consumers of little or no value and prioritize delivery to those who exhibit behaviours of more valuable customers.

How this applies to your strategy

Retargeting customers can increase conversion rates from existing visitors. This can be highly targeted by following users with reminders of the products and prices they have been quoted. This can be highly effective in ensuring your conversion rate is optimized even after the user has dropped out of the funnel.

Retargeting has been given a bad reputation by some early companies who exploited it to give the illusion that their overall display activity performed better than it had. If retargeting data is mixed in as part of the overall performance data for a display campaign it can artificially inflate the click-through rate. This is due to the fact that retargeting is aimed at warm prospects whereas other display advertising is more speculative. It is vitally important to use advertisers' data responsibly.

Retargeting with dynamic creative is very common for e-commerce advertisers, especially those operating in retail and travel sectors, where people commonly shop around for very similar versions of products.

Planning and targeting programmatic display campaigns

Successful display campaigns, like most other marketing channels, revolve around the simple principle of delivering the right message to the right audience at the right time. The balance and importance of these aspects can shift depending on the objectives involved but they always play a part.

Display campaigns rarely use any of these methods in isolation but look at using combinations of targeting to deliver adverts more effectively. This is especially true of programmatic campaign delivery, thanks to technology being able to bring all of this data together. As the technology and data available to us increases in complexity, the way campaigns are planned and executed does likewise.

Targeting display delivery

Audience data

Targeting specific audiences in display chiefly depends on considering who the user is regardless of the content they are consuming. There are several ways of knowing who the audience is and defining who they are, what they like, are motivated by or interested in. There are two main types of audience data: demographical information – who they are, and behavioural information – what they do.

- **Demographic:** This is information about a person and can be inferred from browsing habits or collected from known publicly available information such as consumer credit records.

- **Behavioural:** This data purely observes the type of content consumed and the browsing habits of a person and makes assumptions about that user. Behavioural data tends to typify who users are, what they are interested in and what they may be considering to purchase. For example, browse enough content about a new model of Ford family MPV car and you could be segmented into the following audiences (plus many others besides):

- new car purchaser;
- in market for new car;
- MPV driver;
- brand preference – Ford;
- parent of young family.

Each of these audiences are then made available for advertisers to target campaigns towards.

Contextual targeting

Placing adverts next to appropriate content to ensure the campaign is relevant is typically done by targeting sites and mobile apps as well as specific content or pages within sites and apps. Prior to audience data becoming commonplace websites and apps were used as a proxy for the audience that typically make up their readership. Contextual targeting is still vitally important to advertising and it is extremely common to find part or all of a display campaign being delivered across a list of specific sites.

When targeting websites it is most common to simply list sites that share commonality of content and deliver a proportion of advertising to them. This works well for specialist websites but there is so much traffic that exists on generalist sites – all news and many magazine sites have a deep breadth of content. Contextual accuracy can be achieved by buying only certain sections of a website but this requires activity to be set up with each site in turn.

Keyword contextual targeting

To address this issue keyword contextual targeting (KCT) was developed and is commonplace on sites with a large breadth of content but is now adding benefit to display campaigns by expanding to all websites. KCT allows advertisers to target display advertising space on specific web pages based on the content of that web page regardless of the site that it appears on. There are data companies who by either working in partnership with publishers or by using technology to crawl all web content (just like Google crawls web pages to make them available via searching).

The crawled web pages are semantically analysed and categorized to ascertain the type of content on the page. Then advertisers can target display adverts to appear on pages with content that matches a small set of keywords used to define it. KCT is commonly used in both negative and positive match scenarios. An airline, for example, may use KCT to positively target or negatively suppress its adverts as related to the following:

Table 10.2   Example of keyword contextual targeting

Positive	Negative
Air travel	Plane crash
Holiday	Terrorist attack
City break	Air-fare increases
Business travel	Travel chaos

This is a technique also used in paid search to ensure that the terms that you want to filter out are added to your campaigns. This is important as you can see from the examples in Table 10.2 as it reduces wasted spend on irrelevant terms and also avoids brand association with risky terms.

As with most data targeting methods, the benefit has been amplified by programmatic advertising as it allows advertisers to apply the targeting criteria to the whole of a campaign's activity, across many websites as opposed to having to facilitate this with publishers on an individual basis.

Other targeting techniques

- **Environmental** – this group of targeting options has less to do with the user's interests and media consumption, but provides bigger levers for campaign managers to use to target activity, for factors that may be applicable to campaign delivery despite who the target audience is.

- **Time-based targeting** – this can be specified to get the most from market conditions, seasonality or consumer behaviour. Display adverts can be delivered by hour, day and month, and many advertisers up weight activity to ensure a presence when it is most relevant to consumers. This can be especially useful for sales and events, but also the type of product. Adverts for sleeping aids may be most effective after 11pm, for example, whilst winter coats are likely to be more effective in October than in May.

- **Geo-based** – another essential tool for some advertisers. Display adverts can be restricted to very acute locations if required. In extremis, when targeting mobile devices specifically, display adverts can be targeted to within a small radius of any lat/long coordinates, post or zip codes or cities, towns and regions. Display adverts for all devices can be targeted at village, town, city and county as well as TV and DMA regions. Post or zip codes can also be used to target display campaigns. The accuracy of geo targeting depends on the source of data used and the country a campaign is being delivered in. In the UK, for example, although IP address is readily available information, it rarely correlates accurately to the user's location, so a combination of other factors are used for targeting desktop computers, sometimes including data from websites.

- **Device** – the type of device a user is currently using is also a factor. This can help deliver the right creative format too, but is sometimes brought in to help target adverts and help define users as well.

- **Modelling audiences** – many data points are gathered and/or used in the process of delivering ad campaigns. All of the above mentioned data sets and methodologies, when examined, can yield significant information. Look-alike and act-alike modelling are common terms that refer to a type of statistical analysis that is based in Bayesian Inference Logic. This exists as a way to extend audiences and find people who exhibit the same behaviours as known customers.

  In the simplest form this involves monitoring all the audience segments that users to an advertiser's site (or customer database) belong to from a third-party data company's taxonomy. Once the highly indexing segments of the data provider's taxonomy are identified, they can be positively targeted by a display campaign.

CASE STUDY   Improving campaign performance with data – VisualDNA and PistonHeads.com

A publisher that has its own audience data but improved a campaign being executed on its site by enriching its data with a third-party provider.

The approach

To help power its personalization strategy by enriching its own data, and to reach out to complementary segments, PistonHeads.com (the publisher) decided to trial a rich data and dynamic segmentation opportunity with a third party – VisualDNA – a provider of psychographic audience data. VisualDNA used its analytics platform to help PistonHeads.com understand its audience and extend its reach. The campaign selected for this test was a lead generation for Magnitude Finance, a UK specialist in providing bespoke funding for prestige automotive vehicles.

PistonHeads.com split the first month of its Magnitude Finance campaign into two streams: the first using standard vertical targeting, and the second overlaying VisualDNA's segments. This split allowed the publisher to understand how the test was working versus the standard approach by having a control cell (the standard vertical targeting).

Lee Williams of PistonHeads.com remembers: 'The segmentation was backed by impressively rigorous methodologies, and we could really see our existing segments come to life in the data. Our editors, community manager and sales team all saw a close fit between the segments and the people that we know qualitatively on our site.'

The results

The results were startling: while the average CTR for the standard segments was 0.14 per cent, those overlaid with VisualDNA segments hit 1.15 per cent – an 800 per cent uplift. The campaign generated hundreds of well-qualified lead adverts for Magnitude Finance, driving high conversion rates.

This example proves not only that segmentation can be very powerful and that data itself is a valuable tool for any business but also that implementing a programme of continuous improvement through tactical test-and-learn campaigns will result in an increase in performance over time.

Display campaign measurement

As with all digital channels, display has a plethora of metrics and methods to measure campaign delivery, creative performance, performance against objective and, more recently, how it affects and interacts with other channels. Display advertising is widely critiqued to be the most incorrectly measured digital channel.

The most important rule when measuring any digital activity is to ensure that the metrics meet the brief by providing the relevant insights about the campaign. For example, if an advertiser is using display to increase awareness amongst a specific demographic then measuring penetration of the target audience would be a far more suitable key performance indicator (KPI) than a response-related measurement such as the click-through rate.

One often overlooked fact is that, when delivering campaigns with standard banner advertising, a display campaign has more in common with its billboard and print media cousins than its digital siblings – most digital advertising is centred around eliciting a response from a user and/or reacting to an action performed by a user – paid search, for example, is both responsive to the user's query and its purpose is to gain a click from that user. Display, on the other hand, provides digital advertisers with the ability to proactively target people and the placement of adverts and volume of delivery are controlled by the advertiser.

Display campaign objectives and therefore measurement should be pragmatically seen as appearing at points on a continuum of marketing activity, which leads to as many users as possible becoming customers. Different kinds of display campaigns are themselves operating at different points along that continuum, and campaigns have different objectives and measurements as a result.

An awareness campaign, tasked with informing new prospective clients about a product or service, is best measured with penetration amongst the target audience, than clicks on the advert. The clicks, as a secondary metric, can help return insight about who engaged users are and where they can be found online to help add insight to a campaign. Further along the continuum, closer to users becoming customers, an advertiser may be running a display retargeting campaign, where a click has more value as a way of measuring a campaign's performance.

Display advertising shares some metrics with other digital formats and the most ubiquitous forms of measurement and metrics in display are outlined here:

- **Post-impression/post-view events** – also known as 'view-through' conversions or actions. This is the measurement of any conversion event (sales, visits, sign-ups etc) that happens after users have been exposed to a display advert. This activity can be tracked by the ad server, demand side platform or some analytics packages. This is the most versatile measurement of display as it accounts for the 'halo effect' that display has by influencing users in the future. This form of measurement also helps to compare different campaign activity that happens.

- **Post-click actions** – also known as 'click-through conversions'. This is the measurement of everything that happens directly after a user has clicked on a display advert. Measuring post-click activity can provide valuable insight about how particular placements perform relative to others, which can be a proxy measurement for an advertiser's brand, creative or message strength.

- **Search uplift** – in a multichannel digital world, understanding the effects of one channel on another is important. Outside of the complex world of data-driven attribution, measurement of cross-channel activity becomes more difficult to measure precisely but can provide insight. Looking at the increase in search volumes that occur after display activity begins is a valuable indicator that a display campaign is having an effect on an advertiser's target audience.

- **Increase in site traffic** – as with measuring the increase in searches, looking at the increase in direct site traffic is also an applicable measurement to the effectiveness of display. The most difficult factor in measuring the indirect effects of display, at least without attribution modelling, is the delay between the beginning of a display campaign and seeing the indirect effects. These depend heavily on the type of product and how people's consideration and needs change – in extremis, both the frequency of purchase and the consideration time needed to choose a product are greatly exaggerated in the automotive sector compared with the fast-moving consumer goods (FMCG) sector. So the effectiveness of a toothpaste campaign will see indirect results far more quickly than a car manufacturer. Importantly, an increase in site traffic can be focused on specific actions, such as an increase in traffic to certain areas or an increase in lead generating forms. The measurement can be honed as well – looking at an increase in new visitors, as opposed to returning ones, is a very powerful method of ensuring advertising campaigns are delivering incremental business. A cost per new visitor is also a common metric.

- **Brand uplift/recall surveys** – when a campaign has a specific brand awareness objective, one favoured method of judging success is to run a survey asking users if they can recall the brand or product that has just finished its advertising campaign. The methodology of the campaign is a simple control/expose test that asks both the control and the exposed groups (the users who have been served an advert) whether they know of or recall the brand and product. The difference between the amounts of positive recalls the exposed group yields versus the control group can be a measure of success of the campaign. This form of measurement requires consideration from the outset of any campaign as a control group of users has to be created that display adverts need to be negatively targeted away from for the compare and contrast. It is extremely useful for advertisers who do not have any objective aside from messaging, such as government agencies, who need to be sure their message is seen.

- **Click-through rate (CTR)** – of all the users who have been delivered a display advert, the CTR is the percentage of users who have clicked on the advert. The nature of display means CTR is a potentially dangerous metric when used in isolation. There are a large number of clicks that are accidentally made by users. One judgement of quality of a website from an advertiser's perspective is ensuring that adverts are not too close in proximity to content – a potential problem with touchscreen technology. Therefore, despite wanting to generate clicks with a campaign, they need to be considered with other metrics that can provide the bigger picture.

- **Engagement** – in display advertising engagement metrics most commonly refer to how users are interacting with an ad unit; as such the actual event that counts as an engagement varies with the type of ad. Engagement metrics are associated with rich media – for example, in an expandable banner a user expanding the ad could count as an engagement. For a click-to-play video banner, a user initiating the video would count as an engagement.

- **Format specific metrics** – as rich media display formats become increasingly more sophisticated and functional the amount of measurable actions also increases. Mobile advertising typifies this as many ad units can make use of the functions of the device within the ad unit. Therefore calls, social shares, use of the device's location services to find a nearest store or supplier are all measurable outcomes of user engagement. In tablet and desktop, the functionality of rich media can go further. Car manufacturers often have car configuration tools for users to choose colour, trim, engine and options on a new car. They will also have options to download a brochure or book a test drive, which are all measurable actions alongside the standard display campaign metrics.

- **Return on ad spend (ROAS)** – this is a metric that can be broadly used to look at the effectiveness of display spend. The metric is extremely closely related to ROI calculations but looks at gross revenue generated from a campaign, or part of a campaign as opposed to profit generated. Both ROAS and ROI are useful tools as they are easily understood by lots of client stakeholders, and allow a bipartisan look at the effectiveness of advertising tactics.

- **Video completion rate** – when delivering campaigns with either in-stream or in-banner video the ad-server will provide reporting data about the length of time users have been playing back the video. Normally advertisers are concerned with the number of plays that are started and then the subsequent quartiles until the end of the video – ie a report will usually detail the number of plays initiated (also called views) as well as the number of plays that reached 25 per cent, 50 per cent and 75 per cent of the advert. The most important metric is how many plays were completed. Completed views are expressed as view-through rate (VTR) and are also called completion rate. This is expressed as a percentage, exactly the same as a click-through rate in another digital medium.

- **Video: cost per completed view (CPCV)** – the cost per completed view is an expression of how effective delivery of a video display campaign has been. It is very effective in terms of establishing value across placements, publishers and different types of video advert (in-stream, in-banner and skippable formats) as it measures a common factor across the medium.

- **Viewability** – viewability is a new measurement for display. For each delivered ad impression the viewability rate (or in-view impressions) is calculated as a percentage of all delivered adverts in the campaign or placement. The concept is simple and is essential to the effectiveness of the campaign – the measurement of whether an individual advert made it onto the screen of a user. Virtually all web pages are longer than the screen they are viewed on and usually adverts feature all the way down a web page. Therefore, if a user doesn't finish reading an article, the adverts on the lower part of the page will not be seen, and not be counted towards the in-view impressions served. The definition of a viewable impression is that at least 75 per cent of the area of an advert has to be on the screen of the user for at least one second. This is defined by the IAB and the MRC. However, the methods of calculating this vary between providers and the results of a campaign can vary wildly between different providers. Viewability is really contributing to delivering more effective campaigns as well as highlighting ineffective placements on sites. The latter point allows for publishers to start removing poor placements, which leads to nicer web pages and more effect for the remaining placements.

One key element of looking at campaign data is to make sure the activity fulfilled the initial brief. If a campaign requirement was that it was to focus on Central London, then there needs to be corroboration of that in the reporting. Beyond this, understanding the bigger picture is important and that is where attribution modelling can help. The tracking technology now exists to look at performance across digital channels. For more on tracking and measurement, see Chapter 19.

Summary

Display provides the marketer with a versatile tool that spans the purchase cycle from awareness to advocacy and up-selling. In order to understand this, we have examined types of display, the technology involved, some common approaches to display campaigns and how to effectively target and measure them.

Chapter checklist

- Programmatic advertising ☐
- Types and formats of display advertising ☐
- Key technology in ad delivery ☐
- Types of display campaign ☐
- Planning and targeting programmatic campaigns ☐
- Display campaign measurement ☐

Further reading

- *On Bayesian inference logic*:

Stone, J V (2015) *Bayes' Rules*, Sebtel Press

An implementation guide is available at:
www.koganpage.com/DigitalMarketingStrategy/2

Tailoring your social media strategy 11

What we will cover in this chapter

In this chapter we examine social media – a channel that continues to evolve enormously and has done since its mass adoption in the mid 2000s. We will look at social selling as well as the networks and how to differentiate your strategy across them. We also examine social advertising and measurement. The key areas covered in this chapter are:

- The evolution of social media
- Where to start?
- Types of social media
- The social networks
- Content
- Influencers
- Social advertising
- Measurement

Chapter goals

By the end of this chapter you should understand social media and the challenges and opportunities that both organic and paid social represent. You should understand how content is vital to your strategy and how to measure success on the channel. You should also be able to appreciate social advertising and its effects on SEO.

Social media is a bit of a goliath these days – omnipresent, revered and lamented in equal doses, and most definitely often misunderstood. Social media is generally defined as any website or application that enables users to create and share content, or to participate in social networking. When people think of social media, however, they often think simply of the well-known social networks (Facebook, Twitter, YouTube etc) – these are really just a small part of a much larger channel.

Whilst social media in its broadest sense also includes messaging, we will look at this in the next chapter so will not focus on it here. It is worth noting, however, that social messaging has now overtaken social networks in usage.

The evolution of social media

Your customers, whoever or wherever they are, are likely to be using social media. According to Internet World Stats in December 2017 there were circa 4.1 billion internet users in the world (about 55 per cent of the population) and according to Statista, 2.5 billion of those are using social media – so close to two-thirds of all internet users. These numbers have grown significantly just since the first edition of this book was published when there were 3 billion internet users and 2 billion on social media. This demonstrates the continual growth of this channel although we are beginning to see a plateau in mature countries now. Reason number one for getting involved is to be where your customers are. After all, if you owned a chain of shops and a brand new shopping centre was opened that was attracting phenomenal crowds, you would probably open up there too.

While the irrefutable fact that your audience are definitely 'on social' is a pretty compelling reason, there are others if you need further convincing (or, more likely, you need to convince your board).

Social penetration

As noted above, social is big on a global scale. However, if you are a North American or European reader you might be surprised to learn that by far the biggest social user base is to be found in Asia and the highest penetration of social media is in the Middle East. According to Steven Millward at techinasia.com, China had an estimated 597 million social media users in 2013 with the top 10 sites in China having 3.2 billion users between them (Millward, 2013). The top five countries with the highest penetration, defined as the percentage of the population that are using social media, are

Qatar (99 per cent), United Arab Emirates (99 per cent), Kuwait (98 per cent), Bermuda (98 per cent) and Bahrain (98 per cent) according to the 2018 Digital Year Book from We Are Social and Hootsuite. This presents a significant challenge and opportunity to global businesses that have until now focused on the European and US social networks.

Social and mobile

Social networking is very easy to do on the fly. Indeed, it is an excellent time-killer for the bus/train journey (or if you are a teenager during 'family time'). Social media is therefore ideally suited to mobile and, of course, mobile is on a similar upward trajectory. It is also important to recognize that the vast majority of social media users are engaging through apps, not through desktops or laptops. According to We Are Social, 52 per cent of internet traffic is now mobile and over 95 per cent of Facebook traffic is on mobile or tablet. These numbers are similar across the majority of social networks. Mobile and social are intrinsically linked and it is vital to appreciate this (Brandt, 2015).

Where to start?

As we have discussed throughout the book, your goals on social media, like any other channel, must align with your overall strategy. Specific considerations for social media could be: what are your high-level goals for the channel? What should be your tone of voice? How will you participate? How will you respond? In what languages? On what time zone?

All these questions are crucial, but the single most important thing you can do when setting a social media strategy is to start by listening. Social media monitoring tools such as Brandwatch, Salesforce Marketing Cloud, Hootsuite and Keyhole are indispensable if you want to really understand what people are saying and how they respond to different content/messages.

Having listened and learned you can then start to form what you want to both be and do on social before jumping in. It is absolutely crucial to get your social personality right. It should reflect your customers while also still being true to your brand.

Social personality is a term used to define how you represent yourself on the social networks. The simple truth here is that your social personality should be entirely consistent with your brand personality. Your brand is your personality and, in the same way that you would not expect your friends to have different personalities depending on where they are, you would not expect a company to have different personalities on different channels. Many businesses try to fit in to the channel rather than fitting the channel to their business. This is a mistake. We looked at brand in Chapter 3, so reviewing this is worthwhile here.

Below is a helpful 10 point checklist that you can use either to prepare your social strategy or review your existing delivery:

1 What are your goals?

Growth, awareness, sales, reputation management, customer service, thought leadership, reaching new audiences?

2 Who is your audience?

Young or old? Male or female? Professional or personal? Fun or serious?

3 Where is your audience?

Instagram, Twitter, Forums, Facebook, Snapchat, Pinterest? Mobile or desktop? Office, home or out?

4 When is your audience online?

During work hours? Evenings? Commuter times? When they have down time? When they work? When they are with friends or alone?

5 What are your competitors doing?

As with any strategy you must understand the landscape. Get a view of your competition's presence and strategy. What channels are they on? What are they talking about? Where are they achieving engagement? Use listening tools to understand their plans better.

6 What is your content strategy?

What is your overall content strategy and how does social media fit in? How do you differ content for each network? See Chapter 14 for more on this.

7 What about curation?

As well as creation you can become an engaging hub by sharing others' content that is relevant to your audience. This also builds relationships with those other companies or individuals. What will you share, how often, from whom? Do you have existing partnerships you can leverage?

8 How will you produce this content?

Do you have the necessary resource? Do you have the skill set for design and written content that is optimized for social? See more on this in Chapter 14.

9 How will you manage the channels?

You should consider moderation and administration. You will need to manage profile photos, cover art, contact details, messages that arrive, complaints, questions. If operating at scale this means people and processes must be robust.

10 Establish your success metrics.

You have set your goals but now you must know what success looks like. What are the measures you will use and what is the target? We will look at measurement later in this chapter.

Types of social media

To truly understand social media you need to appreciate the numerous different types. However, this is not, I'm afraid, as easy as it might seem. There are literally thousands of social sites, apps and platforms, and therefore classifying and cataloguing them is incredibly difficult. Add to this that there are probably 10 new social sites/apps created every day – and also that today's popular platform is tomorrow's dud – and this is a bit of a minefield. So in this section I will cover the main types of social media.

Social networking

When most people think social they think of sites such as Facebook, which allows users to post most forms of media and share with a close group of friends or, if they prefer, the whole world. Typically these sorts of sites are categorized as true 'social networks' but the term should be used in a much broader sense. Some social networks in fact encourage face-to-face interaction, Meetup (**www.meetup.com**) being one example, and numerous 'friend finder'/dating applications being others. If your business operates within these markets then you could investigate potential opportunities such as advertising or even sponsoring events, which could be online or even offline.

For your digital strategy these networks can offer significant brand awareness opportunities and direct conversion campaign opportunities. Facebook, for example, offers paid campaigns, company pages and insights to provide analytics on performance. These networks are probably the broadest in terms of opportunity. We will therefore examine some of the leading platforms in more detail later in the chapter.

Blogs and micro-blogging

Blogging is hugely popular. However, the vast majority of blogs are not! While some bloggers have hundreds of thousands of followers, the majority are small hobby sites for close family and friends. The proliferation of blogs is due in part to the relative simplicity of setting one up. Blogging platforms such as Blogger and Wordpress are hugely popular and the majority of domain registration companies will happily bundle in a blog with your domain purchase. While some blogs are global phenomena, for example the Huffington Post despite having some significant drops in traffic, still receives tens of millions of monthly visitors, even these pale into insignificance compared to the largest micro-blogging platform, Twitter, which at the time of writing had 330 million active users (Twitter Q3, 2017) who continue to send hundreds of millions of tweets a month.

Both types, of course, have different purposes and need to be considered differently by marketers. Twitter is great to push out pithy messages and indeed to receive them from your customers. Blogs allow for more detailed consideration and can therefore wield quite considerable power over potential customers. For example, positive reviews on technology, such as on Tech Radar or Pocket-Lint, can have a significant impact on sales. Blogs can offer an opportunity to organizations that have rich content to share or have products and services that can be promoted to highly relevant blog sites. Micro-blogs such as Twitter and Sina Weibo can offer a great deal of advertising potential to an audience that is limited on time and looking for interesting content to share and absorb. You can of course also share your blogs on Twitter – this doesn't have to be an either/or choice.

Media sharing

A number of social platforms have been developed that focus on visual media, the most ubiquitous being video-sharing site YouTube. Also here we can include photo or image-sharing sites such as Flickr. You could argue that Pinterest and Instagram also fall into this category. Instagram has, however, evolved into much more of a social network in its own right and Pinterest is sometimes classified as a bookmarking site. Being able to create adverts that fit with the visual medium is highly relevant for some businesses in areas such as media and fashion. Visual appeal is, however, not limited to these specific platforms. Visual content across social media is universally more engaging. Images, infographics and videos all see higher engagement levels on all platforms than pure text and so this must feature as part of your strategy.

CASE STUDY   Bloom & Wild

Background

Bloom & Wild is a flower delivery company that wanted to attract a wider audience to its fledgling business. As a company that offered a product with great visual appeal, it was clear that Instagram could offer some benefit and so the company decided to promote its business here.

Strategy

Bloom & Wild was a young company at the time and so did not have the budgets that major corporations have. To make the most of the budget, therefore, the company used its existing e-mail list to target a lookalike audience on Instagram. To do this it used Facebook's Power Editor. After some initial tests it became clear that video adverts were delivering the strongest conversion rates. As a result the company optimized its campaign towards video content.

Results

As a result of this activity Bloom & Wild increased bouquet orders by 62 per cent and also experienced a significant increase in new customers commenting on its Instagram profile.

Key lessons

This case study is a great example of how you can use existing data, alongside smart targeting and test-and-learn principles to deliver fantastic success, no matter the size of your budget or resources.

Professional networking

Professional networking sites are, as the name suggests, largely for the business or academic world. LinkedIn is the most widely known and has replaced the rolodex of business cards, the huge benefit being that LinkedIn contacts remain up to date regardless of the number of job switches a person may have. With 350 million registered users it is also a recruiter's dream and has, perhaps inadvertently, helped mobilize the workforce. This can therefore be useful for building your digital team or even sourcing your agency. It is a very powerful space for positioning your brand as a thought leader and enabling your employees to promote your brand and gain their own benefits from this. We will discuss LinkedIn later in the chapter. Also within this category are a number of document-sharing sites, for example Slideshare, which is useful for publishing more formal content and researching an opportunity. This can play a part in your content strategy (see Chapter 14). Here the opportunity is not only to attract new employees but also to disseminate content to other professionals. This can be particularly advantageous in the B2B space, where being a thought leader and gaining trust are vital to success.

Reviews and ratings

Reviews and ratings sites answer a very basic human need – peer approval. We don't like to make mistakes when purchasing goods and services and, in this, peer reviews have always been important. The internet has allowed us to expand our 'peer set' on a global scale, thanks to the plethora of review sites and platforms. One of the best-known review sites is TripAdvisor, which covers over 7.3 million accommodations, places and attractions and operates in 49 markets with over 570 million reviews.

The power of consumer reviews has encouraged brands to offer customers the ability to review their products/services on-site. Third-party platforms such as Trustpilot and Reevoo have been created to fill this demand. In fact almost every industry now has several review sites and most major players have entered this area. You can rate everything from movies to plumbers and televisions to hotels.

Forums

Forums are often considered a little outdated and some of the younger social media professionals might question their inclusion here. However, there are still many highly active forums, albeit usually part of a larger site. Two great examples are Netmums (not to be confused with Mumsnet) and PistonHeads. Although the former is clearly focused on babies and the latter on cars, it is important not to pigeon-hole forums. Consider, for example, the two posts shown in Figures 11.1 and 11.2.

Figure 11.1   Forum post Example 1

exhaust making rattling noises

Hi, When i am driving i can hear a rattling noise which i assume is the exhaust. It does not start off like that, only sometimes. The exhaust does not feel wobbly. It seems to be when i am braking or slowing down. Is it likely to just drop off or could it be something else? I get it serviced every year and it was only done in Sept 07. Could it be that or someting else? Any ideas????☺

thanks,

Figure 11.2   Forum post Example 2

Author	Discussion
	▭quote ▭quote all [news] [report]
Original Poster ◄ 243 posts 97 months	With my 11 week old daugher consuming all my spare time, I am not training anywhere as much as I would like. This has led me to consider ways in which I can train with her (when she is a little older). Has anyone used a running pram before, and if so what are your thoughts/recommendations?
	Initial thought is that it will be strange running with my arms out rather than swinging to my side but I am sure you get used to that?
	Also I'm 6'3" – is there plenty of space to swing my long legs?
	Thanks PH!

Perhaps surprisingly, Example 1 (in Figure 11.1) is from Netmums and Example 2 (in Figure 11.2) is from PistonHeads, demonstrating that forums are more about a collection of like-minded individuals who might well drift off the central forum topic.

Some of these forums such as Ask.fm enable anonymous discussions and questions that are helpful for issues you simply don't want attached to your personal information.

These forums provide an opportunity for your business to engage directly with customers and prospects alike, if you can add genuine value to the conversation. Cynically stepping into the middle of conversations with advertising messages, however, will result in negative brand sentiment as well as potentially resulting in being banned from the forum and even receiving negative PR. If nothing else, forums can be a great way to monitor overall brand sentiment and understand any concerns or complaints.

The sharing economy

This is much more of a shift in consumer behaviour than simply a new type of social media site but it is worth briefly mentioning here.

Sites such as AirBnB, Uber and Taskrabbit are well known and there are many more to enable you to rent out your unused parking spaces, find dog walkers and even swap clothes.

These sites operate through connecting people with needs to those who can supply them, without the need for an intermediary: the power of the internet at its finest. If there is no direct opportunity for your business here then it is at least an inspiration for what we can create in the social space in our own businesses.

The social networks

Facebook – 2.1 billion users

Facebook is of course the most famous, or infamous, of the social networks. With a movie made about its creation, its owner being one of the richest men in the world and the incredible growth it witnessed in its first couple of years, it really has defined the channel. Facebook has an older demographic than platforms such as Snapchat but still has 60 per cent of its users in the 18–34 range.

Facebook has increasingly moved towards monetizing the platform and now, as with most social platforms, it is very difficult to achieve reach through organic posts alone. Paid advertising is very simple and can target a wide range of demographics and interests very effectively. You can also run this advertising across Facebook and Instagram owing to both channels being owned by Facebook. You can also create Pages to promote your business and develop a strong destination as well as serve your clients. Beyond this there are opportunities with the Audience network to reach beyond Facebook to your targeted audience.

For your Facebook strategy it is important to consider that individuals on this platform are here to share moments and stories with family and friends. This is not a business destination and so your messaging and content must fit into this need state. Facebook Insights can help to steer this content strategy. Facebook is an important channel for businesses in the B2C space.

Instagram – 800 million users

Instagram has seen enormous growth in recent years. It is, as we mentioned above, owned by Facebook but this time with a pure visual focus. The leading brands on Instagram take the time to create beautiful photo walls, regular content promotions and use only high-resolution images. With one-third of the most viewed Stories on Instagram coming from businesses it is clear that the opportunity is significant. Instagram users are actually more likely to be influenced by brands for their purchases than ever before.

You should also consider tying your Instagram strategy to your physical brand. Events and brand experiences are great opportunities to feed your Instagram wall. You can also create Stories, something that first appeared on Snapchat but that has since rolled out across many platforms. Stories give you the chance to highlight what is important in your life right now and bring the timely factor into play in a very real sense.

Currently, you cannot add links to your posts but I expect this to change. Your profile for now is therefore crucial. Instagram is an important channel for B2C and B2B businesses that can authentically deliver visual stories.

YouTube – 1.5 billion users

YouTube is now one of the biggest video platforms in the world including television networks, movie production companies and streaming services. The potential here is enormous and the fact it is Google-owned gives you great search marketing opportunity with minimal effort.

YouTube grew through its simplicity and timeliness. As video capture became easier with smartphones, YouTube was the place to go to share your clips. The social networks now generally have a native video offering but YouTube has lost none of its necessity. Funny animal videos played a part in the growth of course but now you can learn to do anything through YouTube. Vloggers continue to grow in volume and specificity and herein lies the opportunity. You can learn much more easily from a video than you can from a written manual. Whether it is learning to change a light bulb, speak a language or play a video game, the How To video has become hugely popular. Reviews of products from trusted Vloggers remain popular and so does entertainment of any kind. Live video is also an important feature as it is on Facebook and other channels.

YouTube is important for every business and you should consider what your strategy is. This is a 'what', not 'if'.

Twitter – 330 million users

Twitter has struggled for growth in the late 2010s. It has failed to monetize in the way other social networks have. It remains a vital channel in the social space and, as the effective inventor of micro-blogging and the creator of the hashtag, it retains its space. Twitter is very much a real-time platform in that people are looking for news and quick facts that are true at that moment. What is my favourite celebrity doing today? What are the news headlines today? What are the latest statistics on social media?

As a result there is real opportunity to create a large and engaged following through regular posting. Your content needs to be more frequent here than on other channels. You should expect to post several times a day here rather than the daily frequency of Facebook or weekly LinkedIn frequency that are perfectly acceptable on those platforms.

Advertising here allows you to promote specific tweets or your profile itself to a targeted audience. You should be aware, however, that there are a great number of fake accounts and multiple accounts for individuals on Twitter. Growing your followers to hit vanity metric targets can be achieved easily but this can damage your social strategy, as your engagement levels will be very low. Twitter advertising can be used very effectively to drive users towards timely events such as sports and television shows. You can also use Insights to understand your successes and failures to improve your strategy as with many other platforms.

Twitter must be managed closely and carefully but can be a significant opportunity to gain mass reach.

Sina Weibo – 376 million users

Sina Weibo is a micro-blogging site specific to China since 2014, known simply as Weibo. The users tend to be coastal and white-collar workers. Whilst Weibo started with a 140-character limit (the same as Twitter) it changed to 2,000 characters back in 2016, before Twitter moved to its new 280-character limit. Weibo has proved very successful in China despite its censorship being beyond what most other social networks experience. The network has encouraged mass usage by celebrities and a great deal of Weibo-originated content has gone viral.

Weibo offers sponsored posts, Weibo Tasks (paid amplification through other accounts) and Fensi Tong – highly targeted advertising. If looking at China as a market, you should consider your Weibo options.

LinkedIn – 260 million users

LinkedIn is one of the longest established social networks. It has long been a useful resource for the professional and is now one of the most popular job boards in the world. It has enabled a great deal more networking and content sharing in recent years and this has significantly increased engagement levels.

Since the sale to Microsoft in 2016 the platform has begun to monetize more dramatically and open up a much wider range of propositions. During this time it has also improved social selling tools. LinkedIn's Sales Navigator is a powerful tool for targeting individuals, keeping up to date on lead and company changes and engaging your prospects to begin the sale process.

LinkedIn also has the opportunity of sponsored content in the news feed of targeted individuals that is common across most social networks. It also offers a lead generation tool that enables companies to directly gain leads through forms hosted by LinkedIn. Expect LinkedIn to continue to develop marketing tools and opportunities as Microsoft continue their monetization strategy at pace.

If professional individuals are key to your success or you operate in the B2B space then LinkedIn is an increasingly important channel.

Social selling

Sales have always been about developing relationships in order to improve conversion rates. Where this may have started with a cold call or visit, or an introduction, it now starts with content. This content can be posted by a salesperson who can then target specific individuals to share this with and over time develop relationships on social channels. This means that, when the time is right, that person is only a digital connection away. These relationships can be taken offline where they become even more powerful but, if this doesn't happen, the relationship can still continue in a powerful way. Salespeople can also use a wealth of tools to find specific individuals in defined jobs at companies in targeted sectors or of specific sizes in specific locations.

For more on social selling see the excellent book, *Social Selling: Techniques to influence buyers and changemakers* by Tim Hughes and Matt Reynolds.

Snapchat – 255 million users

Snapchat saw enormous growth in its early months. It has always been adopted far more by the younger audience than any other network and is therefore heavily youth oriented. They invented Stories, which were hugely popular but were quickly copied by the other networks. Since the IPO it has become clear that Snapchat, whilst heavily adopted, has struggled for growth as its offering has mostly been replicated by the larger networks. If youth marketing is a key focus then you should certainly use Snapchat's advertising mediums. They have a number of innovative opportunities and continue to be an innovative company.

Other significant channels to consider include Pinterest, Tumblr, Flickr, Meetup, Ask.fm, QZone and Reddit, amongst many more.

Alongside these unique elements to each channel it is important that we appreciate that every social network is different. There are different demographics of user, different times that posts are more effective, different types of posts that work. These trends change all the time and so we can't put them onto paper in a book, but you should research and understand the differences so that you can differentiate your content accordingly. You must not simply replicate content across all channels as it will not prove effective everywhere.

Content

Content strategy is looked at in Chapter 14 and this should be your lead here. There are, however, some specific considerations for social media. Video is one of these.

Video remains an exceptionally engaging channel. We have already mentioned YouTube and that most networks now have native video capability. Beyond this you should consider live video. This is an area that has grown enormously and the potential for live reviews, events, tours and news is significant. You must think these through carefully and ensure you genuinely have a story to tell as live commenting needs close moderation and can go horribly wrong if not planned effectively. A powerful and exciting experience that can be provided through social channels very effectively is 360 video. Also consider vertical video here. Traditionally, video is recorded horizontally but social is absorbed through mobile – on vertical screens. The networks continue to optimize for vertical video and you should build this into your plans.

We mentioned earlier that visual content is far more engaging on social media and so you should build in strategies around beautiful imagery, infographics and product shots that tell your story and provide an emotional connection.

Augmented and virtual reality are also powerful opportunities. Even filters – which are common on social media profile photos now, are a type of augmented reality. The Pokemon Go craze and other similar apps are also classic examples but the applications are growing broader every week. Look at opportunities for these to fit with your brand.

Finally, as mentioned above, consider Stories. These are available on Snapchat, Instagram and Facebook. Alongside your standard content strategy, you may want to consider a 'real-time content strategy' that ensures you produce regular timely content for this opportunity.

Social publishing

With the vast quantity of social platforms at your disposal (and, of course, at the disposal of your customers) the job of managing the publication of your social messages is quite daunting. However, as with everything in the social world we are spoilt for choice when it comes to social publishing platforms. Some to consider are Hootsuite, Sprout Social and TweetDeck. These platforms connect with many leading social networks (TweetDeck is specific to Twitter of course). They allow scheduling of posts, monitoring of performance and collaboration.

Influencers

As we have mentioned, social media in its truest sense is about being social. One great example of this is influencers.

Influencers are individuals who literally influence others through having large followings and respected opinions. Brands that partner with influencers have the potential to create strong relationships that can in turn broaden the reach and increase the reputation of a brand and its products or services.

To source influencers, brands simply need to identify them through searching. If you find an individual who has a large following in the field that you operate in and that following is highly engaged in their content then you have found an influencer. There are different levels of influencers and the smaller, more targeted influencers, sometimes referred to as micro-influencers, are often the more successful, if less glamorous targets.

You must consider the fact that influencer marketing is considered paid endorsement in the United States and this may well extend across other countries in the near future.

Figure 11.3 Influence types

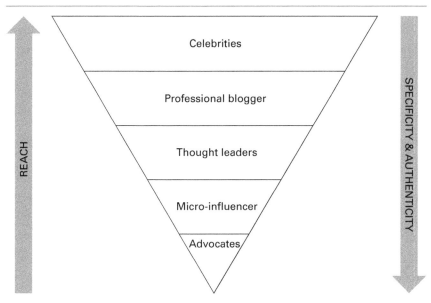

There are three approaches to Influencer marketing and you should consider them all:

1 Marketing **through** influencers, is the techniques of using influencers to promote your product to their dedicated base.

2 Marketing **to** influencers, is the method of promoting your brand to influencers with the aim of raising awareness with influencers rather than with their followers.

3 Marketing **with** influencers is turning influencers into advocates in order to gain better relationships with them and even potentially drive down your costs.

Influencer marketing is an important part of the social strategy for many businesses.

Social advertising

In 2013 Facebook took the brave step of including advertising in the main news feed. Predictably there was a massive backlash (as there had been, and will be in the future, for all major redesigns) but this time Facebook had got it right commercially (and as the platform is so ubiquitous the majority of those who said they would leave the platform just went quiet for a while before returning).

The placement of ads made a difference, as did the targeting, which allows advertisers to create 'look-a-like' groups based on their current customer base. The mix of better targeting and better ad placement has worked wonders for advertisers and, of course, Facebook's bottom line.

It is worth remembering, though, that social ads should not be duplicates of your direct response display ads. Social can absolutely be a direct response channel and indeed is well suited as such for some verticals (fashion, for example). However, the platform is also great for more engaging or even experimental ads – think awesome content that gives users something to share and advocate, not 'just an ad'. We looked at some specific advertising opportunities in the social networks section above and these continue to evolve. Ensure you understand the landscape here as you build out your strategy.

One important point to note here is that the platforms have slowly moved away from including organic brand content in news feeds. This is in the greatest part due to users preferring their families' and friends' content over branded content but it also plays nicely to their commercial goals. It is therefore now vital to have a paid strategy to social. Organic reach is not what it used to be and therefore amplifying it with a paid strategy is close to essential now.

CASE STUDY   State Bicycle Company

Background

State Bicycle Company is an Arizona-based bicycle manufacturer. The company's goal was to use Facebook to familiarize people with its brand and vision in order to increase fan engagement when communicating product releases and events and to drive Facebook followers to buy from its website.

Strategy

To familiarize people with its company, State Bicycle Company first created a Facebook page: a good starting point for any business. From here the company updated its profile picture with the company's logo and added a cover photo featuring an image of one of the new fixed-gear bikes.

The company then added milestones to the page to define key moments, such as 'State Bicycle Co wins Wolfpack Marathon Crash Race'. Milestones are a nice way of highlighting a company's history and telling a story.

The company then ran Facebook Ads to drive bike sales. It was able to use some specific targeting to test correlation between certain likes. For example, it used Broad Category targeting, including 'Arcade Fire', 'M83' and 'Passion Pit' to test a correlation with certain areas of music. It also focused on rival brands and generic keywords such as 'fixies', 'track bikes' and targeted people living in cities with ads promoting specific events.

To increase engagement in its announcements the company hosted frequent photo contests, ran a weekly event called 'Facebook Friday', which included a discount coupon specifically for fans who see their posts on Fridays, and a great deal more. It also used sponsored stories to promote this.

Results

The results of such a well-thought-through and broad strategy were strong. US $500,000 in annual incremental sales now comes from coupon codes and traffic exclusive from Facebook; 12 per cent of traffic to the State Bicycle Company website comes from Facebook. The cost per click on Facebook is one-fifth compared with other advertising platforms and the company saw a tenfold growth in its fan base within 12 months.

Key lessons

Social media success relies on a number of factors, and this company applied them all effectively. It developed clever content ideas that were timely and viral in nature. The content was promoted with sponsored activity and data was used to target the obvious places as well as more creative options. This type of rounded strategy will always give you the best chance of success.

The SEO angle

Much has been written about how social media can help with natural search rankings. We do not know the full details of the search engine algorithms of course but there is a link between social engagement that is related to a site and its search rankings. Perhaps discussed less but very pertinent is that social media is increasingly being used as a discovery tool. It is not uncommon for significant percentages of web traffic to be driven from social channels.

Why? Because people are increasingly using social filtering (ie things tweeted/posted by their friends/connections) as a means of discovering content and brands as well as search engines. For example, prior to the explosive growth of social media since 2007, most internet users would search, primarily through Google, to find something online. Since then, social media has created an increase in the interactions we make with each other on a daily basis and, as a result, we are now far more interested in the recommendations and insights we receive from our network than from internet advertising (hence why influencers are so important). Our networks may even include the brands themselves. These recommendations and insights can in turn steer our brand awareness and consideration.

As we mentioned in Chapter 2, digital is an ecosystem and everything we do on one channel affects the others so consider SEO within your social strategy. Are you linking to your site regularly, are you researching keywords for your content strategy? Are you maximizing your relationships on social channels to expand reach and increase positive noise?

Measurement

The first question to answer when considering measurement approach is what to measure. It is important to think beyond fans or views – while these metrics are interesting the real value is in the quality of the engagement:

- Volume and reach: the quantity and penetration of touchpoints with potential customers.
- Engagement and quality: the quality of interaction with potential customers.

Measuring volume and reach

Typical volume/reach metrics are:

- Brand volume: volume of brand and brand product mentions.
- Market reach: volume of fan/Twitter/subscriber followers (and their followers).
- Twitter followers: volume of Twitter followers on a brand's Twitter profile.
- Facebook fans: volume of Facebook fans on a brand's Facebook page.
- YouTube views: volume of YouTube video views.

And, of course, you can roll out this approach to other platforms that you/ your customers are active on.

Measuring engagement and quality

Typical engagement/quality metrics are:

- Brand conversation: the number of times that individuals are talking repeatedly about a brand, as well as comments and replies on the main social profiles.

- Content dissemination: an aggregated value that measures how brands have engaged with their audience across all the main platforms (to measure whether there is a bias to one or more platform).

- Twitter engagement: the number of posts, shares or retweets related to the brand.

- Facebook engagement: the number of posts or shares related to the brand.

- YouTube engagement: the number of shares of videos and subscribers to the brand channel.

- Overall sentiment: high volume/engagement is one thing but you also need to measure the sentiment: 100,000 comments sounds good, but if 99,000 are negative then you have a problem. All good social media monitoring tools will help measure sentiment.

Creating a social media dashboard

The above metrics require some work to piece together. Tools such as Brandwatch (or other social media monitoring tools), Facebook Insights and Google Analytics will help, but the key is to glue all this data together into a social media dashboard that is meaningful to your business.

This starts, of course, with your objectives – if you know what you expect to achieve from social then you know what to measure.

Data

One other consideration in social media is data. There have been many issues with data leaks and privacy online in the 21st century. New regulations are being put into effect regularly across the world and many are aimed specifically at the large tech businesses and especially social media sites.

Methods such as targeting individuals through interests and uploading client data for lookalike targeting may become more challenging over time.

You must also ensure that you consider the permissions you have from your clients and the permissions social media users have given to the networks before finalizing your plans. If mistakes are made in this area it can cost your business fines that are in the hundreds of millions of dollars or reputational damage that can be even more harmful.

Summary

This chapter looked at the evolution of social media and its meteoric rise in society. We examined how it fits into your digital strategy and some of the challenges with both organic and paid activity. We looked at the different types of social media and how each social network differs. We also looked at how SEO is affected by the signals received from your social media activity, as well as advertising and measurement.

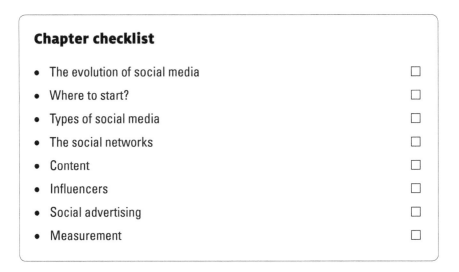

Chapter checklist

- The evolution of social media ☐
- Where to start? ☐
- Types of social media ☐
- The social networks ☐
- Content ☐
- Influencers ☐
- Social advertising ☐
- Measurement ☐

Further reading

- *On social media marketing:*

  Macarthy, A (2018) *500 Social Media Marketing Tips*, CreateSpace Independent Publishing Platform

  McDonald, J (2019) *The Social Media Marketing Workbook*, CreateSpace Independent Publishing Platform

References

Brandt, M (2015) [accessed 1 November 2015] 80% of Twitter's Users are Mobile, Statista [Online] http://www.statista.com/chart/1520/number-of-monthly-active-twitter-users

Millward, S (2013) [accessed 1 November 2015] Check Out the Numbers of China's Top 10 Social Media Sites, *TechInAsia*, 13/03 [Online] https://www.techinasia.com/2013-china-top-10-social-sites-infographic

An implementation guide is available at:
www.koganpage.com/DigitalMarketingStrategy/2

Marketing automation, messaging and e-mail marketing – the unsung heroes

12

What we will cover in this chapter

This chapter looks at e-mail marketing and messaging. These direct channels are increasingly important in the marketing landscape and so we will discuss the key principles of them, considerations around data and what platforms are available to aid your strategy. We will also look at what good e-mail marketing looks like, including testing and measurement. The key areas covered in this chapter are:

- E-mail marketing today
- The 5 Ts of e-mail marketing
- How are businesses using e-mail marketing?
- Account management versus centralized communications
- Follow-up
- Regulation
- Platforms
- Messaging and SMS
- Measurement

> ## Chapter goals
>
> By the end of this chapter you should have a clear view of how to implement an effective e-mail strategy. You should understand the technology landscape and know the KPIs you will need to focus on.

E-mail marketing today

Many organizations now look beyond e-mail as a marketing tool, feeling that it is somehow old news and tainted by the reputation of 'spam', which originally referred to unsolicited e-mail but now is used to describe any unwanted or poor-quality communications. Owing to the filtering tools that every e-mail service, personal or corporate now utilizes, few of us are fully aware of just how much spam is actually being sent to us. Both tools and regulations have gone some distance in recent years to help cleanse and partly solve this issue. Most recently, the GDPR (General Data Protection Regulation), implemented on 25 May 2018 in Europe, has seen significant improvements in data accuracy, permissions and therefore reduced spam for consumers. If it is implemented well, companies should also see an improvement in their core e-mail metrics. Volumes may be down but engagement should be up and, for the more experienced marketers, this has always been the goal. Sending large volumes to a poorly engaged base creates spam, reputational damage and potentially very real technical issues with deliverability, which harms future strategy. Sending to only those who are genuinely interested has quite the reverse effect and is far more efficient for all involved.

> ## GDPR
>
> As part of the General Data Protection Regulation that came into effect in Europe in 2016 and needed to be fully implemented by May 2018, it became essential to ensure your organization has specific permission from an individual to use his or her data for marketing purposes.
>
> Alongside this you must communicate to your customers, prospects or any other individuals and organizations that you wish to communicate with, various information including what personal data you collect, how you

collect it, how you store it and how they can remove their data if required. It is vitally important to appreciate this and companies that get this wrong can expect fines up to 4 per cent of global annual turnover or €20 million.

You should note that GDPR only applies in Europe or in organizations where European data is handled.

Spam aside, the reality is that e-mail marketing remains an incredibly valuable weapon in the marketers' arsenal, provided it is used correctly. And that is the key here. Many people will write off e-mail entirely as a channel and suggest it has been replaced by messaging or SMS but this simply isn't so. Messaging and SMS are far more personal and intrusive than e-mail and so have a very different usage consideration. They are also more timely. E-mails are often acted on many hours or days after they are received whereas direct messages tend to apply to an instant communication, for example a customer service conversation, offer, password reset or news flash.

For some time now, e-mail marketing has been seen as having diminishing value, with a major contributing factor being the rise of social media. Whilst it is obvious that social tools have replaced a lot of what previously would have been communicated via e-mail, be it the social platforms themselves or the above mentioned related messaging apps, you only have to consider how e-mail remains for most organizations the de facto communication method to know that it is important. The volume of e-mail accounts also continues to grow rapidly. According to Statista (2018), the number of e-mail accounts worldwide is due to grow from 4.1 billion in 2014 to 5.6 billion by 2019. We can therefore agree that this channel is not going to die in the near future.

It is important to note, however, that there is a generational factor here. Younger generations will rely more heavily on messaging than older generations, but we must not fall into the trap of thinking younger generations do not use e-mail. In fact, a study by the National Cyber Security Alliance and Microsoft in September 2017 (*Keeping Up with Generation App*) found that whilst 66 per cent of teenagers were using Snapchat and 61 per cent using Facebook, 75 per cent were using Gmail.

It is also worth noting that e-mail has long been the most effective channel. In this I mean that the return on investment (ROI) has always been strong. Studies continue to show that most marketers who use e-mail within their strategy still rate the ROI as the best of all their channels. The opportunity to directly reach large audiences for a very small distribution cost is of course very attractive and the ability to create strong call to actions that fit directly into the end of a conversion funnel is very powerful.

Where SEO, social media and paid advertising, perhaps the more glamorous siblings of e-mail marketing, are focused on attracting new customers and raising awareness, e-mail plays a vital role in maintaining and growing relationships. E-mail therefore remains an important communication tool and part of the marketing mix but only when what the recipient receives is relevant to him or her. If not, then unsubscribes increase, brand perception is affected and overall marketing effectiveness falls.

It is important therefore to consider what good e-mail marketing looks like, whether it is the automated or semi-automated sending of e-mails through an e-mail marketing platform or manually sending an individual e-mail to a prospect or customer.

The 5 Ts of e-mail marketing

There are a number of factors to effective e-mail marketing and I think of these as the 5 Ts of e-mail success. These are:

1 Targeting: Are you reaching the right people with this communication?

2 Timing: Are you reaching them at the right time of day, week, in their relationship?

3 Template: Is the design optimized?

4 Testing: Are you learning? Are you reviewing the data?

5 Tone: Is the content compelling?

Targeting

Good e-mail marketing begins with the quality of the database you have. It could start with deciding on the market you wish to target and the sorts of messaging and themes you want to target them with. If you then have an appropriate database to target with this messaging then you are in a good position; if not, you may need to consider purchasing data sets and there are many suppliers that offer this service. Your own data, if managed correctly is of course far more powerful than a cold list that you have bought of individuals who have no relationship with you.

You should ensure you therefore have a data collection strategy. This could be through maximizing sign-ups when selling products, promoting a newsletter, creating gated content on your website or collecting e-mail addresses at events, amongst many other means.

Gated content

This term refers to content that is behind a virtual gate. This is a technique commonly used online, especially amongst content publishers such as news sites. Some content is shown publicly to the visitor but if they want the full piece of research or the full article they must give their e-mail address as a value exchange. This can be a fantastic way to create a targeted database.

As well as your data in its broadest sense you also need to ensure each message is targeted. You should segment your data effectively and understand the preferences of your audience to ensure users only receive the communications they are interested in. This ensures strong results, low unsubscribes and no brand damage.

Timing

To time your e-mails effectively you need to consider the concept of timing from a few different perspectives. First and most simply – time itself such as day of week or time of day. Second, you need to consider frequency to ensure your audience is not flooded with communications. Third, you should consider frequency across multiple communications. By this I mean not just frequency of your regular newsletter, but frequency across everything. If consumers receive a newsletter once a week maybe they will be happy with that frequency. If, however, they are also receiving 10 other communications then they may well be flooded. Finally, you should consider timing from the perspective of what stage of the customer journey the audience is on. Sending an up-sell message to a customer who has just made a complaint would not be sensible so your data remains critical here.

Template

E-mail design is a fine art. Your first focus should be on ensuring your template works across all devices. This remains a focal point for many organizations and must not be ignored as mobile e-mail will account for 22 to 77 per cent of e-mail opens, depending on your target audience, product and e-mail type according to emailmonday (2018).

Other key design principles include:

Visual hierarchy

Ensure the structure of your e-mail is clear and instantly understandable. This is far more important than beautiful imagery. Fonts, colours, layout all contribute to this.

Call to action

Whatever you want people to do should be instantly recognizable through buttons and clear visual cues. This is of course true across marketing design but remains crucial here. Don't confuse the reader with multiple calls to action.

Visuals

Ensure your imagery and colour palette is representative of your brand of course but also representative of the message you are trying to portray. Positive imagery is almost universally beneficial across design.

Copy

Keep it short and to the point. E-mail is not a channel people want to spend a lengthy time in. If your message is lengthy, use the e-mail to bring them to a nicer home for longer content such as your blog or video content.

Testing

As with any other digital channel, you should be implementing test-and-learn principles throughout. Consider A/B testing a number of factors such as send time and day, imagery, call-to-action button colour and placement, subject line and other variables. To enable this you must ensure you have appropriate analytics in place and tagged links. We will discuss this later in the chapter.

Tone

We discuss content in more detail in Chapter 14 but there are some specific considerations here for e-mail. Dynamic content is an excellent opportunity to personalize communications. If you know the preferences of an individual and have your data in good shape you can potentially insert information related to or based on his or her interests, account activity, behaviours or other factors. This can turn a generic message into something truly personalized without the need to send individual e-mails, and will be a key trend in e-mail marketing over the next few years.

Subject lines are of course another key area of content that applies to e-mail marketing. Your marketing copywriting skills will be tested to their fullest here. You must not try to trick the audience into opening the e-mail, and avoiding terms such as 'free' is advisable as this can be negatively viewed by not just individuals but also spam filters and can therefore impact visibility. There are tools available to optimize subject lines for you. Key considerations here are:

- Short eg 'Build your new smartphone.'
- Actionable eg 'Complete your application.'
- Enticing eg 'What DIY mistakes are you making?'
- Sense of urgency eg 'Dress sale ends at midnight.'
- Localized eg 'Shanghai shoppers prefer this.'
- Consider numbered lists eg 'Top 5 reasons to invest in Europe.'

Tactical e-mail messaging is also important. This is in reference to promoting specific messages. Your e-mail content will fit into your broader content and communications strategies but sometimes you will simply need to generate some leads for your sales teams as they are not hitting targets. This is perfectly acceptable and if your business model makes this likely then you should ensure your comms strategy leaves room for this.

How are businesses using e-mail marketing?

The *Email Marketing Industry Census 2017* by Econsultancy (an important company to familiarize yourself with in the digital space) in association with Adestra, gives a clear view of how companies are using e-mail and their priorities. According to this report, companies are focused on areas such as segmentation, optimizing for mobile devices and list cleansing. We have discussed these already within this chapter. Other uses include encouraging sharing of content on social media, transactional e-mails, remarketing and video content. Each of these is a tactical e-mail to achieve a specific result. Beyond these uses companies also use e-mail for lead nurturing, content personalization, location-based content and behavioural targeting.

As we can see from this list, the opportunities for the e-mail channel are broad and, as an effective ROI channel, it remains a crucial part of the mix of most businesses' marketing strategies. Some of the biggest challenges remain in the fields of personalization and optimization. AI is going some way to fixing this and the landscape is likely therefore to change in the next few years.

CASE STUDY Paper Tiger

Background

Paper Tiger Document Solutions is a Chicago-area document shredding and storage company serving businesses and consumers. Paper Tiger launched a drop-in Saturday shredding service several years ago. Initially, despite the launch being based on demand, this proved unsuccessful and so the company looked to promote further and gain some traction.

Strategy

In 2016, the company's agency, CC communications, named the event 'Shred Fest' and began to promote it in a monthly e-mail campaign. Word of this event spread fast. The company now offers coffee and doughnuts to visitors who get to witness the process and even shows presentations on the journey of the documents post-shredding.

In January 2018 the agency added to the experience by launching a 'Thank You' e-mail campaign that is sent following Shred Fest to attendees who sign up to Paper Tiger's e-mail list. The campaign has a personalized approach (it is sent from the owners and includes their signatures), tells the reader what to expect next (a monthly e-mail) and shares interesting content.

Results

Today the four-hour event draws hundreds of business owners and consumers, and generates 20 times the revenue it did in the beginning. The first 'Thank You' e-mail to Shred Fest attendees generated a 55 per cent open rate and 25 per cent click rate, and the monthly newsletters also deliver strong results.

Key lessons

By developing e-mail communications that are personalized, include interesting content and by only sending to a relevant audience with follow-ups and an indication of what's next, you are giving something of real value to each recipient and ensuring no surprises in the future. This ensures great results and high retention of your e-mail subscriber lists.

Account management versus centralized communications

We mentioned lead nurturing above, and e-mail can be a useful tool to support a sales team, but sales and marketing must be truly aligned to make this work. In theory, putting together a series of e-mails is relatively easy but if your sales team is not aware of e-mails being sent to its accounts serious issues can occur. Customers can ask their account manager about the communication and be greeted with an uncomfortable silence that reflects poorly on your brand. Even worse, your sales team may not have the resource to deal with the increase in opportunities that arise from the e-mail. It is vital therefore, for any companies with this business model, to ensure sales and marketing departments are aligned on e-mail communications as they would be about any other activity likely to affect the other department.

Follow-up

Also critical in e-mail is follow-up. This may be using e-mails to pre-empt and follow up sales activity. It may be using phone calls to follow up e-mails. It may be using other digital channels to do either of the above. This is all part of the integrated strategic approach and you should ensure that you do not consider e-mail in isolation as, when combined with another channel, it can be far more powerful.

Regulation

There are of course many regulations around privacy and data protection and these are likely to continue to roll out over the coming years. We have mentioned the General Data Protection Regulation above and it is important for you to understand the detail of this or the detail of the regulations in your location and industry. This is not something you can afford to ignore in the 21st century. It is also changing at pace and so staying up to speed at least annually is important. You may have internal data protection or legal colleagues who can help you with this. If not I would recommend regular training courses to stay up to speed.

Platforms

When asked to select the three most important features of an e-mail service provider's technology platform, two-thirds (66 per cent) selected marketing automation capability. This has now overtaken user-friendly interface (60 per cent) as the single most important attribute of an ESP (E-mail Service Provider), underscoring the importance that marketers are now attaching to automation. (Econsultancy, 2017)

There are many e-mail platforms available now with a variety of functions. Many are part of a broader marketing technology stack and others are purely focused on e-mail. Some are built to deliver fast and easy access for small businesses whereas others are purely focused on enterprise level implementation. Some of the key names in this space include Salesforce, Adobe, Oracle, Marketo, Mailchimp and Pure360. This list is in no specific order and is neither a set of recommendations nor a complete list, but is more a list of popular and successful players in this space. Your strategy will have its own goals and challenges and you should research the field and select the most appropriate platform considering CRM integration, pricing, integration, data protection, cloud or on-premise preference and other factors.

It does make sense to consider using an e-mail tool that is part of a marketing automation suite that also supports website personalization. In order to personalize a web experience it is necessary to track the interactions a visitor has with a website, and therefore as well as personalizing the web experience, this should also mean you can personalize e-mails using the same analytics data. In this case, consuming specific content on the website can also trigger specific e-mails to individuals, making them aware of an offer or a particularly relevant case study. It may be that a visitor, after spending some time perusing the site and appearing to have particular interests, has been inactive on the site for a few weeks – rules can be put in place that would then automatically send the visitor a personalized e-mail reminding him or her, maybe, that there is still time to enjoy a particular discount.

The journeys, such as that mentioned above, which marketing automation suites provide, can be extremely powerful in delivering timely communications with little effort needed from your marketing department. When selecting a partner therefore you should consider these key factors specific to e-mail:

- Cloud or on-premise based?
- Integration with your marketing technology stack (CMS, CRM, Analytics etc).
- Are automated journeys necessary?
- Cost – integration, set-up, training, ongoing licensing and support.
- Timelines for integration.
- Personalization requirements.
- Easy to use design interface.
- Data management and segmentation.
- Lead scoring opportunity.
- Landing page and form optimization.
- Dynamic content.

Also consider that many marketing automation platforms go beyond e-mail and can also offer website and social media solutions.

Messaging and SMS

We have talked a great deal about e-mail marketing but messaging and SMS are also key direct communication channels and you must consider them within your strategy. This may simply be in terms of customer service, for example deliver updates or product support, but as these channels continue to grow at pace (social messengers are now larger in user numbers than social networks), they will increasingly be used for marketing.

Some of the larger messengers today are WhatsApp, Facebook Messenger (both owned by Facebook), WeChat and QQ Mobile (both developed by Tencent). This differs greatly by region with the first two being largest in Europe and America whilst the latter two are the largest in Asia. Messaging services are also increasingly becoming part of social networks as the two begin to meld.

Businesses have been slow to adapt to the apps and vice versa. Security remains a concern although this is likely to be addressed in the near future. Companies are, however, already using messaging services for a range of purposes. Uses include:

- building lists of people you can directly communicate with through your company messenger account;
- improving your booking process;
- chatbots for servicing;
- live streaming;
- sponsored posts.

The benefits are of course that the channel is direct to consumers who probably have notifications turned on. They are using a platform they are familiar with rather than being forced onto one of your platforms. The messages are instant. These three factors are a powerful combination.

In order to make this channel work as part of your strategy the key factor is relevancy. The story is compelling as to the opportunity here and almost every business should be considering an application of messaging and SMS within their organization but only if relevant. Anything that is not relevant will not only be ignored but will be considered invasive. Messaging is, at its heart, about convenience. You must deliver only what makes a consumer's life easier. Whether that is customer service, booking or live content, it must fit with the channel. If it doesn't then you should consider another channel.

Measurement

Measurement is vital to all channels, and most e-mail tools will allow you to run reports that tell you how many e-mails have been sent, how many were delivered, bouncebacks (e-mails that could not be delivered), opens (although this statistic is often skewed by automated virus checking applications) and how many were actioned (eg clicks). It is vital that results are tracked and considered, but as with all marketing efforts, in the context of an overall strategy and plan.

Bouncebacks

There are two types of bounceback or bounces when sending e-mails.

Hard bounces

This is where the e-mail no longer exists or for some other reason is not reachable. This means your data is wrong or out-dated. You should have a very low percentage of these in your data or you have a serious data quality issue.

Soft bounces

This is where the e-mail was delivered but the recipient is unlikely to have read it. For example, it may be that the server was down or the inbox is full. The percentage should again be low but this would not necessarily mean that your data was poor. If you see an e-mail address returning a soft bounce for a long period of time, however, you may wish to cleanse that data.

Depending on your goal it is unlikely that your goal is open. This suggests that people have an interest in your content and your subject line plays a key role here, as does your data quality. However, you are probably trying to encourage individuals to buy a product or view some content. If they haven't clicked then that would suggest the e-mail itself was poor, the content didn't align with the subject or the offer wasn't interesting enough. Establishing which of these is the case can be done through A/B testing as we mentioned above.

Your key measurements in e-mail marketing are:

- Deliverability – What percentage arrived?
- Open rate – What percentage were opened?
- Click-through rate – What percentage were clicked on?
- Open-to-click rate – What percentage of those opened resulted in a click?
- Action or goal completion – What percentage actually completed the action?
- Unsubscribe rate – What percentage unsubscribed from this e-mail?
- List growth – Size of your list over time.
- CPX – Cost per X.

Where the action or goal is, for example, a purchase, video view, sign up, unsubscribes are a factor of low relevancy. This could be down to low brand engagement, poor targeting, incorrect frequency of communications (too high or too low) or simply a poor e-mail. List growth is not a factor of the e-mail itself but of the strategy you have in place to grow your list. This may include a member-get-member programme, sharing functionality, newsletter sign-up forms or using other marketing channels to grow your list. Cost per X shows the effectiveness of the channel where X may be engagement, sale, lead etc. For a strategy that sends large volumes of e-mails you may also wish to track brand awareness or social mentions to understand the impact your e-mails may be having.

Summary

E-mail marketing remains a highly effective channel and the growth of messaging opens up significant digital direct marketing opportunities. Direct marketing may not be the most glamorous digital channel but it remains, and always will, a strong performer and effective method of reaching engaged and action-oriented consumers.

Chapter checklist

- E-mail marketing today ☐
- The 5 Ts of e-mail marketing ☐
- How are businesses using e-mail marketing? ☐
- Account management versus centralized communications ☐
- Follow-up ☐
- Regulation ☐
- Platforms ☐
- Messaging and SMS ☐
- Measurement ☐

Further reading

- *On e-mail marketing*:

  Brodie, I (2013) *Email Persuasion: Captivate and engage your audience, build authority and generate more sales with email marketing*, Rainmaker Publishing

Littleton, N (2014) *Delivered: The no-nonsense guide to successful email marketing*, Future Visions Creative Ltd

Paulson, M (2015) *Email Marketing Demystified: Build a massive mailing list, write copy that converts and generate more sales*, American Consumer News

References

Econsultancy (2017) [accessed 20 November 2018] Email Marketing Industry Census 2017 [Online] https://econsultancy.com/reports/2017-email-census/

emailmonday (2018) [accessed 20 November 2018] The Ultimate Mobile Email Statistics Overview [Online] https://www.emailmonday.com/mobile-email-usage-statistics/

National Cyber Security Alliance (2017) [accessed 20 November 2018] Keeping Up with Generation App: NCSA parent/teen online safety survey [Online] https://staysafeonline.org/wp-content/uploads/2017/10/Generation-App-Survey-Report-2017.pdf

Statista (2018) [accessed 20 November 2018] Number of Active E-mail Accounts Worldwide from 2014 to 2019 (in millions) [Online] https://www.statista.com/statistics/456519/forecast-number-of-active-email-accounts-worldwide/

An implementation guide is available at:
www.koganpage.com/DigitalMarketingStrategy/2

Lead generation 13
that delivers results

What we will cover in this chapter

Not every business is focused on e-commerce. Lead generation remains a key focus for many businesses, especially those with a business-to-business model. As a result, understanding how to effectively manage leads through digital channels is a vital skillset for the modern marketer. In this chapter we will look at:

- The changing landscape
- Lead scoring
- Lead generation across the digital channels
- Keeping the lead alive
- Measurement

Chapter goals

By the end of this chapter you should understand the core principles of constructing a lead generation process and how this can play out across the digital channels as well as how to measure success.

Lead generation is a fascinating space and one that has changed significantly in the digital era. Before we look at some of these changes and how to implement a successful lead generation strategy, let's take a second to define a lead, as there are many interpretations. When we discuss a lead in this chapter we are defining it as a qualified potential customer, ie an individual who has expressed specific interest in discussing a commercial opportunity with your business. Lead generation is quite simply the process of finding these individuals or encouraging them to find you and gaining an enquiry from them in order to convert them into customers.

The most widely recognized lead generation technique is probably cold calling: a rather irritating and often scattergun approach that relies on the volume of data to ensure success with no regard for the volume of consumers who are left annoyed by the experience. Modern lead generation in the new data rich world is a far more sophisticated machine.

Push versus pull – the changing landscape

As we mentioned above, cold calling was a common approach of lead generation. This relied on buying or otherwise obtaining data and pushing your message out to that audience. However, now that data is available through our own platforms and third-party platforms, we are able to far more effectively target individuals who meet specific criteria and communicate directly with them to build relationships with the right people at the right time. In fact this has even become an expectation. Cold messaging is not just frustrating but is now often considered a sign of laziness, as it is rarely necessary. Potential customers now use their own sources of information to research and this means two things. First, that the consumers are more likely to come to you if their research is positive in your favour; and second, that consumers leave behind signs of where they have been, which can help your targeting.

Understanding this and implementing an effective lead generation strategy can therefore result in more effective marketing metrics, more efficient sales people, stronger conversion, stickier customers and a stronger brand reputation, amongst other factors. This affects how you plan your entire digital marketing strategy including content that leads customers to you and helps them do their research, the way your SEO supports the research phase and much more, but for now let's focus on what this means for lead generation.

Lead scoring

An important part of understanding lead quality is a technique known as lead scoring. This quite simply means giving the leads a score based on key factors to determine the value and likely conversion of those leads. As lead generation is usually a channel that is more closely shared between marketing and sales than most other channels, this system is vital to ensure smooth handovers and positive relationships internally. Some of the factors that may be used to score a lead include:

- at what point in their shopping lifecycle they are (browsing, researching, buying);
- their relationship with your company (existing customer, known prospect, unknown suspect);
- their interactions (e-mail open, event visit, form completion);
- their profile with regard to your targeting (exact target, close fit, no fit).

This method can give a clear picture on the lead quality but there are some disadvantages that must be appreciated.

First, lead scoring can often be misleading. Imagine an individual who is sent an e-mail, which he or she opens and clicks through to your site. This individual has joined two of your mailing lists about your products and regularly engages with your social activity. He or she fits the standard demographic model of your targeting. This seems like a consumer who is on the edge of being a customer and so should be actively pursued. And now what if we told you this was someone looking for a job with you and so was doing research. This is where lead grading comes in.

Lead grading is a technique used to understand the individual in more detail. We see the perceived intent from lead scoring but when we layer over the lead grading we look at factors such as location, job title, company sector and we see a much clearer picture.

You should also consider that different product lines and subsidiaries may need different models. A lead scoring model for garden furniture products may be very different from a model for fencing, although your company may offer both.

Lead generation across the digital channels

Of all the channels for lead generation, including offline channels, content and e-mail marketing remain some of the leaders. Below we examine what you should consider for each channel when building your lead generation strategy.

Content

Content is a very important channel and we discuss content strategy and opportunities in more detail in Chapter 14. Techniques here include:

- highlights of a research paper or report but to request contact details to enable the consumer to read the full report or e-book;
- delivering a deep content strategy with an option to sign up to a newsletter to receive more;
- delivering training courses with the first stages free but sign-up required for the full course;
- product demo sign-ups to enable you to have a direct conversation;
- competitions and contests to win (targeting quality can be compromised here).

Website

Your website must be built to manage the lead generation process effectively. Ensure your site is fast, easy to understand, well signposted and focused on conversion. We talk about UX and design in Chapter 16.

SEO

You can use the content strategies above to build effective SEO strategies. Content is a corner of the SEO triangle, as we saw in Chapter 8, and so ensure that you include SEO thinking when building these plans.

Paid search

Paid search can be used to supplement your SEO or independently to drive specific lead generation campaigns. We discussed this channel more in Chapter 9 and the key principles of clearly communicating the benefit and ensuring highly targeted relevance remain vital here.

Display

You can use display advertising (as discussed in Chapter 10) to target the right individuals through programmatic techniques and bring them into your content or more direct lead generation strategy.

E-mail marketing

It is strongly recommended that you invest in an e-mail platform that enables you to effectively manage your data and deliver targeted e-mail campaigns.

There are many available and we discussed this and how to use e-mail effectively in detail in Chapter 12. Without this you will struggle to build the digital relationships you may need to further the lead relationship.

Social media

Last but by no means least we must look at social media. This channel has become an enormously important one for lead generation. There are countless case studies of success stories and the networks themselves are continuing to monetize their models in favour of this opportunity. Let's remember that we are not considering social media advertising in its purest sense here (see Chapter 11 for this) but specifically lead generation on the channel.

Social media is, at its heart, about relationships and the best lead generation strategies are the same. This is where the synergy lies and why this channel must be part of your plans. We talked specifically about social selling in Chapter 11 and that helped us understand how sales techniques now work with the social media channels. There are also other considerations on social media for lead generation.

LinkedIn is a business tool and so is working hard, especially since the Microsoft acquisition, to enable lead generation for businesses by releasing many tools around targeting, converting and analysing performance. One of these comprises their Lead Gen Forms, which enable users to see a brief overview of some content and then fill out a form to read more. This removes the lengthy journey to the company's website and directs the lead straight to them, thereby both easing the journey for the user and increasing the conversion for the company.

You can also use Google alerts and social media alerts to keep you informed of trending topics and brand mentions. You can use groups to get like-minded people together and feed your content in there to nurture relationships.

You can simply be actively involved in discussions on your key topics. This can result in you becoming a thought leader and a go-to destination for advice, which in turn results in increased sales. Build relationships with influencers and build your own profile to enable cross-sharing and cross-selling opportunities. Use LinkedIn's Sales Navigator tool, which has proved highly effective for many organizations in the social selling space. All of these techniques and more are available to enable you to use social media for lead generation.

CASE STUDY   IR and LinkedIn

Background

LinkedIn offers a specific advertising solution called Lead Generation. This service enables the individuals you target with your advertising on the platform to complete a form without leaving LinkedIn and this generates leads for the business. It has proved very successful for many businesses. IR is a leading global provider of performance management software that has shifted its model from events to content marketing. Its target audience is B2B and primarily large enterprise organizations – a difficult audience to reach.

Strategy

IR had to ensure it was able to tightly target the audience and deliver a strong return on investment. IR therefore used LinkedIn as it was a natural fit owing to the professional audience and precise targeting opportunities. It used skills, interests, group membership and geo-targeting to find the right people. Through this platform it is able to continuously optimize performance and remove any non-performing areas, which ensures the ROI remains strong. After some good results on Sponsored Content the company moved on to LinkedIn Lead Gen Forms and the results were very strong, as users don't have to leave the platform to finish their journey.

Results

IR found that conversion rates from the LinkedIn forms in the first few months were as strong as the landing pages it had been optimizing for over a year. It was clear that this simple channel was a powerful means of delivering high-quality leads.

Key lessons

The ability for users to complete a simple form on a platform that they are already on and that they trust delivers a strong completion rate. Coupled with the tight targeting capabilities, one can quickly deliver a large volume of high-quality leads.

Offline channels

This book focuses on digital channels and so we will not go into offline channels in great detail but, as the subtitle of the book suggests, we always consider the bigger picture. Events can be a highly effective method of generating leads and digital can play a part in this through techniques such as dedicated apps for your events, digital experiences at stands, pre- and post-registration digital communications and much more. You should consider how digital can play a part in your offline channels when it comes to lead generation. No marketing department can function at true effectiveness with the digital and offline channels working independently.

Referrals

Finally, it is vital to consider referrals. They have always played an important role in marketing but even more so since the increase of ratings engines and recommendations. Now people take referrals from strangers, not just from friends and family. You can encourage this by referring and recommending others (some social channels make this very easy). This plays nicely to the ego and, whilst it can be superficial, it often generates results.

Building a referral programme is also a worthwhile technique. Rewarding your customers through a Member-Get-Member approach can generate leads with minimal effort. And don't forget to ask. If you have strong relationships then people will not mind recommending you or introducing you to their network. Don't be afraid but do restrict this to your strongest relationships.

Keeping the lead alive

An important consideration for the lead generation channel is that this is not a one-off exercise. We have already looked at customer lifetime value (CLV) and we will go on to consider CRM and Loyalty in the next chapter, but with lead generation especially this continuous focus is vital.

This is because with a channel such as SEO or social media you can run your strategy and deliver your engagement, traffic, enquiries or sales, but with lead generation simply getting a foot in the door is meaningless if that lead is not nurtured and turned into business. The early stages of the process that we have talked through above are therefore, although important to get right, only the beginning of the story.

Of consumers requesting information on a company, 63 per cent will not purchase for at least three months (Clay, 2018), which goes some way to reinforcing this point. It is therefore important to have a lead nurturing plan in place. This is simply another way of saying CRM. You develop a relationship and continue to keep that relationship warm and engaged until the time is right. This can include product updates, demonstrations, offers, simple check-ins and other non-obtrusive communications to maintain the relationship rather than simply pursue the sale. These can be done through e-mail, messaging or offline channels such as telephone, direct mail or even face to face. See Chapter 17 for more detail on relationship marketing.

Measurement

We will discuss measurement and reporting in Chapter 19. Specifically for lead generation, however, there are some key metrics to consider and some considerations to keep in mind when reviewing your data. Key metrics include:

Lead quality

Here we refer to whether the lead was in fact aligned with the target market. Whether this lead progressed to becoming a customer is not relevant as there are other factors that would affect that such as sales techniques and product quality.

Lead timeliness

For example, was the lead at the right point of the buying cycle when you generated it? Some channels will be more effective than others at this and that should be reviewed. The average time it takes to convert a lead is another way to look at this.

Lead cost

The usual metrics of cost per lead and cost per converted lead will also be key factors in determining success.

Other factors that should be reviewed include:

- What content is delivering the leads?
- Are there specific times, or days that leads convert?
- Are the leads demonstrating behavioural trends (eg mobile usage)?

There are many more and they are dependent on the strategy you employ, but measurement is vital to learning, and therefore vital to the continuous improvement all digital marketers must implement to drive results.

Summary

Lead generation has an important role to play, especially in the B2B space. The shape of this channel has changed materially in the digital age and understanding how content strategy, social media and e-mail marketing play a part is crucial to success. Measurement is also vital. To make this channel work hard you need a full understanding of those areas mentioned above and so you should refer to the relevant chapters in this book.

Chapter checklist

- The changing landscape ☐
- Lead scoring ☐
- Lead generation across the digital channels ☐
- Keeping the lead alive ☐
- Measurement ☐

Further reading

- *On lead generation:*

  Andreeva, K (2016) *Lead Generation: Theory and practice*, CreateSpace Independent Publishing Platform

  Halligan, B and Shah, D (2014) *Inbound Marketing: Attract, engage, and delight*, John Wiley & Sons

  Perry, RL, Sturges, J, Singleton, P, Jordan, K and Fortune, MZ (2015) *Small Business Owner's Guide to Local Lead Generation*, CreateSpace Independent Publishing Platform

  Rothman, D (2014) *Lead Generation For Dummies*, For Dummies

Reference

Clay, R (2018) [accessed 20 November 2018] Why You Must Follow Up Leads, *Marketing Donut* [Online] https://www.marketingdonut.co.uk/sales/sales-techniques-and-negotiations/why-you-must-follow-up-leads

Content strategy – a key pillar of success

14

What we will cover in this chapter

This chapter covers content strategy and how to develop engaging content that fits with your digital strategy. Content is central to success for most digital marketing strategies today as consumers increasingly seek value. Understanding how to effectively employ it is vital. The key areas covered in this chapter are:

- What is content marketing?
- What is content?
- What content types should you use?
- Why content marketing?
- People and process for creating content
- Distribution
- Measuring the value of content
- International content

Chapter goals

By the end of this chapter you should understand how to build an effective content strategy and create engaging content for your customers. You should appreciate how to measure the value of content and how to distribute it effectively. You should understand how to use different types of content and how content works in an international business.

Content marketing has been one of the hottest topics in digital marketing for many years now. That is pretty impressive for a discipline that is hardly new – I would suggest it is at least 100 years old. After all, the *Michelin Guide* ticks a lot of the 'content marketing' boxes (useful, shareable content produced by a corporate) and they have been running since 1900. So content marketing is in fact not the hottest *new* thing in digital marketing – it is the hottest *old* thing in marketing. So lesson one, and perhaps the most important of all the lessons in this chapter, is to remember that it is nothing new. There is no reason to reinvent the wheel: what made good content 100 years ago still makes good content today. The difference is in the execution and delivery.

What is content marketing?

Well, for a start it is very broad: as we will see later, 'content' can take many forms. There are already hundreds of definitions for content marketing, in fact Google has 692 million results for the search term 'definition of content marketing' and those of you who have read the first edition of this book will spot that this number is a significant leap from the 53 million results just three years ago. So rather than an encyclopaedia definition let's look at how an established content marketer would assess whether content is 'great' or not. Great content needs to be all of the following:

- credible;
- shareable;
- useful or fun;
- interesting;
- relevant;
- timely;
- different;
- on brand and authentic.

The unfortunate truth is that quite a lot of content produced fails to hit many of the above and unless it does it is unlikely to succeed. Given this, these pillars of great content warrant further consideration:

Credible Audiences are fickle, they always have been (even Shakespeare complained about it) and always will be. One sure-fire way to turn an audience off is to present them with content that lacks credibility. In short, they have to believe it. This does not mean that they require a robust data set to be behind every statement made but it does mean that the statements made need to be substantiated enough to be believable. Take one of the many quizzes that appear on Facebook, for example, that purport to identify what type of person you are. A recent example was a quiz that 'estimated' your IQ by asking 10 questions. Of course 10 questions was not enough for anyone to truly believe the result was accurate but it was enough for the result to have enough credibility for the audience it was directed at (ie someone in 'fun' not 'work' mode). As part of your strategy you can create credibility through establishing the profile of the author as an expert (including a biography), through including facts and references from well-known sources or through ensuring that your content is authentic to your brand by only speaking on subjects that are relevant to your expertise.

Shareable Great content only becomes great if lots of people consume it, or rather if a significant percentage of the target audience do. To achieve this, it needs to be shareable. If all the other content pillars are met then the content should be shareable by default, but the acid test for any content that you or your team produce should be this question: 'will my audience want to share this?' While some consumers will go to great efforts to share good content (note that copy, paste, insert = great effort in the digital age) it is also good practice to make it easy for consumers to share your content via quick links to the most relevant platforms for sharing (eg Facebook, LinkedIn, Google+). A great way to make content shareable that is relevant to many industries is offering tips and advice. If you can create 'how to' videos or useful guides that help consumers learn how to achieve something then you will find that this content can be very shareable.

Useful or fun Content is useful or fun if it passes the 'so what?' test. Take the *Michelin Guide*, of its time a fairly unique publication that was highly useful. Fun speaks for itself; however, what is and is not fun is heavily dependent on your target audience. I have friends who love an LOL cat; I hate LOL cats; my mum doesn't know what an LOL cat is. The 'how to' guides above are a good example of useful but what about fun? Can you create an engaging game or fun tool that helps users to achieve something? This route can help customers to find a result they are looking for whilst also enjoying the process, making it both useful and fun.

Interesting There is some definite crossover between 'useful/fun' and interesting. However, it is still an important pillar in its own right. For example, it may be useful to know that you bought bread every time you went shopping this year but it is not particularly interesting. But how do we define whether something is interesting or not? After all, it is very subjective. A great measure is whether the content is interesting enough to be remarkable, ie it is worth making a remark about. This is a similar principle to one of the rules of good PR. Just because you find something interesting does not mean that your audience will – so, as with anything in marketing, consider it from the consumer's perspective.

Relevant Relevancy is probably the most crucial content pillar. As we will cover in depth later in this chapter you cannot start to create content until you understand your audience. You need to know what makes them tick and ensure all the content you produce is relevant to them. For example, if you are a manufacturer of chairs then creating content around basketball is likely to be beyond what is relevant to your business. If you can create a link between chairs and basketball then you can create relevant content and tap into both, but if there is no link then your content will be irrelevant and not engaging.

Timely Not all content is reliant on being released at a specific time, but when content (as with anything in life) is in the right place at the right time, it works far more effectively. We will look at how you can maximize this in the planning section later in this chapter.

Different Great content needs to be different. It does not necessarily need to be unique; there is absolutely nothing wrong with taking a good idea and making it your own. There are hundreds of guides to the best bars in Barcelona but that should not stop you creating your own: just be sure to create one that differentiates itself from the rest. Of course it is more difficult to cut through in a crowded market, so the closer to unique you can get, the better. The best check for the 'different' pillar is to ask two questions, 'has this been done before?' and if so, 'is my idea differentiated enough to cut through with my audience?'

On brand and authentic It is very easy to get carried away with content. I have witnessed some brainstorming sessions both at agency and client side that have resulted in some amazing content ideas but the end result is zero progress. Why? The group forgot about the brand. Companies spend millions crafting their brand and, whether written down or not, there are generally a number of dos and a lot of don'ts. In addition, think about your audience again. Consumers of content expect to see a link between the content and the brand. Authenticity is very important now and consumers will very quickly see through attempts for brands to enter into spaces where they simply have no right to be. So if Ferrari produces an interactive guide to Formula 1 their consumers would see the connection. However, should they create a list of the best ice cream in the world, the authenticity would be zero.

Some strong content examples

There are many opportunities to maximize the above principles through great content. Below are some opportunities you should consider building into your content strategy.

Live content

Live streaming and experiences are now quite common and can be very engaging. These apply very well to the principles above but must be executed well. In fact I saw a live video stream today from a major publisher. It had great engagement; however, it broke many of the principles above. It was not clear why they were streaming the view of a famous international location. It was a controversial location yet no one was moderating comments or answering questions. It therefore had only two themes of engagement: 1) arguments about the controversial subject; 2) questions about what this was and why they were broadcasting it. Live experiences can be excellent but you must plan them effectively.

Immersive experiences

With VR and AR we have fantastic opportunities to bring experiences to our customers rather than the other way around. You should be considering any relevant examples for this or you will get left behind. Do not create them for the sake of it, however, or they will be inauthentic and poorly received.

Spoken words

With the Internet of Things, podcasts and audiobooks now gaining enormous popularity, you should consider the audio angle. Could some of your written content become spoken and can this be achieved through IoT devices or smartphones? With 5G technology approaching, download speeds will vastly improve and device amalgamation is highly likely as some of you may have heard me speak about in the past. Consider your audio strategy now.

Tools

These remain a great way of attracting a relevant audience to your platforms. Many financial organizations use mortgage calculators, pension planners, investment return models and tax calculators to attract new customers. You should consider any angles here.

Imagery

Infographics continue to perform well on social media and imagery also continues to outperform pure text. You must have an approach to producing branded design work quickly and beautifully if you are to succeed in your content strategy.

Written copy

Whilst we have said that video, audio and imagery are the future, the written word is not dead and that does not look like happening any time soon. We still love to read and it remains a medium that is easier to engage with. No need for headphones, good bandwidth or privacy, for example. Do not fall into the trap of neglecting your written content in favour of the richer experiences.

What is content?

This may seem like a stupid question, but in fact many types of content are often overlooked.

So what is content? In a nutshell, content is anything that can help engage the end users of your product or service. It can be consumed both on and off your website and in any medium that is capable of delivering a message (so it is much wider reaching than just the written word). Content can include videos, infographics, imagery, tools such as calculators, e-books, blogs, virtual reality experiences, live streaming, podcasts and a great deal more. The opportunities to create and distribute content are getting greater all the time. Figure 14.1 shows a sample of channels now available to the marketer and how this has grown since the early digital age.

What content types should you use?

There are no hard and fast rules as to what types of content you should use. However, there are some general rules of engagement when it comes to selecting the content type, or types, to use:

Figure 14.1   Content distribution channel growth

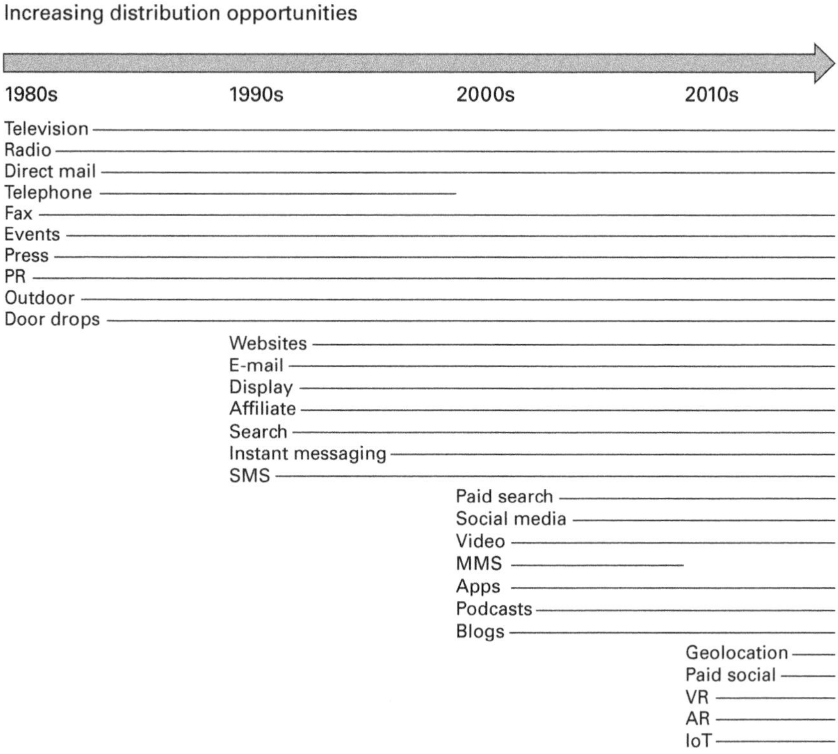

Increasing distribution opportunities

1980s	1990s	2000s	2010s

Television
Radio
Direct mail
Telephone
Fax
Events
Press
PR
Outdoor
Door drops
Websites
E-mail
Display
Affiliate
Search
Instant messaging
SMS
Paid search
Social media
Video
MMS
Apps
Podcasts
Blogs
Geolocation
Paid social
VR
AR
IoT

- *Target audience.* Who exactly do you want to consume the content? It goes without saying that this is dependent on your brand and products but there is also more detail you should consider. For example, your target audience for this specific content may be a subset of your overall audience. If you sell 10 products and one of them is most suitable for older consumers then testimonials and white papers might make great sense, as an older audience will more often look for trust and proof points. How to define your target audience is covered in detail later in the chapter.

- *Buying cycle.* At what stage of the buying cycle are the audience you want to connect with? Again there are no hard rules here, but give it consideration. If you are mainly trying to target consumers who are at the 'decision stage' (the moment of decision) then detailed product information on-site and analyst reports/white papers might make sense. During the 'consideration stage' (still shopping around) case studies and testimonials could be the best choice.

- *Think plural.* If you have a great content idea that ticks all the content marketing pillars then don't necessarily limit yourself to one content type.

An infographic can make a great presentation and vice versa. If you have points that you are making within a slide show that you will share online then can these points become an infographic... and can that infographic fuel a white paper... and can that white paper be shortened into an article... and can that article be further shortened into a blog post... and so on.

- *Don't just take the easy street.* Publishing content on your website is easy and certainly makes sense. Indeed your website should be your home for content (see the section on search engine optimization in Chapter 8) but, unless you have a household name, the unfortunate truth for many businesses is that only a fraction of your target audience will be visiting your site. What this does enable, however, is your SEO, social media and e-mail marketing strategies as they all rely on your content strategy and deliver traffic to your site.

Why content marketing?

So we now know what content marketing is, and we know it is an extremely popular discipline at the moment. But why is this? What is all the fuss about?

While there are likely many contributing factors to the meteoric rise in popularity of content marketing I would suggest two primary factors that are driving the groundswell: 1) changing consumer behaviour; 2) Google.

Changing consumer behaviour

The process for selecting which good/service to buy has not changed much from a high-level point of view. It still starts with awareness and ends with evaluation/decision and the key elements remain unchanged. In short, we tend to like to do some research and know what others think.

What has changed is how we go about doing this. The internet has been around for longer than most think (it went public in 1989) but it arguably only started to realize real commercial potential at the turn of the 21st century. If we consider some of the basic elements of the buying cycle (Table 14.1) we can see how the internet has had a dramatic effect on consumer behaviour.

The real tipping point was when big brands realized that consumers were turning to the internet in ever increasing numbers to research (and buy) products/services. Millennials and Generation Z are especially influenced by social media. In fact, according to Retail Dive, Instagram was the primary

Table 14.1 Buying cycle

Steps in the Buying Cycle	Pre-2000	Post-2000
Awareness	In-store, TV/radio commercials	The multitude of additional advertising formats online from pre-rolls to advertorials
Research the product/service	Magazines, brokers	Manufacturer sites, retailers' sites, blogs, YouTube videos, comparison sites
Peer reviews	Word of mouth (small network)	Numerous online review sites and systems (wide network)
Final decision	Done in isolation or with one or two trusted peers/family members	

influencer for millennials with 74 per cent saying they had been influenced by Instagram when making a purchase. For GenZ it is more likely to be Snapchat than for any other generation and here 21 per cent were influenced.

Google

The role that content plays in SEO has been discussed at length since the dawn of Google. Whilst content was always a notable ranking factor, Google's relationship with content in the early days was questionable at best. In Google's eyes, it wasn't the quality of the content that was important, just that you had it. Indeed it was not that long ago that keyword-stuffed content was the 'best' content in Google's eyes. In other words, we had SEO technicians writing content and leaving professional content writers out in the cold.

Over time, we have seen Google placing a greater reliance on content factors in determining a site's credentials to rank. We have gone from simply keyword-heavy, electronically-spun paragraphs to a situation where quality, context, relevancy, format, social shares, bounce rates and time on page are all considerable factors. As an example of how extensive this has become, Stickyeyes, a UK digital agency, monitors around 150 known 'ranking factors' using their proprietary software, Roadmap. This effectively tries to 'decode' the Google algorithm by identifying correlations between ranking factors and ranking positions. What Roadmap demonstrates is a clear correlation between good content and strong rankings. Through this platform they achieve a 97 per cent correlation between an increased 'time on site' and Google ranking positions. Overall, sites ranking in the number one position had an average time on site in excess of 263 seconds (Figure 14.2).

We see a similar correlation with bounce rate. In this instance, the sites with the lowest bounce rates attract the strongest rankings. Both average time on site and bounce rate are strong indicators that the content on a site

Figure 14.2   Time spent on site

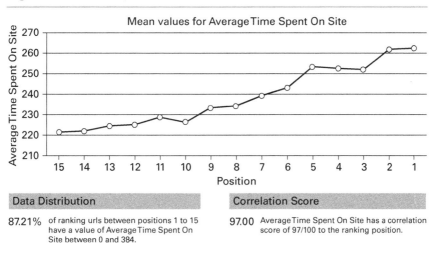

Data Distribution	Correlation Score
87.21% of ranking urls between positions 1 to 15 have a value of Average Time Spent On Site between 0 and 384.	**97.00** Average Time Spent On Site has a correlation score of 97/100 to the ranking position.

SOURCE Stickyeyes

Figure 14.3   Bounce rate

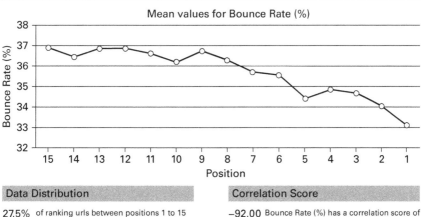

Data Distribution	Correlation Score
27.5% of ranking urls between positions 1 to 15 have a value of Bounce Rate (%) between 30 and 40.	**−92.00** Bounce Rate (%) has a correlation score of 92/100 to the ranking position.

SOURCE Stickyeyes

is compelling and engaging enough to encourage users to seek more, or to navigate deeper into a site.

These correlations are a growing trend, signalling that Google is very much focused on rewarding content above many other known ranking factors. This is good news for the content experts. Only a few years ago journalists and copywriters seemed to have a bleak future, the print industry continued to decline and the new digital world seemed to have less need for them. We have now turned full circle and in most decent digital marketing agencies, especially those with an SEO focus, you will find as many content experts as developers.

People and process for creating content

So content is important. Consumers increasingly demand it and the most dominant search engine in the majority of markets favours quality content. In this section we cover what people and processes you need to create content.

People

Conceptually, content is not that difficult to grasp. There is a lot of common sense involved. Unfortunately, many brands still struggle, and continue to get content marketing wrong, because they have wrongly determined who is responsible for content marketing within the business.

It starts at the top. Many brands and organizations continue to operate in silos. They have PR sitting on the upper floors, the SEO teams halfway up the building and, as ever, IT down in the basement. When an organization has different teams working individually, often to different performance metrics, it becomes incredibly difficult to develop a culture that allows content to thrive.

Content marketing is a form of marketing that touches every department, not just a handful of creatives and copywriters. It needs strategists and analysts to understand the market, branding teams to understand the customer psyche, marketers to create the idea, copywriters to produce the content, search marketers to understand the impact on SEO, PR to identify earned media opportunities and IT to make sure that it all works together. And that is just for a purely digital campaign. Content marketing only works when the walls between teams are broken down and silos are removed, allowing teams to collaborate freely and work to a single, customer-centric goal. That is a culture that has to come from the chief marketing officer

(CMO), or even the CEO. And it is this person who is ultimately responsible for content marketing in a brand. Without a clear focus and a culture that encourages collaboration, making content marketing work becomes infinitely more difficult.

CASE STUDY   Adidas

Background

A great example of a brand that has got content marketing right is Adidas.

Strategy

In March 2014 the Adidas Group, which encompasses both the Adidas and Reebok brands, announced that it had year-long plans to create 'digital newsrooms' for its brands. The move was part of a long-term strategy to capitalize on hot trends and build on 'moments of celebration and acknowledgement'. Adidas states on its website that it wants to own the stories that global superstars create and capitalize on the action in real time. It also states that it wants to be seen as pivotal to the success of players and remain in the focus of sports fans watching in a range of locations around the world.

Key lessons

So what makes their approach different? The key factors of the digital newsroom concept that you can learn from as a marketer are:

- People: lots of them. Adidas has invested heavily in a skilled team from both online and offline backgrounds.

- A wealth of content: Adidas sucks up as much sporting and related content as possible. The majority has nothing exciting about it, the key is finding the needles in the haystack. And as Nike and Puma have similar set-ups there is also a race to find those needles first.

- Speed: in the newsroom set-up speed does not mean quick, it means immediate. To be truly effective a content team needs to be 'switched on' for the events that its audience cares about, be ready to act and have the resource to spring into action when the biggest stories break.

- Trust: marketers regularly come up against hurdles that prevent them from producing fast, groundbreaking content. From slow sign-off procedures and legal compliance, through to overzealous brand protection and a lack of resource, many creative content teams find themselves stifled, unable to publish content until it is too late. To be immediate the reins need to be loosened, or perhaps even cut. This does not mean that you can let your creative team go wild and publish what they want, it does mean you need to define the boundaries very clearly.

While the newsroom concept will be a step too far for many organizations, the key principles can and should be adopted by any company that is taking content marketing seriously. Recent stats from the United States suggest that most companies still need to work out exactly what they are doing with their content marketing from an organizational structure point of view.

Processes

Once you have the organizational structure and people in place it is time to create a plan and set of clearly defined processes. Most companies don't have this in place; according to the Content Marketing Institute only 37 per cent of content marketers have a documented strategy whereas 62 per cent of the most successful content marketing organizations have this in place. The figure of 37 per cent is up by 10 per cent from three years earlier, but there is still clearly some way to go. (Content Marketing Institute, 2018).

Figure 14.4 B2C content marketing

45% of US B2C content marketers have a dedicated content marketing group. [Source: *Content Marketing Institute*, October 2014]

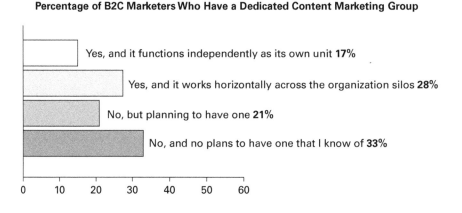

Percentage of B2C Marketers Who Have a Dedicated Content Marketing Group

Yes, and it functions independently as its own unit **17%**

Yes, and it works horizontally across the organization silos **28%**

No, but planning to have one **21%**

No, and no plans to have one that I know of **33%**

Figure 14.5   B2C content marketing

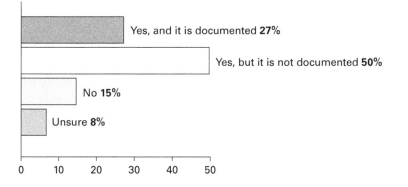

27% of US B2C content marketers have a documented strategy. [Source: *Content Marketing Institute*, October 2014]

Percentage of B2C Marketers Who Have a Content Marketing Strategy

The key stages to create content are:

- objectives and strategy;
- data analysis and target groups;
- ideation;
- creation and planning.

Objectives and strategy

One of the biggest mistakes organizations make when starting down the content journey is to jump straight to creating content. This is typically for one of the following reasons:

- Someone in a position of authority is shouting, 'I want content and I want it now.'
- The content creator assumes that they know their brand/audience well enough so why not just get started.
- Jumping straight into creating content is easier (and potentially more fun).

As tempting as it might be to do this it is crucial to start with setting your objectives and strategy. Jay Baer summed this up very nicely: 'Content helps achieve business objectives, not content objectives' (Baer, 2012).

So objectives and strategies need to start with what your business wants to achieve. For example, if the focus is on retaining and growing existing customers then the content requirements will be very different to a focus on attracting new customers. Broadly speaking, content marketing strategies can be linked to the sales lifecycle and therefore typical objectives are to:

- Create awareness: increase visibility of the product service.
- Change perception: change views on the product service (for example following a product recall).
- Create engagement: increase interactions with the brand and website.
- Drive transactions: increase leads and conversions.
- Increase retention: improve loyalty and customer satisfaction.

An alternative and perhaps simpler approach is to classify the objectives into brand engagement or demand generation:

- Brand engagement:
  - thought leadership;
  - improve brand perception;
  - increase loyalty;
  - create brand advocates.
- Demand generation:
  - increase traffic;
  - generate leads;
  - nurture leads.

Of course, brand engagement and demand generation are far from mutually exclusive. It stands to reason that creating lots of brand advocates is a sure-fire way to generate demand.

Finally, it is important to agree up front whether the content required is functional, engaging or both:

- *Functional content*: this is the content that sits on your site and performs a very functional role, typically to help you sell your products/services. A good example is product descriptions or user reviews. This content is often overlooked as it is not the 'sexy' content that gets presented at digital marketing award ceremonies. It is, however, the most crucial to get right as good functional content helps you to convert browsers into customers and also has a significant impact on natural search rankings.

- *Engaging content*: this is the content that is typically used to communicate information to your target audience in an interesting and engaging manner. The purpose of this content is to encourage people to talk about it digitally (across the web and social media) and naturally link to it. As well as enhancing your brand, this content can also help to improve your natural search performance as it garners links from authoritative sites. Typically this content sits off-site although it may well have its home on-site.

Having defined your high-level strategy and objectives the next step is to perform some detailed analysis to inform the brief.

Data/analysis and target groups

Having set the high-level strategy you then need to perform analysis to inform the content approach. The most important consideration by far is your target audience; however, there are also a number of other data points/tools that are worthy of consideration first:

- Brand guidelines: most sizeable companies have brand guidelines and good content marketers know them inside out. As well as providing creative cues and tone-of-voice guidance they should also give a good idea of the acceptable boundaries for the brand.

- Competitor analysis: what are your competitors doing? This market intelligence is crucial for a number of reasons. It will give you an idea of what content is being consumed, where it is being consumed and crucially what content already exists so that you do not simply replicate it.

- Customer interviews/focus groups/surveys: ask your customers what content they consume, where and why. Also ask what they would like. But ask with caution... one of the smartest marketers I ever met gave me some sage advice when he said, 'What people say they do and what they actually do can be very different.' So ask away but do not rely 100 per cent on this; make sure you test the hypothesis that your face-to-face research is telling you, by looking at real data.

- Analytics: utilize your own analytics to ascertain the most valuable content you already have.

- Keyword analysis: utilizing Google Keyword Optimizer, or other third-party tools such as Moz (Moz.com) you can get a good idea of what your customers are searching for. See Chapter 8, which discusses SEO, for more details on keyword analysis.

Target groups

Unfortunately many brand marketers still are under the illusion that customers love their brand. The unfortunate truth is that your customers do not care about you. They do not care about your products, your history, your service or that you even exist. They only care about themselves.

So why would those people care about your content? The reality is that no one craves branded content, so the only branded content that achieves any recognition whatsoever is the content that fills a need or that solves a problem. As a brand, you need to make yourself and your content relevant.

Overcoming this challenge requires a deep understanding of your target audiences, the challenges they face and how they interact with brands online. It comes down to three key questions:

1 What is your audience's problem?
   If your product or service does not solve a problem, it is extremely difficult to create content that is going to grab their attention. Do your audiences have a problem that they need to address, do they want to do something differently or do they simply want to be entertained? Whatever those challenges are, understand the pain points of your audiences and articulate how your product or service solves them.

2 Where are your audiences digitally active?
   Different audience groups are active in different places online. Younger audiences may be more active on social media and mobile devices, whilst older audiences may prefer to consume digital content on specialist blogs or mainstream media sites using desktop PCs. Consider where your audiences are likely to be most digitally active, who they are most likely to be influenced by and where they are likely to consume content. Consumer analysis tools, such as Hitwise or GlobalWebIndex, are incredibly powerful at identifying where your target audiences spend their time online, giving your brand a clear indication on how you should shape and distribute your content.

3 How do they like to be communicated with?
   Knowing where your audience is, is one thing; knowing how to communicate with them is quite another. Different audiences consume content in different ways and different formats. Some prefer long-form written copy, other audiences may prefer infographics or video content. Again, Hitwise and GlobalWebIndex are extremely useful sources for this insight, informing the format that is likely to be most effective for your content.

Pulling it all together

Ideation

Having defined the strategy and objectives, performed the research and gained a detailed understanding of the target groups it is time to move to ideation. Of course this can, and often is, done by one person but if you want to create a number of great content ideas quickly then it is preferable to use a group. Anyone, within reason, can contribute to an ideation session. The only prerequisite is they must be privy to all the previous research. Indeed an ideal session starts with an overview of objectives, research performed and the target audience. While it is perfectly reasonable to simply sit a group of people in a room and see what emerges, a more structured approach is recommended. Brainstorming is one method but, as it is commonly used and understood, I will suggest an alternative and lesser known approach – brainwriting.

Brainwriting was developed by Bernd Rohrbach in 1968 and allows a small group (six participants and a moderator) to create 108 ideas in just 30 minutes. The approach is as follows:

- Ensure all participants are fully briefed on the goals of the session and any background research.

- Create a 'problem statement'. For example, 'We want to drive awareness of our new product.'

- The 'problem statement' is written on top of worksheets (a grid where the heading of the columns are Idea 1, Idea 2 and Idea 3) handed out to all participants.

- Each participant is then given five minutes to complete the first row with three ideas on how to solve the problem.

- The sheets are then passed to the right and the process is repeated, with each participant being free to gain inspiration from the new ideas presented.

- The process ends after six rounds and the worksheet should be filled with 108 ideas.

The ideas are then quickly screened to remove any duplicates and then the group decides on the best ideas to develop further.

Creation and planning

Having decided on the broad content theme(s) you want to create it is time to plan out the creation. Whether the content is to be created in-house or by an agency, a detailed brief is required. The good news is that all the hard work of the previous steps gives you the essence of a great brief. One model I have developed for content planning is The Content Bubble (see Figure 14.6). This model is a useful guide for creating content that resonates with your audience whilst ensuring you consider a wide range of angles.

In the smallest bubble you look at content that is relevant to your content. In the middle bubble you consider content that applies to the sector you operate within, and in the largest bubble you examine content opportunities in the broadest sense. The smaller the bubble, the smaller the opportunity for content but the more directly relevant it will be and vice versa.

To put this into context, your smallest bubble would include content such as company news, product information, company events and offers. The middle bubble may include industry events or regulatory changes. The largest bubble can then include anything from a new world leader to a sports event.

The critical part of the smallest bubble is to ensure that your content, which is already highly relevant, is of interest and engaging to your audience and is not too internally focused. With the largest bubble you have the opposite challenge as it is very likely to be an interesting subject but you need to find a way to get an angle on that subject from your company's perspective. A bank has no right to offer commentary on a baseball game unless it can find a financial angle to it. Finding these angles is crucial to your content strategy and ensures you retain authenticity and resonance in every piece.

Figure 14.6   The Content Bubble

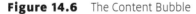

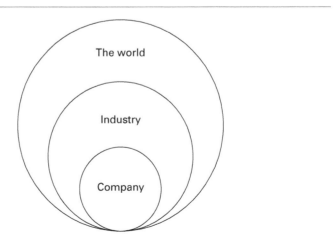

The world

Industry

Company

Alongside The Content Bubble it is essential to understand the reactive and proactive sides to content planning.

Reactive content

For all the best planning in the world you will still find there is a need to quickly produce content to react to an event or news story. You may find that your national sports team performs dramatically better or less well than expected, that a surprising political outcome occurs or there is a sudden death of someone famous and relevant to your business. There is, of course, nothing you can do to fully predict this but there are processes you can put in place to enable you to move quickly.

These include:

- If you are producing content on the outcome and it seems quite clear what it will be you should still ensure you have the backbone of an alternative story. For example, if you expect Brazil to beat Luxembourg in a soccer game then you may focus on writing a piece in advance but should still have a framework for if the opposite happens to enable you to deliver it quickly without having wasted too much effort if it doesn't happen, which is more likely (sorry Luxembourg).

- You should ensure your team is able to work the hours they may need to. This may involve ensuring all content writers have remote access to all relevant systems (your CMS, for example), all vacation is covered by an alternative writer/producer and you have a plan for out-of-hours working, be it compensation or time in lieu.

- You should also have fast approval processes in place. This may simply involve a management sign-off, or it may be more complex needing global approvers from various teams such as compliance, brand or legal. The ideal plan here is to create a self-sign-off process. This involves agreement with all key stakeholders that the writer can approve the piece as long as it meets certain criteria. Those criteria may include not mentioning any specific product, any pricing or any customer details, for example.

With these considerations in place you can enable your company to move fast which can be the difference between your reactive content being engaging and it failing, which is a factor in your thought leadership positioning.

Proactive planning

For proactive planning we use The Content Bubble to give us a view of the pieces we can cover and from this we construct a content calendar. This calendar should include a view of every piece we are producing and how it is being distributed. It should be used to see a long-term view of our strategy but also a locked-down view of the next few weeks. We will talk specifically about this below.

The other piece that is essential to proactive planning is a calendar of relevant world events. In a similar vein to The Content Bubble this should also be split into company, industry and world. Within this calendar we list everything we know that is going to happen over the next 12 months and we then use this to plan out relevant stories at the right time. If we know an art fair is coming we can produce a piece about how art makes a difference to a home on our home improvement blog including a mention of the fair. This ensures relevance, which helps us with SEO, PR and our positioning as a content leader in this field.

As we mentioned, alongside this event calendar it is essential to implement a content calendar to keep track of all the briefs. A simple Excel sheet will do, the core elements being:

- publish date;
- location/media/channel;
- author;
- designer;
- audience/target persona;
- title;
- synopsis;
- assets required;
- dependencies.

It is also important to consider that your content calendar should not just cover your digital channels. It must incorporate anything that is happening across your business including events and printed brochures or newsletters. It should also note when any above-the-line campaigns are running, what they are saying and on what channels. Your consumers see only one brand and that is therefore how you must plan.

For more complex strategies you may need to include splits by country, region, company, brand or other factors dependent on how centralized your content team is within your organization. It is worth mentioning at this point that whilst centralization can have cost savings and consistency benefits it is crucial that your content remains personalized and targeted and not too homogeneous.

All content calendars should also include, or at least be reviewed alongside, a calendar of potential areas of interest. This is as discussed above in the proactive planning section.

In addition to the content calendar the content owner should also have a content editing checklist to ensure that the end deliverable meets the brief.

When developing your content calendar, sometimes known as an editorial calendar, you should look to exploit content opportunities from three perspectives. As you can see in Figure 14.6 you should first look internally, then within your industry and finally more broadly.

Company

Consider your company content. This could be research papers, corporate news, personnel changes, events, product releases – items that are directly relevant to your company. This is the easiest to understand and plan for.

Industry

Here you look at what is directly relevant to the space you operate in. For example, in the automotive industry this could be petrol prices, self-driving car trends, new licence plates and other external factors that are clearly directly relevant to you and your customers. As this category is broader there are more content opportunities.

The world

In this broadest category you ignore your company and industry and focus on what is relevant to your customers. This could be a football World Cup, Christmas, current affairs or similar area that will resonate with the individuals. The important factor here is that you find a way authentically to get involved. That earlier automotive company could not authentically talk about the football World Cup unless it was a sponsor. To do so it would need to find a content angle. For example, the company could consider the top car brand in each of the countries competing in that World Cup and show how, if they all competed directly their own brand would win. There is almost always an angle to be found and in this broadest category there are plenty of opportunities to choose from.

Distribution

No matter how good the content is, creating traction in a crowded market is a key stage in delivering success. We looked at how we can maximize this through planning above and now we will look at some channel considerations using a mix of three channel types: owned, earned and paid (Figure 14.7).

Figure 14.7   Three channel types: owned, earned and paid

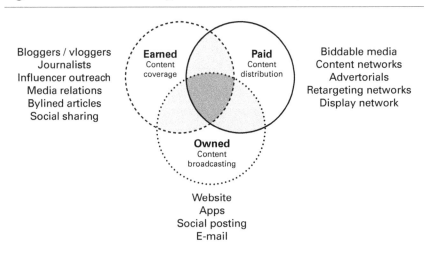

Bloggers / vloggers
Journalists
Influencer outreach
Media relations
Bylined articles
Social sharing

Biddable media
Content networks
Advertorials
Retargeting networks
Display network

Earned
Content
coverage

Paid
Content
distribution

Owned
Content
broadcasting

Website
Apps
Social posting
E-mail

Owned

These are the channels that are fully controlled and owned by you. They can drive early groundswell and engagement with any content-led campaigns. The obvious owned channel is your website, but also give consideration to your social channels and how the content you have created can be leveraged on these channels (although note that social channels now invariably need paid placements to kick start). It is also easy to forget about your e-mail database, bearing in mind that the content message might need to be tweaked for existing versus potential customers.

Earned

These are channels that you cannot buy exposure on, but you can earn it by providing value to the user. This requires a concerted effort to sell your content to journalists, bloggers, social media users and website owners. If you have done your audience research and followed a structured approach to content strategy and ideation you should find that your content resonates. While earned media exposure can be performed in-house it is common for brands to turn to specialists for this service who have both the contacts and tools at hand to make the task easier.

Paid

These are the channels that typically involve some form of media or partner spend in return for exposure for your campaigns. They are also often the most overlooked, as digital marketers tend to wrongly associate paid channels as acquisition-only channels. While they are highly effective for driving traffic for e-commerce they can also help to generate groundswell for content. Examples of paid media uses include:

- a paid search advert on Google to promote a new white paper;
- use of platforms such as Outbrain or Taboola (both content distribution platforms that tend to serve content on major publisher websites) to push out a fun/novel piece of content;
- Facebook advertising to a targeted demographic of early adopters;
- LinkedIn advertising to promote a webinar;
- display adverts to launch a new app.

It is worth noting at this point that social sits in the owned, earned and paid sections. The unfortunate truth is that in order to genuinely leverage social you now need to pay to reach people – including your own fans. That does not mean you should avoid non-paid posts; rather, if you really want to engage people via social you will need to consider paid placements as well.

Measuring the value of content

Given that content can have many guises and the objectives can be quite different there is no one standard measurement approach or tool set. Below is a list of common metrics used; which ones you utilize will depend on the content being measured and the objectives for that content.

It is advisable at this stage to refer to Chapter 19 to understand social metrics in the context of your analytics and to avoid focusing on vanity metrics.

Volume and reach metrics

These metrics look at the volume of touchpoints with an audience as well as the quantity of campaign/channel-driven goals. Examples include:

- Social reach and followers: is your social reach/followers increasing?
- Impressions: how many impressions did your content receive?
- Media coverage gained: what coverage was gained? What is the reach of the publications that have published the content?
- Social mentions: how many times has your content been mentioned on social channels?

- Links back to your site obtained: time-poor consumers of content will of course be more inclined to visit your site if a link is provided in the content. In addition, links from quality sites also bring SEO benefits.

View-through rate (VTR)

This is a measure of what percentage of the view was watched. Many platforms will provide this and it is essential in measuring the engagement of the video. Simply starting to watch a video does not show whether it was engaging. You may also want to consider removing any intros, credits or disclosures from this metric to get a true picture.

Engagement and consumption metrics

These metrics look at the quality of customer interaction and discussion, as well as how campaign or channel content is consumed. Examples include:

- Content interaction: how many page views/downloads has the content generated? What are the bounce rates for the content? What are the views and what is the view-through rate for your videos? (Bounce rate is the percentage of users who visit a page and then immediately leave.)
- Social triggers: retweets, shares and posts.
- Social engagement: this is where content is actively promoted by the consumer and, more than just a like or a share, there is real engagement. For example, adding comments to a post. Linked to this, and a more sophisticated measure, is amplification. Amplification measures the real value of the social sharing by considering the audience of the person sharing a piece of content. For example, a share by Katy Perry, who has over 60 million followers on Twitter, is likely to be more valuable than a share by this book's author (depending on the context!).

Acquisition and value metrics

These metrics look at traffic acquisition as well as the full range of sales and revenue metrics:

- How many conversions/leads have been generated?
- What is the attributable sales volume and revenue?
- What is the cost per lead/action/sale?

Depending on your content objectives, a combination of the above metrics should provide the analysis you need to ascertain what content is working and what is not.

Measuring failure

This is an important consideration for content marketing. When it comes to making engaging content you should expect, and indeed celebrate, failure. That is not to say that if you produce 100 pieces of content you think are engaging and they all fail you should be happy, but it is important to recognize that not everything you produce will work. In fact if everything is working you might ask whether you are pushing the boundaries enough.

The key to success is to have your measurement in place. Understanding the features of each piece of content and how you have distributed it will help you to understand the reasons for failure when it happens. For example, the subject of your content, the author, which social channels were used, on what day and time and whether it was imagery, copy or video will all be factors in success or failure, so being able to analyse these is important to being able to refine your content strategy over time.

CASE STUDY   Hertz Europe

Background

Hertz is a well-known global car rental company. However, in recent years the brand had come under pressure from low-cost operators, particularly in the holiday rentals market.

Strategy

To counter this competitive pressure, Hertz commissioned a detailed analysis of the European vehicle hire market to identify where they could steal a march on their competitors in six European territories. This analysis revealed a gap in both functional and engaging content compared to the competition. The lack of content was hurting the brand both in terms of SEO performance for non-brand terms, especially location-based and in terms of conversion. The challenge was deploying a huge quantity of functional content in an incredibly short space of time, as well as developing creative content concepts to support rankings growth for both local and core keyword terms.

Their solution was a major deployment of both functional and creative content. Whilst Hertz's organic rankings were relatively strong on generic keyword terms, by virtue of the strength of the brand, there were a number of key opportunities to drive improvements for localized keyword search terms. These city- or region-specific keyword terms had significantly lower volumes, but would drive considerably better conversion rates due to the intent of the searcher. For example, a person searching for 'Car hire Malaga' is certainly showing purchase intent.

The result was the creation of over 11,000 pages of localized content across the six international domains covering every town, city and region served by Hertz. Of course this was a mammoth task; however, Hertz followed a logical and audience-centric approach, which made the production process relatively seamless. Crucially, the focus was on added-value content; a side result was SEO benefit.

This functional content was supported by creative, engaging content campaigns that aimed to inspire people to explore a Hertz location. From encouraging leading journalists to try new experiences with a Hertz van, and sharing great walking destinations outside of Edinburgh, through to ghost hunting in St Pancras and finding vintage fashion in Islington, north London, the creative content would reach new audiences and enhance Hertz's online reach.

Results

Outstanding revenue growth across six European markets. The localized content strategy delivered outstanding returns on investment for Hertz, with both booking and revenue growth exceeding all expectations. The creative content helped Hertz to secure excellent levels of coverage, and high-quality referrals, from leading publications across Europe. This included the *Telegraph*, *TNT Magazine*, *Scottish Daily Record* and the *Herald* in the UK, as well as *Le Parisien*, *Grazia*, *GQ* and the Huffington Post across Europe. The localized content strategy resulted in significant rankings uplift for city- and region-specific search terms. These pages, which contained useful information regarding the destination in question for the end user, supported revenue growth in all six of the core European markets. This ranged from growth of 11.06 per cent year on year (YoY) in the UK, up to 121.13 per cent YoY revenue growth in the Italian market.

Key lessons

- Hertz's adoption of a content-led strategy helped to drive significant improvements in all markets through solid research, broad and relevant content that was well distributed.

- The key content goals, discussed above, were all met and this is ultimately why their strategy was so successful.

International content

While the processes remain the same, regardless of the market, there are some key considerations for international content marketing that need to form part of your content briefs:

- Are the personas different? Your segments and personas may be similar in another culture but with small differences or they may be completely different.
- Are the platforms different? For example, the dominant search engine in Russia is Yandex and in China is Baidu. The dominant micro-blogging site in China is Sina Weibo, not Twitter.
- Cultural differences? This is particularly the case when it comes to using humour. What is considered funny in one country might be highly offensive in another. We looked at cultural differences in Chapter 3.
- Legal implications? For example, in China the content on Baidu is controlled to keep in line with the country's laws. Privacy laws differ in countries and regions, as do laws around the freedom of speech and the right to be forgotten. Ensure that you understand the relevant laws and how they apply to your strategy.
- Seasonal events? Thanksgiving, Chinese New Year and Bonfire Night, for example, are all very significant celebrations in their home countries but much less so elsewhere. On the other hand, events such as St Patrick's Day and Christmas are often celebrated in countries that have no specific tie to the celebration but that still enjoy taking part.
- Localization: while it may be tempting simply to get your content translated, you may well lose the intended audience if you do. Having your content written and reviewed by local native speakers will ensure that it is both culturally and linguistically accurate.
- Mobile: mobile penetration and operating system popularity also change significantly by country. Where some countries primarily use iPhones, others focus on Android and others are very low on mobile penetration overall. This difference also changes other factors such as platforms mentioned above. Yandex is the largest search engine in Russia but if you look solely at Android it is Google.

Audit checklist

A three-step content audit checklist is available to download at:
www.koganpage.com/DigitalMarketingStrategy/2

Conducting a content audit is one of the most critical aspects of content marketing, but it is also one of the most difficult. This guide will take you through the three major stages of a content audit, highlighting what to look for and how to find the insight that you need to make the best possible decisions. This online resource will help you to develop your content strategy.

Summary

Content has many forms and is much more than just the written word. It can be both functional (descriptive content) and engaging (designed to provoke interest or a reaction) and its meteoric rise is largely down to changing consumer behaviour and Google's emphasis on ranking sites that provide great content. In order to resonate with the intended audience it is important to consider the content pillars. Content should be:

- credible;
- shareable;
- useful or fun;
- interesting;
- relevant;
- timely;
- different;
- on brand and authentic.

Creating great content is not easy. First and foremost it requires the right people and the right organizational structure; without this the content produced is unlikely to be the best it can be or reach its potential. Content production starts with setting high-level objectives and strategy. Having defined this it is important to analyse the data you have, review competitive output and, crucially, define your target audience using personas. Ideation can then begin and brainwriting is a great way to create over 100 ideas in under 30 minutes. Content creation is, however, only half of the challenge.

Content becomes successful when it is planned and distributed well. You should use The Content Bubble and create both proactive and reactive processes to manage your content effectively. In order to maximize coverage it is important to consider all channels:

- Owned: the channels you own – for example, your website, your social channels (to a degree), your e-mail database.
- Earned: the coverage that money cannot buy; often editorial in nature, social media and closely linked to traditional PR.
- Paid: bought coverage has a role to play, in particular to help initially seed content on publisher sites or socially.

In order to measure content effectively we need to consider three key elements:

- volume and reach;
- engagement and consumption;
- acquisition and value.

Finally, creating content for international markets requires a very local approach; a simple translation will likely do more harm than good.

Chapter checklist

- What is content marketing? ☐
- What is content? ☐
- What content types should you use? ☐
- Why content marketing? ☐
- People and process for creating content ☐
- Distribution ☐
- Measuring the value of content ☐
- International content ☐

Further reading

- *On content marketing:*
  Norris, D (2016) *Content Machine: Use content marketing to build a 7-figure business with zero advertising,* Dan Norris
  Scott, EJ (2018) *Content Marketing Book: 3 manuscripts in 1, easy and inexpensive content marketing strategies to make a huge impact on your business,* CreateSpace Independent Publishing Platform

- *On content strategy:*
  Casey, M (2015) *The Content Strategy Toolkit,* New Riders. This includes the research phase, creation of your strategy, gaining buy-in and delivery of your strategy.

- *On storytelling:*
  Jutkowitz, A (2017) *The Strategic Storyteller: Content marketing in the age of the educated consumer,* John Wiley & Sons

References

Baer, J (2012) [accessed 1 November 2015] A Field Guide to the Four Types of Content Marketing Metrics [Online] http://www.convinceandconvert.com/content-marketing/a-field-guide-to-the-4-types-of-content-marketing-metrics/
Content Marketing Institute (2018) [accessed 19 November 2018] Annual Research: Content Marketing Budgets, Benchmarks and Trends [Online] http://contentmarketinginstitute.com/research/

An implementation guide is available at:
www.koganpage.com/DigitalMarketingStrategy/2

Personalizing the customer journey and digital experience

15

What we will cover in this chapter

This chapter covers personalization, the options available to digital marketers and some of the challenges involved. Technology has enabled personalization to become quite sophisticated and it is increasingly an expectation so we will discuss how to maximize the benefit. The key areas covered in this chapter are:

- What is personalization?
- Defining true personalization
- User-defined personalization
- Behavioural personalization
- Tactical personalization
- Single customer view

Chapter goals

By the end of this chapter you should have an understanding of the benefits and types of personalization. You should understand the concept of the single customer view and the differences between personalization and segmentation.

What is personalization?

In Chapter 17 we will look at loyalty, retention and CRM marketing from a digital perspective. A successful CRM or loyalty programme has always relied on delivering highly relevant messages at the right time. This is increasingly becoming a consumer's expectation of marketing as a whole but especially on the digital channels, from UX to advertising and of course e-mail, and so personalization is therefore growing in importance every day. Thankfully, technology has developed to a level where the possibilities are broader than ever. With the rapid growth of artificial intelligence (AI) the options for personalization are increasing every day.

Taking a personal approach has always been the best way to get your message across. Whether you are communicating with your customers or just chatting to your friends, no matter who the audience, putting your message into terms that are relevant for them will make your message stronger and clearer. It has long been a key factor in highly successful marketing campaigns, and direct marketing saw a significant growth in the late 20th century as a result of this type of communication becoming more and more accessible. The growth of digital has increasingly allowed us to do more, and we are now at an exciting stage where the realms of possibility are immense and the questions are more *how* and *when* than *why*. Recent data suggests that personalization, which was a priority when I wrote the first edition of this book, is even more crucial to success today. The '2018 Trends in Personalization' survey by Evergage in fact stated: 'Marketers overwhelmingly agree (98 per cent) that personalization helps advance customer relationships, with 74 per cent claiming it has a "strong" or "extreme" impact' and 'nearly 9 out of 10 (88 per cent) state that their customers and prospects expect a personalized experience' (Evergage, 2018).

CASE STUDY   Amazon

Background

Amazon is famous for its personalization and has been using a product curation and recommendation algorithm for many years. It has been hailed as one of the first to play heavily in this space and we can continue to learn from it, although more sophistication will be required as it moves forward.

Strategy

Amazon has worked hard to understand its consumers through data and makes recommendations based on a number of factors. Clearly there is a correlation between personalized recommendations and increased sales. This can be in the form of direct purchases through the recommendation itself, sharing products with friends (as friends often share similar interests to you) or in increased usage of the app owing to the likelihood that you will find what you want with ease (even if you didn't know you wanted it).

Amazon personalizes through a number of routes and this is an important lesson. Personalization is not simply adding a name but true personalization in the digital age is about understanding your user and giving him or her a unique offering. Amazon's recommendations include:

- people like you bought…;
- recommendations for you;
- your Dash buttons (a product Amazon promotes);
- continue searching for…;
- categories you regularly search in;
- review your purchase;
- inspired by your shopping trends;
- inspired by your wish lists;
- customers who viewed this item also bought…;
- frequently bought together;
- and many more that rely on data and trends.

Results

The results are clear. Today Amazon is one of the largest businesses in the world and this is in no small part due to its use of digital personalization. The power of this tool, if implemented as fully and effectively as Amazon did, is enormous.

Key lessons

All businesses today should have a clear data strategy and their data managed effectively. It is totally unacceptable to be in any other position. Using this data then to create effective personalization strategies is a must within any digital strategy and should be central to everything you do from content to platforms.

Defining true personalization

So what do we mean by true personalization? Well, there are many ways to ensure that your message is tailored to the individual and we have been using many of these for decades. Including the individual's name in the salutation 'Dear Mr Doe' or 'Hi John' is probably the most common. There is also the practice of pulling a fact about your customer from the database and inserting it into the communication such as 'Because we know you love *skiing,* we'd like to tell you about this great alpine vacation offer'. These are all great methods but they do not go quite deep enough to be really tailored.

Segmentation can be used, as discussed in Chapter 1, and this certainly helps to ensure that your message remains relevant whilst keeping down the logistics and costs of fulfilment. This is not personalization, however. Treating people exactly the same as other people due to a few common factors is never going to fully resonate with everyone. Take the television commercials from eHarmony in the UK in the mid 2010s. The commercials reference the fact that the two individuals on screen have some similar interests, for example being the same age, living in the same town or loving food – and that for some websites that is enough to make them a match. We see that one of the individuals is a young man or woman and the other is a camel, boar or other ridiculous match. This is a good (and fairly funny) way of bringing to life the fact that segmentation is not the answer if you really want your customers to get a truly personalized service.

There are two key methods of personalization that get us to the goal. In simple terms, you can let the individual tell you what they want (user-defined personalization) or you learn what they want (behavioural personalization). Let's look at these in more detail.

User-defined personalization

This method simply allows the individual to tell us what they want. The danger with many segmentation and even personalization models is that the decisions about what someone wants are made based on trends, assumptions and other indications, which may not be representative of that individual. The user-defined model ensures that this risk disappears. This method relies on the individual being prepared to provide you with data that allows you to tailor your communications to them. This may include their demographics, interests, routines and much more. This can be done through any channel such as an online form or preference centre, phone call or even by post. This method would seem on the surface to be fairly black and white. A consumer tells us what they want and we give it to them. Surely you cannot get more personalized than that? Well, actually you can and there are a number of challenges with this method.

First, you need to collect this information. If someone is unwilling to provide you with this then your entire personalization model collapses. This results in some of your customers receiving personalized comms and some receiving generic comms. This may result in you needing to run two separate comms programmes – one for the personalized approach and one generic for everyone else. You will then need to ensure that this thinking is built into all of your marketing decisions, which is slightly messy and can lead to mistakes. This includes duplicating and complicating such complex areas as your content strategy, your contact strategy and your key website landing pages as well as separating data and reporting, which can be incredibly complex.

Second, you rely on the data being accurate. If, for example, you force all of your customers to give you this data then there is a strong chance, as with any mandatory field online, that a percentage of individuals will provide fake data as they do not want to give you what you are looking for. Birth dates, interests, occupations, even gender could be incorrect. This can then become hugely embarrassing and even brand damaging when you send a ladies beauty voucher out to a 78-year-old man with a message that reads 'Happy 40th Birthday Janice'.

Third, you are also assuming that people know themselves. Anyone with children will know that the answer you get from someone's mouth, no matter how genuine they think it is, is not always representative of the true picture. We all have our aspirations and beliefs in who we are and who we want to be. Pride sometimes overtakes reality and memory is not always reliable. There are reasons why someone may give you a genuine answer, but not necessarily a correct one. Adam may, for example, have been a keen cyclist many years ago with a plan to get back into it, so he still considers cycling to be one of his main hobbies. It has been over 10 years since he last sat on a bike but time has flown and it doesn't seem that long to him. Adam fills out a research form at his local supermarket and lists cycling as a hobby. The supermarket then starts to send Adam local cycle-route maps and vouchers for cycling products, which go unused. One of their other rewards programmes is around food, however, which Adam genuinely would have used but he doesn't consider himself a foodie even though he eats out at least three times a week.

There are many studies on human psychology that make fascinating reading to illustrate this point. Notably, the Dunning-Kruger effect in which an individual believes themselves to be far better at a skill than is actually the truth (I think we all know someone like this).

So the user-defined personalization model does have some strong advantages, but you will need to be sure of the completeness and accuracy of your data. Behavioural personalization can help by augmenting your user-defined data.

Behavioural personalization

We are at a stage now where we can learn from the behaviours of our customers and serve them with the right messages at the right time. This is the ultimate goal of direct marketing and something that is now very much a possibility.

Big data is another of the buzzwords in digital marketing today and also one of the biggest challenges for many organizations. Data is one of the largest assets a company can have, alongside its people, and the sheer volume of data obtainable from web analytics, purchase funnels, research, call-centre operations, finance and many other areas creates a complex web of possibilities. We look at big data in more detail in Chapter 19 but it is worth noting that organizing and maintaining the quality of your data is vital to success in personalization and your wider marketing strategy.

Behavioural personalization takes indications of an individual's behaviour from signals received through various data collection points such as visiting a website, opening an e-mail, engaging with some content or even visiting specific areas of a store. This data can then be fed into a model that can make decisions in real time. The possibilities for this are truly endless. Do you offer a great deal to a customer who has come to your site several times and added items to the shopping basket but never bought? Do you personalize every e-mail journey so that the content is only relevant to an individual and only sent at the time they like to open their e-mails? Do you message your customers directly to their phone once they reach an area of your store because you know they have interacted with that area of your website?

This opportunity means that consumers can start to receive only the marketing information that is relevant to them. Spam becomes a thing of the past and marketing effectiveness levels soar. Surely this is the future and it is understandable why so many marketers are excited about it. However, behavioural personalization does come with challenges. First, using the data correctly is vital to success. It is likely that the data will be correct (unless there has been a tagging error or similar) but how you use that data is important and so having a strategy for this is the key to success. It is often the way that, when presented with new technology and a large list of options, we as marketers can be guilty of getting a little overexcited and doing things because we can, rather than because we should. The one thing to always keep in mind in marketing is to think of the customer first. This is easier said than done and whilst many individuals and companies claim to do this it is often not the case. Is what you are doing actually going to benefit them? If so, then you probably have a sensible strategy as long as you can make it work for your business.

Not only do you need a strategy but you also need to be able to interpret the data and make the right decisions from what you see. In order to do this, you will need to make certain assumptions and it is these assumptions and interpretations that can render high-quality data worthless. Where the user-defined personalization model excels is that we know the data is correct from the consumer's point of view as they have given it to us. With the behavioural model we are trusting our view of this data. Imagine, for example, that we see a user, Miss Kennedy, repeatedly visit our site and add cycling gear to the basket but then decide not to buy. What do we know from this? Is Miss Kennedy a keen cyclist who is undecided about the products or our brand? Is Miss Kennedy thinking about getting into cycling but is not sure? Is Miss Kennedy considering buying cycling gear as a present for friends or family? Is Miss Kennedy experiencing technical difficulties or a user experience issue when trying to buy? The answer could be any of these, or a thousand others – it might even be Miss Kennedy's 14-year-old son who is using her user ID. Without the individual supplying us with data we have to be careful what assumptions we make.

Finally, privacy is an ongoing challenge in this area. The amount of data being collected now is simply enormous and the ethics of what we should know about people, even in anonymized form, is constantly being questioned. Many brands have been damaged by trying to own too much of our data in recent years and this has resulted in a number of public exposures and scandals for such high-profile businesses as Sony and Facebook. One such example is Disney, who back in May 2011 allowed their Playdom business to enable children to post their full names and locations online. This is a violation of the Children's Online Privacy Protection Act (COPPA) and as a result they were fined £3 million (Marsan, 2012). Consumers are becoming increasingly savvy about giving away their data, and regulation continues to restrict the ability for organizations to obtain and use this data. GDPR in Europe in 2018 is a good example of this and should be understood by all marketers, not just those in Europe, as it has wide-reaching implications.

Ofcom's 'Adults Media Use and Attitudes Report 2014' found that 42 per cent of internet users are 'happy to provide personal information online to companies as long as they get what they want in return'. In their 2018 report this number had dropped to around 33 per cent and was contingent on certain conditions being met. It is possible, however, that businesses may have to purchase this data from consumers in the future – after all, it is an asset.

The future of behavioural personalization is very strong and it offers the best result for both organizations and consumers, but there is still a difficult path ahead before this becomes comfortable.

It's not either/or

One thing to remember with the models above is that you do not necessarily have to choose. Both models have their merits and there are times and places for both. Behavioural personalization is the more modern approach, but that does not make it better for any given scenario. For example, you may want to ask your customers to tell you which e-mail programmes they want to be a part of, and what content they are interested in so that you don't need to serve them some irrelevant content for three months whilst you work this out (by which time they may have become frustrated and unsubscribed). You may wish, however, for their experience on your website to adapt to their behaviours.

Bad personalization: Facebook mood experiment

This specific experiment was carried out back in 2014 but it remains a fantastic example of how not to use personalization. I have included this as a bad example of personalization. Not because the mechanism failed but because the experiment was poorly received by many as being deceptive and it therefore cost Facebook a degree of trust that it may never regain from those users who left the network. A poll on the *Guardian* newspaper's website in the UK suggested that 84 per cent of respondents had lost trust in Facebook with 6 per cent considering closing their page (Fishwick, 2014).

The experiment manipulated the feeds that users saw in order to try to control their moods – and then reviewed their posts to see if their mood had indeed been affected. This concept caused anger as people generally felt that a corporation had no right to conduct psychological experiments on people for their own benefit and without permission from the participants. This was an effective delivery of the personalization strategy but a poorly thought through experiment for the user.

Tactical personalization

Not all personalization has to include data collection and be part of a complex strategy. Sometimes a level of personalization can simply offer a user something unique and enticing. For example, if you allow your customer to alter the design of your product or change the background image of the app they are using then are you really going to gain a great deal of insight about them? No, but you are offering a level of value that the customer may appreciate.

Single customer view

A single customer view is a full and complete picture of your customer that is created by combining all data from across your organization into one holistic view. It is challenging but can be incredibly rewarding.

There is a need to increasingly move away from treating different areas of the customer journey separately and this is worth considering when building your personalization strategy. Working in silos is something that has caused many businesses to fail and this is never more true than with customer experience. If you understand your customer with a single customer view (SCV) then you must personalize your experience at every touchpoint wherever possible. This includes your website, e-mail programme, call-centre operations and even social media customer services. Many businesses have been moving towards developing an SCV over recent years and never has it been more urgent than now. The reason for this is because social media and review sites make it abundantly clear when an organization is bad at this. If you are perceived as delivering poor or inconsistent customer service then your business will suffer. Aside from the visible ratings you will find that your customers will also vote with their feet. According to Esteban Kolsky, CEO of ThinkJar, only 1 out of 26 unhappy customers complain; the rest simply leave. Also, those who are receiving a more personalized service are likely to stay with your business and may even become advocates.

CASE STUDY   Coca-Cola

Background

In 2011 Coca-Cola launched its famous 'Share a Coke' campaign in Australia, the aim being to reach millennials. Each bottle contained one of the most popular first names assigned to that generation. This has since expanded to more than 1,000 names and many other variations as it takes on a global reach with regional variations.

Strategy

This personalization is delivered on a physical product, not through a digital channel; however, the effect was broad. This case study is therefore less about digital implementation and more about marketing integration. The title of this book includes the subtitle 'an integrated approach to online marketing' and this is where we focus here. Coca-Cola's naming strategy was one that clearly had the potential to go viral.

Social media, content, imagery and much more was developed around this. By integrating its efforts Coca-Cola was able to take an engaging campaign and send it viral through multiple channels. The power of personalization was the driver behind the success but the integration of marketing across all channels with digital playing a key role, was what helped this to become a sensation.

Results

According to www.coca-cola.co.uk, in 2014 alone there were 998 million impressions on Twitter and 235,000 tweets from 111,000 fans with the hashtag #ShareaCoke. This led to more than 150 million personalized bottles being sold, over 730,000 glass bottles being personalized via the e-commerce store and 17,000 virtual name bottles being shared online across Europe.

Key lessons

Personalization doesn't have to be implemented digitally to be part of your digital strategy. Physical implementation can actually give far more impact as it is less expected. Using digital as part of an integrated strategy to support your physical marketing, however, is essential. You must not draw a line between the two – marketing is one department, one strategy, and digital should be considered across all of it.

Summary

In this chapter we have looked at what personalization is and how modern techniques allow businesses to go far beyond segmentation and simplified personalization techniques. We looked at user-defined and behavioural personalization and how the two techniques differ, but also how they are not mutually exclusive. Finally we considered the single customer view and its increasing importance in delivering a consistent message to your customers.

Chapter checklist

- What is personalization? ☐
- Defining true personalization ☐
- User-defined personalization ☐
- Behavioural personalization ☐
- Tactical personalization ☐
- Single customer view ☐

Further reading

- *On the Dunning-Kruger effect*:

  McRaney, D (2012) *You Are Not So Smart: Why your memory is mostly fiction, why you have too many friends on Facebook and 46 other ways you're deluding yourself*, Oneworld Publications

- *On personalization*:

  Berndt, J (2015) *Personalization Mechanics: Targeted content for web teams of all sizes,* TBG Books

  Wirth, K and Sweet, K (2017) *One-to-One Personalization in the Age of Machine Learning: Harnessing data to power great customer experiences*, BookBaby

References

Evergage (2018) [accessed 20 November 2018] 2018 Trends in Personalization [Online] https://www.evergage.com/wp-content/uploads/2018/04/Evergage-2018-Trends-in-Personalization-Survey.pdf

Fishwick, C (2014) [accessed 1 November 2015] Facebook's Secret Mood Experiment: Have You Lost Trust in the Social Network?, 30/06 *The Guardian* [Online] http://www.theguardian.com/technology/poll/2014/jun/30/facebook-secret-mood-experiment-social-network

Marsan, C D (2012) [accessed 1 November 2015] 15 Worst Internet Privacy Scandals of All Time, 26/01 *Network World* [Online] http://www.networkworld.com/article/2185187/security/15-worst-internet-privacy-scandals-of-all-time.html

PART FOUR
Conversion, retention and measurement

Effective design, 16
e-commerce and
user experience
(UX)

What we will cover in this chapter

In this chapter we look at user experience (UX) and how to apply this to digital design in order to provide fantastic experiences for consumers and to hit the goals of your strategy.

The key areas covered in this chapter are:

- User experience
- UX research
- Design thinking

Chapter goals

By the end of this chapter you should understand the important role of user experience design in your digital marketing strategy, as well as on your website or other digital platforms. You will understand the research element of UX design that can help throughout the entire cycle of your digital marketing strategy and how design thinking can be applied to maximize the impact of your platforms.

User experience (UX)

If your digital marketing approach is delivering as planned you will be acquiring more traffic, and the user experience of your digital estate will therefore be critical to encourage your visitors to take the actions your strategy is designed to facilitate. Good UX is fundamental to this. User experience and the design of your users' experience should not be divorced from your digital marketing strategy.

User experience is – as its name suggests – how people experience your digital properties (apps, websites and an emergent range of devices like Alexa) and therefore needs to be closely aligned to your marketing strategy and also to your brand values. If your brand is premium and makes promises about offering superior service, you cannot offer a clunky digital experience without undermining your reputation.

Wikipedia gives us a lovely definition of user experience in a rich snippet amid Google's search results: 'The overall experience of a person using a product such as a website or computer application, especially in terms of how easy or pleasing it is to use'. This is a very nice way of phrasing it.

User experience designers typically focus on the structure, navigation and interactions of a digital property. Depending on the scale of a project or size of a project team, there can be a number of differing design disciplines supporting the creation of digital experiences.

UX is often the lead discipline on digital projects, frequently owning the process of defining the user journey – in other words, the steps that an idealized customer (typically referred to as a persona) takes to become aware of your product or service, interact with your business and then hopefully complete a purchase or equivalent action.

No two customer journeys are the same, and they are often heavily idealized – however, when both quantitative and qualitative data is available, an accurate approximation can be arrived at allowing the UX designer to create an effective experience.

While we may have the goal of selling certain products or services to prospects and customers, the prospects or customers will themselves have goals they want to accomplish through their digital interactions. These can be subconscious, such as 'distract myself' for two minutes while browsing Facebook at work, through to more substantial goals such as evaluate a given product against a competitor offering.

The job of the UX designer is to create an excellent experience regardless of the user goal.

Your research and data is critical to surface these goals and then feed them into the UX process – designing the structure and navigation for a website, whether e-commerce-based or not, becomes a lot easier when you broadly understand where traffic is coming from, what the people comprising that traffic might be like and what they want to accomplish.

Google's rich snippet on UX

A rich snippet is a piece of structured data that Google can read and insert into your search results. This could be product information, reviews, price, availability, recipes, event times and locations or app information. These give the user greater information to make a decision and give your results more stand-out.

Roles and responsibilities

Having asserted that UX is frequently the lead discipline in contemporary web and digital projects, it's worth quickly looking at the other disciplines that might be in the mix according to the scale of the project.

Every project or team will be slightly different, but the important take-away from the following list is the increasing specialization of roles within digital. Specialization is increasing, but at the same time it is getting harder to draw tight delineations between some of the disciplines.

This means digital is increasingly a 'team sport', and executing your digital marketing strategy will need a number of people who may sit within other parts of your business (eg IT) or who have job titles that might not have existed five or 10 years ago (eg content designer).

Marketing roles have always involved a degree of orchestration, and the rise of digital, with its new specialisms, is continuing this trend.

A website or digital marketing team might include some or all of the roles detailed in Table 16.1.

The importance of context

The user's context has become vitally important because of the proliferation of devices that people use to access the internet and the fact that digital is becoming the primary channel for so much of our lives. Understanding how, where and when your users are interacting with you is vital to providing them with the best experience.

Table 16.1   Website/digital marketing team roles and job descriptions

Role	Headline Job Description
User experience designer or architect	Defining the user journey, designing the structure, navigation of and often interactions with digital experiences
Creative or visual designer	Working with the UX designer to define the look and feel of an experience – a creative might define how something looks, and the UX designer how it works
Interaction designer	Some large businesses or project teams might include a User Interface or Interaction Designer who considers the behaviour of the digital product or service. There can be significant overlap with UX and visual design
Service designer	Designs some or all of the service or proposition at the heart of the strategy in collaboration with the customer. Differs from UX in considering multiple touchpoints (digital, call centre and physical) and how to make a multichannel experience feel seamless
Content strategist/designer	Content strategy and design are differing but related disciplines concerned with serving visitors the right content, in the right way and at the right time. Think (beyond just words) what content will best meet a user's need?
Copywriter	Like the other disciplines, copywriting is fragmented into conceptual/creative, long-form and UX – but ultimately it is all about elegant sentence construction
Developers – front-end and back-end	Front-end developers write the code that works in the user's browser or app (and may frequently be able to design as well) Back-end developers write the code that powers the systems the website or app sits on
Business analyst	Gets into the detail of requirements gathering – which can mean the requirements of the business or the technology to deliver a certain experience

(*Continued*)

Table 16.1 (*Continued*)

Role	Headline Job Description
Project manager and/or scrum master	Project managers – and scrum masters in the Agile world – help to keep everything moving and make sure the right people are involved at the right time. For more detail on agile methodologies see Chapter 6
Data analyst	Digital offers an abundance of data, and most teams benefit from having someone to make sure the right metrics are being tracked and to interpret the data being generated
User researchers	User researchers should bring qualitative data to the table to balance the quantitative data
Search engine optimization/ Pay per click specialist	It's not just about acquiring traffic, but the right traffic, and a skilled SEO and/or PPC practitioner can help. SEO input on technical hygiene factors (eg how redirects are handled) is critical to avoid Google penalties
Optimization specialist	Will be thinking obsessively about the conversion rate on your site, and the ways that it can be improved. They will be key when it comes to testing
Personalization or messaging specialist	Delivery of targeted messages and personalized content is growing with the rise of tools like Adobe's Marketing Cloud and Sitecore's Experience Cloud. Larger teams will benefit from having a personalization specialist to define the dynamic messages used
Product owner/manager	This is typically a client-side role and the product owner/manager defines what experience the business intends to offer in pursuit of its objectives
Strategists (of varying flavours)	Strategists tend to be agency-side roles and often perform a role that is essentially similar to that of the product owner/manager

We can no longer assume that because we have built a great website we will satisfy all users. Mobile users will have a different view, will interact through touch rather than a keyboard or mouse, may be interrupted by calls or messages and are more likely to be looking to absorb content rather than make a purchase compared to desktop users. Appreciating these contextual differences is crucial to creating a great experience.

We work on the internet. We buy on the internet. We communicate on the internet. We entertain ourselves on the internet. We find love on the internet. We book holidays and manage our finances on the internet. We get things done on the internet.

US research house Forrester issued a report in March 2014 entitled 'The Future of Business is Digital' (Forrester, 2014). In itself that title is nothing groundbreaking, but the message from the report was clear: 'You must harness digital technologies, both to deliver a superior customer experience and to drive the agility and operational efficiency you need to stay competitive'.

Ernst & Young went further in a report called 'The Digitisation of Everything' (Ernst & Young, 2011): 'The real imperative in a world where "everything" is digitised is that businesses need to pursue innovation to disrupt their business model before the competition does. Without innovation strategies, companies will lose their competitive advantage in an increasingly commoditised world'.

It is therefore clear that companies must understand their consumers' context in the digital age if they are to win and serve customers effectively.

In the days of what Seth Godin, author of *The Purple Cow* (Godin, 2005), calls the TV-Industrial Complex, marketing was relatively straightforward. Godin's premise is that you paid for some advertising and you blasted your message at people. They consumed that message passively as there was no return path and you could hit millions of people at once because there was a limited number of outlets or channels available to you as the marketer.

Think of your own habits here: When did you last watch TV? When did you last watch terrestrial, scheduled TV on your living room TV without a laptop, tablet or mobile device in your hands at the same time? Were you watching a previously recorded show, streaming something through Netflix, or watching a movie you had downloaded? Do you pay a subscription for that or did you purchase the show? Did you watch adverts before or during the show? Were you watching on a TV, tablet, phone or another device?

Be honest – when did you last give your full attention to a single task? As marketers we all want to believe that we are sufficiently compelling that our customers will concentrate when they interact with us. But as we don't do that with the brands we interact with, why should anyone do that with our brand?

We can cut through some of this complexity and say the role of UX is to mediate between the company that wants its customers or prospects to take a particular action, and those customers who just want to solve a problem (in the broadest sense). Therefore, a core goal of your marketing strategy – to be delivered by UX – is to be easy for your customers.

UX research

Traditionally, markets and customers were segmented on the basis of demographics. However, as discussed in Chapter 4, those approaches are no longer the ultimate answer to the question of who your customers are, as needs and behaviours make much better starting places for innovation. This points to one of the most important considerations in building digital products – ensuring that you never make assumptions. It is vital that a business takes every opportunity to fully understand its intended users and find out what they really want and how they behave.

The best practice approach of UX today involves using tools such as heatmap software, user interviews and even ethnographic models of observation. Truly, the best experiences are created when a designer has been able to put themselves in someone else's shoes.

Tools used for UX research

Heatmap software

A tool that shows where users moved and hovered their mouse on your site, which gives an indication of the appeal of the elements of the page.

Usability testing

Research that works directly with users, letting them test your UX. This gives you an opportunity to learn where there are challenges and areas for improvement.

Eyeball tracking

Often used in usability testing to monitor exactly where a user is looking whilst they interact with the page(s) being tested.

Multivariant or split A/B testing

A testing method easily implemented on to a website to enable multiple versions of a page to run simultaneously and determine a best performer.

Web analytics

Commonly used across all websites to provide detailed data on visitor behaviours.

The two faces of UX

There are two distinct areas of activity falling under the broad banner of UX and they can be separated as follows:

- **Tactical or technical UX:** this is where the core principles of good interaction design are applied and where considerations like conversion optimization will come to the fore. Good interaction design is ensuring that every interaction is well thought through to serve the user in the simplest and most effective way possible. Conversion optimization focuses on ensuring that users find their way to the end of the goal without dropping out of the conversion funnel.

- **Strategic or human UX:** this is where we get into the realm of insight and brand. The role of UX at this elevation is to uncover the needs of people and to design an experience that meets those needs in a way that is congruent with the brand.

Tactical or technical UX – making the internet better one click at a time

Conversion is the primary metric for a business operating an e-commerce website.

The conversion rate – the ratio at which people who visit a site buy something – is probably one of the most studied marketing metrics available.

Data is analysed to assess every on-page element and typically a UX designer will be involved to construct differing permutations of the page that can be tested. This method of multivariant or split A/B testing is now routine in e-commerce and high-traffic environments to establish what page elements really influence conversion.

Split A/B testing simply tests version one against version two to determine a winner. Multivariant testing uses the same principle but with more variants and deeper results.

That conversion rate can have a significant impact on a company is self-evident but the scale of the impact can sometimes surprise.

CASE STUDY Uber

Background

Uber is, by now, a very well known global brand after its phenomenal growth between launch in 2009 and 2015. Its app is often hailed (please excuse the pun) as being very simple and therefore a great example of effective user experience. That much is true, but the goal was to take something that is actually quite complex and make it seem simple. This is the goal of good UX and Uber has succeeded here.

Strategy

Uber had to give a great deal of information to users but in a format that was intuitive and beautiful. This is something that most app designers struggle to deliver. It was not enough to create icons and make numbers bigger or more colourful. The app needed to be easy to understand and use. Most travel apps for trains and flights are full of forms and are not only ugly but frustrating and slow to use. Uber needed to be different.

The key here is that this was not about being minimal, it was about being complex but in a well-designed interface that delights. Uber therefore delivered a platform that could visually show you where a driver was, click to see their ratings and communicate with the driver directly. You could see an eta and simply move your pickup location on an interactive map. You would know the car and licence plate and even see the driver's route to you in real time. This is not simple at all – it is in fact a lot of complex information, but all displayed beautifully and quickly with an easy-to-use interface. That is great UX design.

Results

The results speak for themselves. Uber achieved its growth for many reasons including pricing and aggressive expansion, but the UX Uber delivered created a great deal of word of mouth and was a significant part of its growth story. This should not be underestimated.

Key lessons

UX is all about the experience, not the interface, but the latter leads to the former. In Uber's case it made something as simple as calling a taxi feel fun and cool. Simplification is not the goal here. Deliver a complex solution if that is what is needed to give users everything they require, but complex does not have to result in a difficult-to-use interface and so good UX design principles are key to success.

Strategic or human UX – bringing brands to life through experience design

We have already examined how important research is to the experience design process. Another factor is brand, because of how it can influence the end solution.

When thinking through your digital marketing strategy it is important to be honest (on the basis of good research) about what problem your product or services addresses for your target audience. The days when slick advertising, big marketing budgets or hard-working content could make up for a poor value proposition are surely coming to an end.

Be open-minded and the research from your UX people can open up all sorts of new opportunities for your business, or stop you from making terrible mistakes.

But this demands a culture shift – to think about brand as an experience that you offer to your prospects and customers, rather than as a set of key messages to repeat endlessly.

To become more digitally evolved, a brand must become a meaningful, tangible expression of the company that can be lived through every channel and form of interaction with consumers.

Design thinking

Underpinning customer-centric experience or design is the transformative power of design thinking. Workshops with Post-its, Sharpies and whiteboards have become de rigueur in digital circles and brainstorming, and they remain a technique that delivers results. These workshops can be challenging, however, and make some people uncomfortable or even self-conscious. Indeed the

Figure 16.1   The double-diamond approach

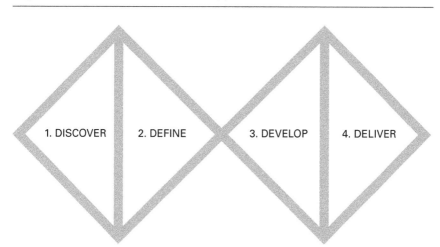

very nature of taking a group of people out of their comfort zone is intrinsically disarming. Tim Brown, the mercurial chief executive officer (CEO) of IDEO, said: 'Insofar as it is open-ended, open-minded, and iterative a process fed by design thinking will feel chaotic to those experiencing it for the first time.' He goes on to say, however, that 'over the life of a project, it invariably comes to make sense and achieves results that differ markedly from the linear, milestone-based processes that define traditional business practices' (Brown, 2009). There is much more to design thinking than running workshops, although they are tangible artefacts that often spring to mind when thinking of this discipline. In 2005 the British Design Council released the double-diamond approach as a way to neatly encapsulate the differing phases of divergent and convergent thinking necessary for design thinking (Figure 16.1).

The double diamond was born to represent the strategic design processes used at companies as diverse as Lego, Alessi, Microsoft and Virgin Atlantic Airways and is formed of four broad phases: discover, define, develop, deliver. Many designers have tweaked the process to their own needs, as is often the case with developed models, but the outline still gives shape to the core components. These are research, agreeing objectives or the problem to be solved, ideation and iteration of possible solutions, and then delivery of a finished product:

1 *Discover*: this is crucial to understand your users, challenges and therefore the design principles you need to work with.

2 *Define*: from the discovery phase we then need to build out what the problems that need to be solved are and the opportunities that are open to us.

3 *Develop*: this then needs to be developed, through the use of ideation, into a set of design principles to solve these problems.

4 *Deliver*: finally, these solutions need to be put in place in order to complete the design process.

A piece of research entitled 'Closing the Delivery Gap' from Bain & Company in 2005 stated that 80 per cent of companies believe they provide superior services, while only eight per cent of their customers agreed with them (Allen *et al*, 2005). This gap may (or may not) have narrowed in the intervening years, but it speaks to the difficulty that many large businesses have in getting a rounded understanding of their customers – despite the fortunes they spend with agencies on research.

Design thinking – and its core tenet of co-creation – may help that expectation gap narrow as businesses and customers work together to create the right products and services. More importantly, the research, the workshopping and the prototyping that design thinking advocates should be carried out hand-in-hand with the customer – the act of co-creating, co-designing a new service or product with the very people who will be buying it or consuming it is, by its very nature, transformative for most companies.

Summary

In this chapter we have examined the criticality of good user experience design to your overall digital marketing strategy and the importance of context when creating digital experiences for the people you want to engage with.

We have examined roles and responsibilities in the design process, and considered a number of UX research techniques, including ethnography. We have considered design thinking and the double-diamond approach.

We have also seen that UX can be considered to have two faces – one being strategic and the other more tactical.

Chapter checklist

- User experience ☐
- UX research ☐
- Design thinking ☐

Further reading

- *On ethnography*:

  Hammersley, M and Atkinson, P (2007) *Ethnography: Principles in practice*, Routledge

  Murchison, J (2010) *Ethnography Essentials*, John Wiley & Sons

- *On user experience*:

  Buley, L (2013) *The User Experience Team of One: A research and design survival guide*, Rosenfeld Media

  Unger, R (2012) *A Project Guide to UX Design: For user experience designers in the field or in the making*, New Riders

References

Allen, J, Frederick, F, Reichheld, B H and Markey, R (2005) [accessed 8 February 2019] Closing the Delivery Gap: How to achieve true customer-led growth, Bain & Company [Online] https://www.bain.com/insights/closing-the-delivery-gap-newsletter/

Brown, T (2009) *Change...By Design*, Harper Business

Ernst & Young (2011) [accessed 1 November 2015] The Digitisation of Everything [Online] www.ey.com/.../The_digitisation_of_everything.../EY_Digitisation_of_e...

Forrester (2014) [accessed 1 November 2015] The Future of Business is Digital, *Fenwick and Gill*, 03/10 [Online] https://www.forrester.com/The+Future+Of+Business+Is+Digital/fulltext/-/E-RES115520

Godin, S (2005) *The Purple Cow: Transform your business by being remarkable*, Penguin

An implementation guide is available at:
www.koganpage.com/DigitalMarketingStrategy/2

Managing loyalty, CRM and data

17

What we will cover in this chapter

This chapter looks at the digital methods that can be used to retain customers through effective relationship marketing and loyalty strategies including how to use data and technology effectively to accomplish this. The key areas covered in this chapter are:

- Defining CRM and retention
- Contact strategy
- Cross-selling and up-selling
- Predictive analytics
- Technology platforms
- Loyalty

Chapter goals

By the end of this chapter you should understand the core features of CRM programmes and how contact strategies play a part in shaping them. You should have an appreciation of cross-selling and up-selling techniques and an understanding of how predictive models play a part in retention decision making. You should also appreciate how CRM systems play a part in the process. Finally, you will have an understanding of loyalty programmes as well as the data and technology used to drive all of the above.

Defining CRM

It is a well-known adage that it is cheaper to keep a customer than to acquire one, and so for many businesses, retention is key to profitability and growth. Whether your business has a membership, renewal-based, relationship-led or single sale model you will still most often be looking for your customers to stay loyal to your brand and keep purchasing from you as often as possible. This is where CRM and retention strategies come in. CRM is about developing a relationship with your customers so that they want to stay. Retention is about changing the mindset of customers who want to leave. CRM is therefore a proactive strategy (we are looking to turn an existing negative situation into a positive outcome) whereas retention is a reactive strategy (we are reacting to the negative situation that has arisen). Neither retention nor CRM are new or unique to digital but they are often overlooked when digital strategies are being developed, as digital is often seen as your acquisition channels and your website experience. This is not the case and there is a great deal of depth to digital CRM and retention.

CRM is often mistakenly thought of as the system used to manage your customer contact details and perhaps the scheduling of interactions with them. Whilst these systems are CRM systems, they are not the definition of CRM itself, which is the far broader essence of developing truly value-adding relationships with your customers. There are several factors that are vital to success in CRM and retention. Below is a guide to how these are covered in this book. You should use the following to inform your understanding and implementation of CRM:

1 Personalization: it is vital when developing a relationship with a customer that you demonstrate an understanding of who they are and what they are looking for from you. We looked at this in greater detail in Chapter 15.

2 Segmentation and profiling are important to ensure that communications are not sent out in bulk. Spam e-mails from reputable companies are less common than they used to be as strategies have developed, but they certainly have not disappeared altogether and will not for many years. We looked at segmentation and profiles in Chapter 1.

3 Content: to create a compelling CRM strategy you need to have something compelling to discuss with your customers on a regular basis. This content needs to resonate with each customer and give them some form of added value. To do this effectively you need a content strategy, which we looked at in Chapter 14.

4 Insight: we cannot hope to understand how to build a compelling CRM strategy or how to retain customers if we don't understand them. Insight and research are vital to understanding the needs, aspirations, beliefs and other factors that cannot be obtained purely through the data itself. We looked at this in Chapter 3.

Finally, another factor that plays a large part in customer satisfaction and retention rates:

5 Customer service: this has changed significantly in the last 10 years with the direct access to organizations that customers now have through social media. We look at this separately in Chapter 18.

Principles

The goal of an effective CRM strategy is to ensure that your customers feel they are getting value for money and have a positive relationship with your brand. As a result they would have to think very hard before going elsewhere. This does not only result in increased retention rates but can also allow you to raise your prices without affecting existing retention rates as customers recognize the value in staying with your brand.

The core principles of CRM all relate to creating brilliant relationships with your customers and they can be broken down as follows:

- *Frequency*: this is a difficult principle to get right. How often do you contact your customers? Each customer may have a different opinion of this. Ultimately this comes down to what you have to say to them: if there is no value in what you are saying then you should not communicate with them. Never contact a customer just to meet a schedule you have built if you have nothing valuable to say. For example, monthly newsletters will be fine if you have news to provide. Daily cross-selling e-mails are highly unlikely to be popular for most companies.

- *Timeliness*: are you talking to the customer at the right time? How do you know when this right time is? Understanding the customer and their behaviours will help you to deliver messages they want when they want them and will also mean increases in sales. Understanding your analytics and consumer mindset through data is vital to getting this right.

- *Accuracy*: is your data accurate? This means that you need to keep your data cleansed, ensure it is being correctly used in your communications and also check that data from time to time through appends. A fantastic CRM strategy can be ruined if the communications are being sent to the wrong individuals, or if, for example, John Smith is being referred to in the salutation as Mr S John.

- *Relevancy*: does your message truly resonate with the customer? If your customer is interested in fishing, for example, does your CRM programme talk to them about fishing products or do they simply receive the same e-mails as everyone else, which also include jet skiing and dance music?

- *Personalization*: if your customer has shown an interest in certain areas or displays certain behaviours then are you responding to that? Does the customer only open e-mails in the evening? Do they only ever click on the first item? Do they only like to hear from a specific sales person?

- *Value*: are you offering true value? What is the customer getting from your communications that they cannot get elsewhere? Are you delivering your company's unique selling proposition (USP) or brand values through your communications?

- *Channel*: how do you reach this individual? Do they prefer e-mail, SMS, instant messaging or phone?

Whilst demand for value is a constant and the above principles apply to all CRM programmes, there are some differences in CRM depending on your business model. Below we look at some of the differences between B2B and B2C CRM:

- *Scale*: B2C companies are more likely to need to develop large and often complex CRM programmes with advanced systems to ensure that they are able to manage a large number of customers, potentially across a number of programmes. B2B companies tend to have smaller databases and fewer, but higher value, sales. They do, however, frequently need more data on each individual as the relationships are often more personal.

- *Frequency*: B2C customer touchpoints are often single, short touches whereas B2B relationships are often developed over a longer period of time.

- *Interaction*: B2B relationships tend to be primarily one-on-one and so personalities can play a major part, whereas B2C customers have a relationship with your brand rather than an individual and so your brand is your personality.

- *Goals*: B2B CRM is often about increasing and automating sales, whereas B2C is more regularly about decreasing churn and increasing up-sell.

Now that we understand the differences between CRM and retention and the key principles involved, we can move on to look at contact strategy – an essential part of any communications plan.

Contact strategy

One of the principles we looked at above is frequency: the number of times you contact your customer in any given period. This can be a very difficult area to get right and will almost certainly evolve over time. You may also run several CRM and retention programmes together and alongside a number of other marketing and customer-led communications, and so the frequency of communications can be quite significant and getting this balance right is crucial.

We mentioned spam above and, whilst this is less common than it used to be, it is still easy to be perceived by customers, if you are not careful, as sending spam. Whereas spam used to be perceived as e-mails coming to you from companies that had obtained your e-mail address without your permission, it is now much more broadly recognized as any unwanted e-mail. This means in practical terms that should a customer actively sign up to your e-mail newsletters but then find them irrelevant or too frequent they may begin to perceive it as spam. In the purest definition of the word this would not be spam, but it is the perception that matters as that is what the customer makes their decision on.

With regulation becoming ever more stringent to ensure consumer privacy and data control, for example GDPR in Europe, it is vital that you consider your data collection, retention and targeting carefully. This is common sense in marketing anyway and always has been but now regulation will be driving your behaviour if common sense does not. For more on GDPR see Chapter 5.

There are three forms of marketing communications that most businesses follow: single campaigns, repeat campaigns and contact strategy, as set out below.

Single campaigns

These consist of the business running a campaign before moving on to a completely separate campaign. This is, in most industries, no longer a sensible marketing strategy. Each communication begins from a standing start and has no relationship with the previous communication, therefore it offers very little consistency to the communications and fails to tell a compelling story. This method will offer a spike in response and potentially sales but will offer very little if any ongoing activity and no halo effect on other activity (Figure 17.1).

Figure 17.1   Single-campaign response curve

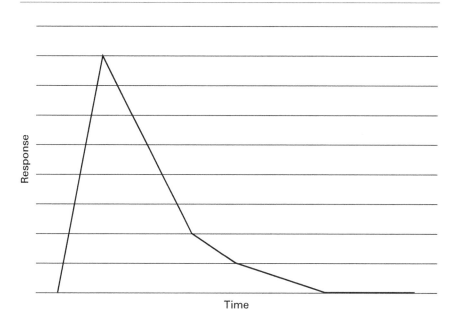

Halo effect

The halo effect is a term coined by Edward Thorndike who originally used it to refer to people. The term now more broadly refers to any form of bias based on positive feelings from elsewhere. This is often seen when reviewing above-the-line advertising, as consumers are more likely to respond to a communication from a brand that they recognize through advertising they have previously seen. If a consumer recognizes a brand, campaign or proposition they are more likely to respond to it and this plays a part in the success of contact strategies.

From a digital perspective, if you were to search for banks in the UK you would see paid search adverts and organic listings for a range of companies. These might include Barclays, Virgin, HSBC and many other leading financial brands. You are aware of these because you have seen their advertisements on television, in the press and elsewhere. You may also see advertisements for brands you have never heard of that have equally good, or even better offers on the services you are shopping for. Who do you click on? Well the fact is that a significant percentage of users will click on the brands they have seen in other adverts – and this is the halo effect. A digital marketer can take advantage of this through above-the-line advertising such as display or social media advertising, or simply through integrating creative with the offline above-the-line marketing.

Repeat campaigns

This is where a company repeats the same campaign(s) regularly over a period of time to encourage further sales (Figure 17.2). This ensures that the message begins to be seen by those who may have originally ignored it. It becomes more recognizable over time. It does, however, also become tired very quickly and so can become an irritant for some ('If I didn't interact with it the first time why do you keep showing it to me?'). It is also not going to convert anyone who has already converted and so the results will tail off over the period.

Contact strategy

Through developing a contact strategy your business can develop a meaningful programme of communications that take the customer on a journey and offer real value (Figure 17.3). This means that the consumer will get new and real value from every communication and may even begin to look forward to receiving the next communication. This is not just about sales or keeping customers but is about a journey.

Figure 17.2   Repeat-campaign response curve

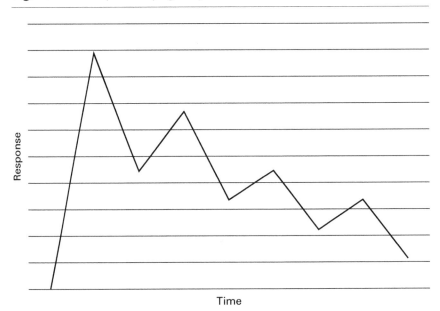

Figure 17.3 Contact-strategy response curve

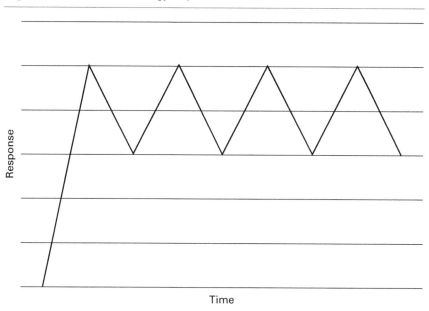

Types of messaging

There are many forms that messages within your contact strategy can take and these should be appropriate to your proposition, business, industry and consumer. Given below are some examples of types of communications that can form a contact strategy:

Warm-up

Warm-up e-mails can be anything from an introduction to a series of compelling content such as 'How To' guides to a preview of an upcoming product or series. These e-mails, similarly to teaser campaigns, can give the customer a sense of anticipation and this will in turn heighten their appetite for your next communication, which strengthens your overall contact strategy. A communication that is expected is far more likely to be opened, read and interacted with than one that is unexpected.

Example 'Your series of guides on how to get the most from your new drum kit will be starting next week. Get a sneak peak of lesson one by clicking here.'

Follow-up

The follow-up communication is effectively the opposite of the warm-up. These can be very common in B2B contact strategies. Where the customer has received a phone call or e-mail on a specific subject, following it up after a short period of time can be crucial to closing a sale or capturing the purchase moment. The crucial detail here is the timing. If your initial contact has sparked an interest for the customer but they need to do their own independent research or review their finances, for example, then contacting them too early can be a significant irritation. Contacting them too late, however, may result in a missed opportunity as their online activity can be seen and acted upon by a competitor.

Example 'Thank you Jane for popping in to see us last week about getting a new laptop. If you need more information to help you decide we have these great guides and a help centre to answer your questions. If you need to chat to anyone you can call us any time on XXX XXXX XXX.'

Surprise and delight

This form of communication is value in its purest form. The purpose of a surprise and delight message is to do exactly as it says. There is no sales message here, no data capture and no directly commercial element. A surprise and delight message is something that gives some value to your customer that they will really appreciate. You may, for example, offer your customers a discount on their birthday to say thank you. This is one of the rare opportunities when something that appears too good to be true is actually true. It does of course create a good feeling about your customer service and brand that increases retention rates. It may also increase word-of-mouth advertising and result in positive discussions in public forums and even PR – so the advantages are clear.

Example 'Happy birthday Li-Wei. We just wanted to say that we love having you as a customer, so to say thank you on this special day we're adding a bottle of wine to your next order to enjoy with your birthday dinner. Have a great day!'

Reward

This is similar to surprise and delight in that you are rewarding your customers, but this time it is clear that you are rewarding them for a specific behaviour. This may be a gift or some valuable information that is hard to find, and it would be in exchange for buying a product or reaching a certain milestone as a customer.

Example 'Hi Juan Carlos. We just wanted to say thank you for taking the time to complete our survey last month. These results really help us to improve our service, so next time you come to see us you can use this token to get 50 per cent off whatever you buy up to £100. We look forward to seeing you again soon.'

Win-back

This is actually an acquisition message rather than CRM as the customer has left and you are trying to win them back. It does, however, have a blurred line with CRM as you have an existing relationship with them, albeit ending. You have knowledge of their behaviours and can therefore engage them in a contact strategy to bring them back to the business.

Example 'Dear Celeste. We're very sorry to see you go. It's not you, it's us. We're all very upset here in the office but we wanted you to know that if you're willing to give us another chance one day then we hope this voucher for 25 per cent off will help.'

There are many more forms of communication and it is a valuable exercise to think about the different forms of communication that can fill your contact strategy.

Cross-selling and up-selling

Cross-selling and up-selling are two common forms of maximizing revenue from your customers and they continue to play an important part in many business strategies.

Cross-selling is where you encourage your customers to purchase another one of your products. If, for example, you are a retailer and a customer has recently bought a winter coat, perhaps you could encourage them to buy some matching gloves or a scarf that complements the look. This shows an understanding of the underlying need of the customer and presents an opportunity for revenue.

Up-selling is the method of encouraging a customer to upgrade their product to the next level. This may, for example, be a customer who has recently purchased a 'Bronze Level' cover from your motor breakdown company and you notice that they have historically had numerous issues with their car at home, which is only covered on the 'Silver Level' cover. Explaining this to the customer and trying to up-sell this product is both of value to the customer and to the company and so is a relevant up-sell opportunity.

Cross-selling and up-selling are ultimately reliant on what is known as collaborative filtering, which is a method of predictive analytics. With CRM and retention strategies, predictive analytics can be very powerful. We look at these below.

Predictive analytics

One of the vital areas of information for CRM and retention strategies is predictive analytics. Whilst retention is a reactive process, being able to predict behaviours and therefore anticipate customers leaving is very powerful. Also being able to understand customer behaviour and therefore make advance decisions is equally effective. In this section we look at two predictive analytics models that are relevant to retention strategies: propensity models and collaborative filtering.

Propensity models

Propensity models are probably the most commonly known form of predictive analytics as they are commonly used in businesses to predict future customer behaviour based on known information. Propensity modelling can be used for many purposes, including predicting engagement and conversion, but we are most interested here in its use for retention.

By understanding which customers leave and then the behaviours they commonly exhibit before they leave we are able to see a potential issue before it happens. We can then introduce a specific contact strategy to softly warm this person back to our product or brand and therefore decrease churn and increase retention.

One specific form of this for retention purposes is 'next best action'. This is where a propensity model is used to assess the next conversation to have with the consumer. It is used in numerous scenarios such as up-selling, converting and saving customers. If a customer is looking to leave then your website (or customer service representative) may have a series of choices that can be made about how to save them. They could be offered a discount or even free products or services. The propensity model is designed to try the next action necessary to save this profile or individual – not jumping straight to the expensive option, which may be unnecessary.

Collaborative filtering

As mentioned above, many businesses now use recommendations to encourage customers to purchase other products from them – something that was pioneered by Amazon. This method is called collaborative filtering. The reason for this name is simple. Recommendations are being made by using filtered data from many users, or a collaboration of users.

By using the data of many people's behaviours we can effectively segment behaviours into many buckets and therefore many tailored recommendations from the outputs. As well as continuing to be used by Amazon it is also used by many other businesses in a wide range of industries, such as Netflix's movie recommendations based on social connectivity and Apple's genius recommendations.

Technology platforms

There are many CRM systems on the market today and they continue to improve and become more sophisticated. Many, however, are not used to their full potential. In 2003, a report by the global IT research and advisory company Gartner estimated that 41.9 per cent of CRM software goes undeployed (Gartner, 2003) whilst the same company's 2013 report showed that over 20 billion US dollars are spent on CRM software worldwide (Gartner, 2014). The software itself remains an important part of the overall strategy, but implementing it and using it correctly are equally important. The features that you should expect from your CRM software are as follows, although the importance of each will depend on the priorities of your strategy:

- Customer support automation: the function that allows users to centralize, manage and automate customer support. This can include capturing e-mail and web interactions, sharing a knowledge base and self-service portals.

- Marketing automation: this includes creation and managing marketing campaigns in an automated fashion, therefore retaining consistency and reducing resource requirements. Separate marketing automation platforms are now commonplace and integrate with CRM systems. We looked at these in Chapter 12.

- Reporting: a report on all of the activity that is managed through the CRM system, including marketing, sales and service.

- Sales force automation: primarily but not solely for the B2B user, this feature manages sales funnels, contract management, lead scoring, sales forecasting and much more.

- Contact centre support: some systems also combine CRM functionality with specific contact centre features such as interactive voice response (IVR) menus, missed call management and skill-based routing to enable the systems to be fully integrated with call-centre environments.

Other features such as workflow management, e-mail integration, data management and inventory management may also be useful for your specific needs and should be considered.

There are many systems available on the market today such as Salesforce, Microsoft Dynamics, Oracle, Adobe, SAP, Zoho, SugarCRM, Sage and many more. These are not recommendations and you should conduct your own procurement exercise to fully understand your needs alongside the propositions of the potential suppliers available.

AI is now playing a part in CRM as in many other areas of digital marketing, as we have discussed throughout the book. Specifically to CRM, machine learning and AI are being used in many of the leading CRM platforms.

Some of these developments include predictive calendars that can inform you of relevant information prior to an event, AI that searches for trends, account insights, chatbots, social media conversation analysis, image classification, sales opportunity analysis, product recommendations, content personalization and other uses. New developments are continually underway.

This use of AI enables the digital marketer to have a wealth of relevant data and automated processes with which to deliver tailored marketing with minimal administration. This trend will only continue and should now be considered an essential part of the digital marketing ecosystem and technology stack. No digital marketing strategy is complete without AI built into it and especially into the CRM channel.

The Internet of Things (IoT) is another technology development that has grown substantially in recent years. The opportunity here for CRM is in integrating with your experiences. Your experiences should, where possible, integrate with an IoT device and this enables insights, predictive offerings and personalized servicing. Being able to communicate directly with a client in real time in their home enables a great deal of CRM opportunity but this must be developed with a clear client-first approach to avoid disappointment and invasive communication.

Loyalty

Finally in this chapter we look at loyalty. Much of what we have discussed in this chapter is about encouraging loyalty, but loyalty itself is a specific area of CRM that needs to be looked at independently.

The ladder of loyalty

The ladder of loyalty is a model often referred to within marketing as it shows the five stages that a consumer steps through to become loyal to a brand (Figure 17.4). They are:

1 *Suspect*: no relationship with the brand; no reason to suggest they would or would not buy from you.

2 *Prospect*: shown some indication of interest such as visit, free subscription or enquiry.

3 *Customer*: has purchased from you and so has a basic relationship with your business.

4 *Client*: has developed a deeper relationship with you through repeat purchases but not necessarily a fan of your business.

5 *Advocate*: is showing signs of recommending you and is highly unlikely to stop shopping with you unless something drastic happens.

Other steps can be added to the ladder such as members, evangelists, shoppers. There are many interpretations that you can apply to your individual business, but the above list covers the core stages.

Figure 17.4   The ladder of loyalty

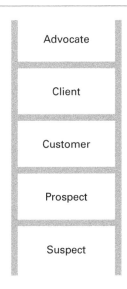

In order to guide the consumer up this ladder you will need to be successful in all areas of your strategy, from targeted acquisition and personalized content strategy through to social CRM and analytics.

Loyalty programmes

Loyalty programmes remain a strong method of forcing loyalty. Where advocacy and brand loyalty may sway a consumer towards choosing to visit one website over another from the search engine results, a loyalty programme can ensure that the consumer does not search at all but goes directly to the website. Loyalty can be a powerful thing: I myself spent many hours as a child being forced to travel around the roads of England, running desperately low on fuel, so that my father could find the right brand of petrol station to get his loyalty points from. There have been many highly successful loyalty programmes in the last 20 years such as Tesco, Nectar, Walgreen's, Canadian Tire, Flybuys, Boots, Payback and many more. These can be referred to as loyalty, reward, club, discount or points cards. Ultimately they all have the same purpose – to offer the consumer a high perceived value from regularly shopping at one brand and in turn to receive higher average sales and revenue per customer. The key here is the term 'perceived' value. This can be the ultimate decision as to whether a loyalty programme works or fails.

High-value loyalty

This type of programme offers items, services or discounts to the customer that are of a high value. This can lead to a significant increase in average sales per customer and retention rates but it can be costly to offer these rewards, especially as many of your customers would probably have shopped with your store anyway. That factor, combined with the cost of promoting and running the scheme, has in the past resulted in criticism for loyalty schemes.

High perceived-value loyalty

This type of programme is focused more on making the customer think that the items are of value whereas they may actually cost the company very little. This means that the cost of running the programme can be kept low and the customers will still show increased shopping behaviours. It can, however, result in criticism for not offering enough value to the customer.

An example of this is buying a product in bulk and then adding it to your product for free or for a small increase in price. This could be a voucher or a service such as insurance.

The key to success is to ensure that the customer is offered some real value but not at the expense of the financial rewards of the scheme. This can take some significant adjustment of the programme over time and it is therefore wise to be as flexible with your loyalty scheme as possible at launch, and to build up the scheme slowly.

Summary

In this chapter we looked at what CRM and retention strategies are and how you can use them as part of your digital marketing strategy to deliver increased revenues and improved customer satisfaction. We looked at the benefits of a contact strategy and the principles therein, as well as methods of cross-selling and up-selling to maximize commercial opportunities from your sales funnels. Predictive analytics in terms of both propensity modelling and collaborative modelling have shown us how we can use data to make smart decisions and enable us to decrease churn and increase sales. We have looked briefly at some of the functions of an effective CRM and, finally, we looked at loyalty programmes and the power they can have to encourage customers to return more often and spend more money.

Chapter checklist

- Defining CRM and retention ☐
- Contact strategy ☐
- Cross-selling and up-selling ☐
- Predictive analytics ☐
- Technology platforms ☐
- Loyalty ☐

Further reading

- *On subscription marketing*:

  Janzer, A (2015) *Subscription Marketing*, Cuesta Park Consulting.
  Anne also goes into great detail on providing and nurturing value,
  as well as how to put your strategies into action.

References

Gartner (2003) [accessed 1 November 2015] 42 Percent of CRM Software Goes
  Unused', 28/02 [Online] https://www.gartner.com/doc/387369/gartner-survey--
  percent-crm
Gartner (2009) [accessed 1 November 2015] Gartner Says Companies Need to
  Pursue Four Steps to Harness Social Computing in CRM, 19/02 [Online]
  http://www.gartner.com/newsroom/id/889712
Gartner (2014) [accessed 1 November 2015] Gartner Says Customer Relationship
  Management Software Market Grew 13.7 Percent in 2013, 06/05 [Online]
  http://www.gartner.com/newsroom/id/2730317

An implementation guide is available at:
www.koganpage.com/DigitalMarketingStrategy/2

Providing a smooth online service and customer experience

18

What we will cover in this chapter

This chapter looks at customer service through the lens of digital. This has been a growing challenge and opportunity in recent years. The key areas covered in this chapter are:

- Customer service principles
- Service channels
- Social customer service
- Measurement

Chapter goals

By the end of this chapter you should understand best-practice customer service principles and channels. You should have an appreciation of social customer service and how to measure effective customer service. You should understand specific digital challenges and opportunities in serving your customers as part of your strategy.

Many years ago marketing was purely about growing your company whilst customer service was about solving customer issues. The increased focus on customer satisfaction and the increasing power of the consumer in the 21st century has led to much more of a service element to marketing. Also, the growth of social media has led to a need to directly interact with consumers in two-way conversations whilst pushing marketing content out on the same channel.

All of this means that the content strategy you have must fit with your service goals and your customer service principles must support the messaging from your content. Your website must also fit with your service goals. For example, will you be including online chat functionality or simply promoting your call-centre telephone number? Do you need a secure messaging function within your customer logged-in experience? All of these questions change your UX.

We can quickly see that customer service and marketing now overlap a great deal and so understanding how to build this into your digital marketing strategy is important.

Customer service principles

One of the key messages of this book is that digital is an integrated part of your strategy and must not be a separate silo within your business. That principle does not apply anywhere more than with customer service. Whether your customers are coming to you with questions or with complaints they will expect to be treated well and served quickly by experts – at this stage more than any other.

Within your digital strategy you have opportunities to talk directly with customers through social media, which is now an expectation of many consumers. You are able to provide real-time online help and information and all without the need for the consumer to go through a phone system. This is no longer an add-on to a customer service strategy, but is an essential part of it.

In order to understand how to achieve this within the digital arena we first need to understand how to achieve the best possible customer service levels and to do this we will review the key service principles (Figure 18.1).

Understand your customer

We have discussed throughout the book how important it is to understand the consumer and your customers. This primarily involves research, insight and analytics, which together give you a broad mix of data and direct

Figure 18.1 Customer service principles

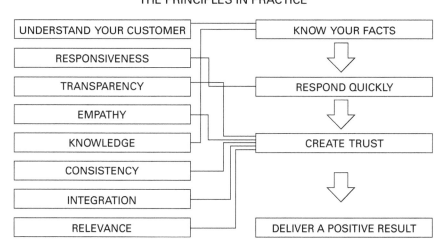

THE PRINCIPLES IN PRACTICE

UNDERSTAND YOUR CUSTOMER	KNOW YOUR FACTS
RESPONSIVENESS	
TRANSPARENCY	RESPOND QUICKLY
EMPATHY	
KNOWLEDGE	CREATE TRUST
CONSISTENCY	
INTEGRATION	
RELEVANCE	DELIVER A POSITIVE RESULT

feedback to shape your strategy. Part of this data must be understanding the views and opinions of your customers. This can be broken down into two core areas: trends and individual customers.

Trends

Trends give us a broad view of the common issues that customers experience and can also show us where we have been doing a great job. Analysing your data to understand how customers are behaving at key touchpoints and what feedback is being received via your call centre, service e-mail or other communication method is crucial to understanding the trends. Only by finding the common factors that your customers are struggling with will you be able to prioritize the work and truly understand how to help them.

Trends can come from your data, for example you may find that customers from Germany are struggling to pay their annual fee online as they are dropping out of the funnel at a very high rate on the payment screen. This could be due to a technical error on the German version of your website or it could be that German consumers do not use credit cards as widely as your UK customers and so you need to offer another payment method. Seeing this trend can enable you to tackle it and improve your customer satisfaction levels.

Trends can also arise directly from your customers' feedback. This may be through any of the open communication channels such as e-mail or social media. Looking for the common themes here can be harder than through data analytics, but by understanding what the trending areas of complaint are you can focus your efforts towards those.

Individual customers

Whilst trend analysis is important, it is also vitally important to demonstrate an understanding of each customer individually and this is increasingly becoming an expectation rather than simply a desire of customers. We looked at personalization in Chapter 15 and that principle remains relevant here.

Ensuring your systems allow you to know your customer is a challenge that large businesses have always faced, as knowing each individual customer personally is impossible for most businesses when operating at scale. There are many software solutions that store all conversations and interactions in one place with features such as complaint monitoring, known issue management, knowledge base and social media integration. These features can be very powerful when used in conjunction with a customer database.

Ultimately, understanding your customer is the most important stage in delivering excellent customer service.

Responsiveness

One area of frustration for customers that has increased significantly in the digital age is the time taken for organizations to respond. Consumers are less patient than they used to be and have higher expectations when it comes to response. You need to be prepared to structure your business to enable fast response and therefore meet the demands of your customers.

There are a number of ways that we can at least acknowledge a message straight away and be proactive in responding to our customers. A quick response with an appropriate and, where possible, personalized message can make the difference between dealing with a simple complaint quickly and it escalating into a serious issue.

For example: 'Thank you for your message Linda. Below is a copy of what you sent us for your records and we will get back to you within two hours. If you have any questions in the meantime please call us on XXX XXXX XXX.'

Even if Linda is not happy with the two-hour time frame at least she knows what the time frame is and her expectations have been set. This can reduce complaints.

Transparency

Another area that has continued to face increasing scrutiny in the 21st century is transparency or, put another way, openness.

Transparency should always be a core principle of customer service. Consumers are more cynical than ever and a great deal of information on businesses such as turnover and management teams is available online. Regulators are also being far more aggressive in punishing organizations and releasing information when decisions are made that have a negative effect on consumers. When something goes wrong it is often quickly publicized and can even go viral.

Toyota

Toyota in the United States, in 2010, took what was generally considered too long to respond to a crisis regarding a vehicle defect. By the time their head of sales for the United States publicly responded they had already recalled 2.3 million vehicles and their president had issued a 75-second apology. The recall cost Toyota $21 billion in market value. The slow response may have cost them much more through a loss of trust in the brand.

Transparency has never been more important.

Empathy

The tone of voice used in marketing communications is an essential part of delivering on the principle of empathy. This should be driven from your brand and must be consistent across your organization. To explain this, given below is an example of how tone may differ.

Company customer service tone of voice

- A friendly, conversational tone: 'We're sorry you didn't love your experience. We're going to return your money right away.'

- A formal tone: 'Apologies that your experience was sub-standard. Your account will be refunded within the next 24 hours.'

Your tone comes through such important elements as vocabulary, humour and storytelling. It can be more powerful than many people would imagine. Your tone of voice can build trust and demonstrate understanding. It can be a key factor in creating advocacy, as some consumers will feel that you speak like one of their friends – and how you say things resonates with them.

Decide how correct you want your language to be. For example, if you are writing in English are you willing to split an infinitive? Are you willing to start a sentence with 'And' or 'However'. Are you willing to use slang, jargon or profanity (tread very carefully with the latter)? These techniques break English language rules but can be powerful in marketing copy.

Empathy itself is vital as a customer who does not feel that you understand them (even if you do) will become frustrated. The line here is in showing that you understand the customer and can empathize with their position but ensuring that you do not go so far as to agree with any views that may show your business to have been negligent or not to have operated according to the customer's best interest. There may be extreme cases where this is true, but admitting this in a customer service environment can lead to escalation of an otherwise relatively minor issue.

Knowledge

This area is very different from knowing your customer. Knowledge in this sense is related to knowing your business and so looking inwards rather than out. Another frustration that customers can have when speaking to your agents or using your website for help is that the knowledge isn't there. Needing help with a product or service can be frustrating and speaking to someone at the company, either on the phone or digitally, can exacerbate the issue if they do not know more than you do. Therefore ensuring your online information is up to date and correct is vital as is ensuring that all staff are experts in the field they are responding to.

Consistency

We have all experienced issues where we phone a company and speak to a department that gives us an answer and then redirects us to another department that gives us a completely different answer; perhaps even the same person in the same department giving us different answers on different days. This can seem like being stuck in an endless loop and be extremely frustrating. It is important that your service approach, language, training, documentation, service levels, systems and all other factors are aligned into one consistent approach no matter what the channel. Taking a channel agnostic approach is essential as it ensures that you put the customer and the process before the channel and not vice versa. In order to achieve this you will need to build a set of processes and procedures that create consistency across your service touchpoints. You will need to set your tone of voice, your processes for handling certain types of calls, your systems used for decision making and record keeping.

Integration

Integrating your customer service with your broader business is crucial. This also includes integrating your digital service with your broader service. It can be tempting to buy some new customer support software and integrate it into one area of your business to show everyone else what is possible. Whilst this can be a good technique for creating competition and therefore raising the game of other departments, it can create a disconnect for customers as they receive very different levels of service in very different areas of your business, which again can cause frustration. Integrating into your existing systems is of course also a practical process in terms of cost and efficiency savings.

Relevance (eg channel)

Finally, relevance is important. Pushing customers through a process that they do not want to follow, in order to hit certain targets, can be counterintuitive. Ensuring that your customers have a choice of channels to use and can therefore contact you through the method that they wish will be far more productive and create better and faster resolutions. It is worth adding a note here that, although the above principle is true, it can create significant cost savings to have a purely digital customer service process and remove or significantly reduce call-centre service if this is appropriate for your customers. This model is fairly common today and, whilst it can cause frustration for some customers, it can be an entirely valid strategy if implemented correctly.

Service channels

There are many channels available for digital customer service but some are often overlooked. Not all channels are appropriate to all organizations. For example, an e-commerce site may offer a live chat facility to enable people to get quick answers but this would not be appropriate for a B2B manufacturing business where customers have dedicated relationship managers. This comes back to the relevance principle mentioned above.

Online content

There is a great deal that organizations can do to proactively solve customer service demands simply by answering common questions and providing information openly. As we mentioned above, by understanding our customers we can deliver what we know they want without the need for those customers to get in contact with us. This information can come in a number of forms but must at all times be fresh. This means that providing product specifications, guides, 'how to' videos, FAQs and much more can be useful, but if these are not updated regularly then they become a customer issue rather than resolution.

There is also far less value in online documentation if customers do not know it is there. You should ensure that customers are made aware of your 'help zone' when they become customers and you could consider promoting it to customers on a regular basis or including it within your newsletter. If you keep the content really fresh, with monthly guides on how to use your products or services, then customers may proactively seek out your content. This all reduces e-mails, calls and chat requests, which keeps your customers satisfied and keeps your resource requirements low.

Keep in mind that online content does not strictly mean your website. Many customers will start by searching to find the content they want. This could be Google or any other engine. Your help content should therefore be search engine optimized but should also reside on YouTube and other locations likely to help your customers find the information they need. Remember the full digital ecosystem when distributing your help content.

Live chat

Live chat, sometimes known as web chat, allows your customers to use an online chat window to talk directly to your customer service representatives. This is text based and should not be confused with video chat. This method, whilst digital, still has a traditional offline service approach in that you need agents to hold the conversation and these agents need to have good product knowledge, access to a customer service system and to follow all of the principles we mentioned above.

There are some distinct advantages and disadvantages to live chat versus the traditional call-centre approach and, whilst they are not mutually exclusive, this is a useful lens to use when assessing the channel:

- *Advantages to live chat*:
  - Not always on: it can be switched off or changed into a contact form when you do not have the capacity to be able to handle the volume.
  - Copy and paste: you can send direct links to helpful areas of the site rather than having to talk the customer through how to navigate to somewhere.

- Knowledge: as well as accessing a knowledge base, an agent has the ability to ask their colleagues without having to put the customer on hold.
- Language: the issue of regional accents disappears through text-based communication. This can remove what can be an issue for some customers.
- Multitasking: agents are sometimes able to help multiple customers at once without each customer knowing, which can be far more efficient.

- *Disadvantages to live chat*:
  - Appropriate: it may not be appropriate for your audience. Almost all people are comfortable using a phone but some are still not comfortable using digital technology.
  - Patience: if you do not respond quickly the customer is likely to have less patience than if you do not answer the phone quickly.
  - Mobile: whilst calling someone from a mobile is very simple, live chat does not always function well from a user experience perspective . This is primarily because much of the software has not yet been optimized to as broad a range of devices as is necessary. Whilst this is improving, it remains an issue.

Based on the above list of advantages it can be seen why live chat can be a very powerful tool if used with an appropriate audience.

Chatbots

As artificial intelligence continues to improve, increasing numbers of chatbots are being used for customer service. These chatbots are often intelligent enough to be able to solve a high percentage of issues for customers without the need for a human to get involved. This sits somewhere between the online content and live chat model as it is online content that is provided by a machine.

According to Accenture (2016), 80 per cent of customer engagements can be handled by bots. As a result this trend is likely to continue and we will see more usage of visual IVR rather than audio IVR. IVR is 'interactive voice response' and has been common in customer service for decades. You would recognize it from the phone channel as 'press 1 for sales, press 2 for customer services' etc. Visual IVRs are for your chat screens and can reroute a significant percentage of calls to chatbots and reduce resource requirements.

Voice

We will also see increasing usage of voice for customer service. This is an interesting trend, helped by the IoT (Internet of Things) revolution and smart home assistants such as Amazon Echo. Whilst we have discussed above the fact that we are moving away from phone conversations with humans, we are not entirely moving away from voice. Chatbots and live chat are part of the journey but voice help through IoT devices is also growing and this should be considered in your strategy.

Messaging

We will discuss social media below but messaging is a specific area of focus for digital customer service. This has grown enormously in recent years and the platforms are having to adopt to ensure they can provide the relevant security to enable this opportunity for large brands. You can now use messaging apps to order your coffee and be notified when it is ready to pick up or integrate it with your music streaming service, but customer service is a different proposition for the channel. Being able to deal with your customer services issues directly through your favoured messaging app is a smooth experience and one that can be hugely beneficial to both the consumer and the business, but it is not the same as chatting to a friend or ordering a coffee.

A report by Forrester entitled 'The Future of Messaging Apps' clearly explains the importance of this channel (Husson *et al*, 2016) . First, messaging apps have a very high frequency of use. Second, there is a high emotional connection as with any direct line of communication, and third, they are convenient. These three factors are a powerful combination and so platforms such as WhatsApp, Facebook Messenger and WeChat should be in your plans. We already looked at them from a promotional perspective in Chapter 12 but don't leave them out of your service strategy.

Forums

Forums have been around for many years and remain an important part of the internet. As we continue to drive towards creating digital communities the forums remain a powerful tool for sharing information and helping others. They can also be an incredibly powerful tool for reducing contacts from customers by proactively solving problems. Some consumers can have as much, if not more, knowledge of your products or services than your customer service representatives. At the very least they can offer a different perspective – that of the practical use by a peer. Your representative, no matter how talented, can never offer a truly independent opinion in the customer's mind. Forums have one common feature that is simultaneously the major advantage and the major disadvantage. This is that there is little input needed from your organization. You may steer the categories and some of the subjects but you will not be originating the content that is posted. This means that there is no need to produce the content or manage it on an ongoing basis. This clearly creates a significant efficiency saving and ensures that you have helped your customers to find the answers they need with very little direct effort. This sounds too good to be true.

As with most things that sound too good to be true – it is. The other side of this feature is that anything can be posted to your message board. This could include profanities, spam, details of any serious issues that you would rather keep between yourself and the one customer in question, and even illegal content. This is where moderation needs to play a role. Moderating a forum can be an intensive use of resource, dependent on the size and type of content. They therefore need to be moderated effectively. Below are some good principles for moderating a forum to ensure that your brand and broader content and experience are not affected by these issues.

Transparency

As with the customer service principle we mentioned above, this is important. You must not delete content simply because you don't like it or you disagree with it. Keeping the forum open and honest is vital to its success. You should, however, engage with the user and try to take the issue offline to be solved.

Rules

Develop a set of rules for your forum that are clearly promoted to ensure everyone who signs up has read and accepted them. This is not a way of guaranteeing the correct use of the forum but is a way of removing the content that does not follow the rules, without causing any complaints. First, however, it is important to try to get the user to remove the post themselves before you take further action; this will help to maintain a personal approach.

Stay involved

Take part in discussions and try to help and guide wherever possible. Do not get into disagreements in the forum but try to add value and steer conversations away from negative views towards positive outcomes.

E-mail

E-mail customer service has been used for many years now and remains a common method of communication for many. It allows customers to take their time to build their argument and attach relevant information. It also reduces the need for a conversation, which many customers will find difficult due to the potentially confrontational nature of a complaint. From an organization's perspective it allows you to assess the information provided and return a response within a prescribed time frame, which can be helpful. It also maintains a written history of the conversation. It can be argued that many digital channels offer these same features but, though that is true, e-mail is the channel that has been established for much longer than most digital service channels and so is the one that almost all customers will feel most comfortable with if their need is not urgent. What is important within e-mail, however, is managing response time frames and this can be done effectively through automated messaging.

Once an e-mail is sent, the sender has no way of knowing what will happen next. It is vital therefore that when the customer sends you an e-mail, either directly or through submitting an online form, they receive a response that sets their expectations. These e-mails should state the time frame of response and also what the customer submitted and any details such as the date and time. This e-mail should be personalized and where possible should include details about who will be making contact with them, so as to set up a personal relationship. Having some set replies for specific areas ready to send out can be hugely advantageous in ensuring consistency and saving time. These are sometimes referred to as 'canned replies'. These can simply be copied and pasted into the e-mails to answer the relevant queries. It is vital, however, that these are read through and checked to ensure they still seem personal and contextual before being sent. We discussed tone of voice above and, again, that is highly relevant here. Ensuring that your e-mails are friendly, positive and simple (without being patronizing) is vital. You can, and should where relevant, also include links to key documents and relevant locations on your site that the customer can visit to solve their issue.

Finally, ensure you are always moving towards, demonstrating and speaking of an end resolution so that, with each e-mail in the chain, the customer feels that progress is being made. We discussed e-mail as a channel in more detail in Chapter 12 so please refer back to this for further detail.

Callbacks

Callbacks remain a common form of customer service for those customers who are not looking for an immediate response. They can, therefore, be frustrating for those customers who need help quickly but are presented with no other options. Callbacks have the advantage of enabling customer service departments to manage the call levels entirely as they wish but clearly take this control away from the customer. Best practice is to include a time frame for when this call will occur and this should be precise. If it is possible for your organization to manage your call times to within half an hour then this would be a good aim for businesses where customers are looking for a quick response. Where the response can be slower, ie a matter of days, then simply suggesting time frames such as morning, afternoon or evening are normally acceptable and allow for simpler management within the service centre. This channel should not be your only service route, however, as that would be a poor experience for most consumers.

Co-browsing

In simple terms co-browsing is two or more people accessing the same web pages at the same time and this duplication of experience allows a customer service agent to understand a customer's needs better. The difference between this and screen sharing is that co-browsing is both looking at the same page at the same time whereas screen sharing is one user looking at the other's screen. This can be especially helpful in helping a user to complete an action such as a purchase and it offers a more personal experience than a simple phone call or live chat. It is often used when a conversation is proving difficult without being able to see where the user is struggling. It can therefore deliver stronger results than other channels alone.

There is another opportunity with co-browsing – the ability to up-sell – but this would, however, be inappropriate in the majority of service situations. Whilst helping to guide a user through a process you have the opportunity to talk to them about the decisions they make and this may help them to realize that they should be purchasing something that they had disregarded when browsing alone. This should not be a primary goal of co-browsing but it can be an advantage.

CASE STUDY HSBC

Background

HSBC, a major global bank, placed customers at the heart of an agile project to improve customer experience and set new standards for project delivery. Using technology provided by the company Vizolution, the bank set up a digitally assisted phone conversation – one that was as easy as the branch experience, but more efficient.

Strategy

Through this platform customers were able to complete and sign applications electronically, quickly, and see all information required by regulators. These platforms can be difficult to implement; in large organizations it can also often be difficult to gain internal confidence in such platforms. HSBC therefore first implemented a low-risk proof of concept, which gathered evidence in order to build confidence. This customer service improvement has now been rolled out to 15 further UK workstreams and will support a new global banking proposition. Advisors are excited and a new Centre of Excellence is building capability for the future.

Results

This implementation of a digital platform to deliver improved client experience resulted in processing costs reducing by more than 8 per cent per application and process times dropped between 45 per cent and 93 per cent (from initial application to final resolution). In addition, 95 per cent of customers found the system easy to use, with 93 per cent agent satisfaction. On top of these fantastic customer service outcomes, the new system also resulted in a 20 per cent increase in conversion in telephony lending applications.

Key lessons

Using digital platforms to solve customer experience challenges can radically improve customer service metrics. Enabling people to self-serve is a simple but effective way of doing this and can sometimes achieve results beyond what you might expect.

Social customer service

One area of digital customer service that continues to undergo a major transformation is that of social customer service. One of the major differences between social customer service and other channels is that it is often initiated and sometimes continued in a very public channel. Responses are demanded quickly, as in other channels, and the principles above all still apply.

One of the key challenges is around the process of social media within your organization. Social is often managed by either the PR or marketing team (which may be one and the same) who are unlikely to have the skill set or capacity to handle the customer service elements. Therefore, should there be a dedicated customer service Twitter handle, for example? Customers cannot be guaranteed to use this handle so in practical terms this is difficult to manage. Should marketing therefore pass on the messages to customer service? Well, this seems in fact like a resource drain on a marketing department. As social media increasingly becomes a two-way communication for organizations rather than a 'push' message channel, ownership is moving away from marketing. Once companies reach maturity with social media they will be using the channel as an integrated part of their customer service process, which would include use within the contact centre.

Another challenge is amplification. When a complaint is made on social media it has the opportunity to be picked up by friends and other followers. It may go viral and can then even become newsworthy. This can be brand damaging or, alternatively, it can be an opportunity. An excellent example of how to turn this challenge into an opportunity was when, in 2014, United Airlines lost Rory McIlroy's golf clubs immediately prior to a tournament.

Rory McIlroy's golf clubs

After the US Open in June 2014, Rory McIlroy flew out of Newark and headed for Dublin, Ireland. When he arrived he discovered that his clubs had not arrived with him. As he was flying there to play in the Irish Open his clubs were fairly important. As a result, Rory took to Twitter with the following tweet:

@McIlroyRory: 'Hey @united landed in Dublin yesterday morning from Newark and still no golf clubs... Sort of need them this week... Can someone help!?'

This received 3,700 retweets and 3,200 favourites. It could have been very bad news for United Airlines. Receiving that level of exposure of a mistake with a much-loved celebrity could have been brand damaging. United, however, followed all of the good customer service principles we listed above and responded quickly and delivered a result fast. In less than two hours United responded with this:

@united: '@McIlroyRory We have good news. Your clubs will be in tomorrow and we will deliver them to the tournament for you. ^JH'

This then received 160 retweets and 116 favourites. Clearly that is not to the extent of Rory's tweet, which perhaps is to be expected, but it then became newsworthy and was highlighted by many websites as a great example of how to get social customer service right. United, through understanding their customer, having empathy and responding quickly turned around a negative situation into a positive.

We have looked above at how responsiveness is vital as a customer service principle and this is very true within social customer service – people expect and even demand a response within minutes rather than hours or days. There are now more and more businesses doing this well and the barriers to exit continue to shrink in many markets, so responsiveness is crucial.

Social media can, however, result in more resolutions per hour for an agent than calls and therefore lowers cost per interaction, which is a vital metric within a customer service environment.

We also looked in Chapter 11 at social listening and one area to use that to our advantage is for customer service. By simply tracking your brand name on Twitter for example (with or without the @) and including common misspellings, as you would when determining an SEO keyword strategy, you can monitor and respond to mentions across the social landscape whether they be negative or positive. The latter point is an important one to remember. Acknowledging positive comments can be just as powerful as responding to negative ones.

New technology

Alongside the above considerations it is also important to consider the fast pace of change of technology and how this can be used to aid your customer service journey.

AI, as we have mentioned throughout the book, is improving at pace. It is now at a point where it can recognize emotional signals. This can be used for several purposes but one of the most beneficial is customer service. Using AI to detect the emotion of an individual can help you enormously in positioning your response. This is not just in typed messages but even on phone calls with prompts to Customer Service Agents.

We will discuss data visualization in the next chapter. It is also relevant here in that there is a great deal of data that is relevant to a service communication and it can be hard to pull together into anything coherent. Using visualization techniques you can take this data and simplify the graphical representation, therefore enabling agents to quickly find the issues and resolve them.

Measurement

In Chapter 19 we explore how to effectively measure your digital marketing but we will look here at specific measurements for customer service, as they are unique.

Content engagement

One of the channels we mentioned above was online content and we need a measurement for how this is performing. This can differ dependent on how your content is managed, organized and consumed, but the constant is engagement. This could be the number of times your help video is viewed or watched all the way to the end (view-through rate or VTR). It could be visits to a page, shares of a piece of helpful content or guide downloads. You may have 'like' buttons on your blog or forum or comment posts. You may also want to monitor this for logged-in customers versus public visits to understand differing trends in customer needs. All of these interactions can give us a view as to engagement with the content you are serving to your customers and therefore how useful it is proving in helping customers with issues or concerns. You will need to consider what the relevant measures are for your content – these should play a part on your customer service dashboard but are often overlooked. This should be measured through your web and social analytics platforms.

Hold time and abandonment

This applies not just to call centres but also to any live interaction with an agent and so live chat is a good example here. As we mentioned above, a significant percentage of customers will expect you to respond immediately and so understanding that demand and how your business is meeting it is crucial to measuring success. This should be measured through your phone systems.

Response time

This measure is primarily in relation to channels such as social media and e-mail. With social media you should be looking to respond within a number of minutes that is appropriate to your market. For e-mail this could be hours or days. This should be reviewed on a regular basis for response times; documentation should be kept electronically to enable future improvements.

First-contact resolution

This is another measure that is common in both offline and digital channels and refers to the quality of your response. The above 'response time' measures how fast you are but fast, poor responses are not helpful so we need a quality measure. The measure is therefore what percentage of resolutions are provided at the first contact. For example, if I contact a business that has a secure login area because I have lost my password, will you provide me with a reset or reminder straight away or will you need to pass me to someone else, or perhaps even forget to send me the e-mail?

Net promoter score (NPS)

There are many methods of gaining customer feedback and one measure that also enables you to have a quick view of how you perform as an organization is net promoter score (NPS). NPS is a concept developed by Reichheld in his 2003 *Harvard Business Review* article 'The one number you need to grow'. The article has certainly had mixed reviews but has been widely used by many organizations as a guide to general customer sentiment. This measure works by simply asking customers to score your organization out of 10 in response to the question 'How likely are you to recommend X' where X is what you are looking to measure. People who score 9 or 10 are considered promoters, 7 or 8 are passives and all others (6 and below) are detractors (Figure 18.2).

Figure 18.2 Net promoter score

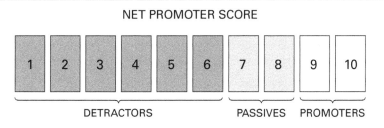

By averaging out the score you can understand whether your business is primarily delivering satisfactory outcomes for customers or not.

This can then be applied to specific areas of your business such as your customer service. Customers can be asked to score the service they have received out of 10 and an NPS score can be determined as a result. Some believe that NPS can give a result that is below that of other satisfaction surveys and can therefore paint an inaccurate picture; and the different interpretations of scoring in different cultures affects global results. There are also no details behind the score so understanding the motivations for the scoring would require further research. Whilst there are challenges such as this it is fair to say that NPS will give a sensible guide as to the satisfaction of customers of many businesses. Other measures such as customer lifetime value (see Chapter 1) and retention or churn (see Chapter 17) should also be considered.

Summary

The key to digital customer service is to retain the many decades of learning about best-practice customer service from the more established channels and to integrate digital into your existing processes. In this chapter we explored what these principles are and how we can apply them to digital servicing. This includes the challenges of social customer service, chatbots, messaging and measuring success in customer service. It is vital that when building your digital strategy you consider some of the technical implementation and integration challenges around some of the channels listed above. It is therefore also essential to ensure that you implement only the channels that are most appropriate to your customers – and you can only achieve that by truly understanding them.

Chapter checklist

- Customer service principles ☐
- Service channels ☐
- Social customer service ☐
- Measurement ☐

Further reading

- *On customer service strategies*:

  Heppell, M (2015) *Five Star Service: How to deliver exceptional customer service*, FT Press

  Stevens, D (2010) *Brilliant Customer Service*, Prentice Hall

  Watkinson, M (2013) *The Ten Principles Behind Great Customer Experiences*, FT Press

References

Accenture (2016) [accessed 20 November 2018] Chatbots in Customer Service [Online] https://www.accenture.com/t00010101T000000__w__/br-pt/_acnme-dia/PDF-45/Accenture-Chatbots-Customer-Service.pdf

Husson, T, Wang, X and McQuivey, J L *et al* (2016) [accessed 12 February 2019] The Future of Messaging Apps: With Bots and Intelligent Agents, New Conversation Interfaces Will Change Your Relationship with Customers, Forrester [Online] https://www.forrester.com/report/The+Future+Of+Messaging+Apps/-/E-RES133304?docid=133304

Reichheld, F F (2003) The One Number You Need to Grow, *Harvard Business Review* (December)

Measuring success through data analytics and reporting

19

What we will cover in this chapter

This chapter covers how to build effective measures for digital marketing success, the tools needed to track your achievements and how to communicate them consistently as part of the story of your digital strategy. The key areas covered in this chapter are:

- The data landscape
- The reliability of data-based decisions
- What are analytics?
- Tools and technology
- Attribution modelling
- Reporting

Chapter goals

By the end of this chapter you should understand the importance of analytics and key techniques in developing your reporting structure. You should understand attribution modelling and have an appreciation of data-based decision reliability. You will understand tag- and server-based analytics as well as social and web analytics.

The data landscape

The final part of developing your strategy is also quite possibly the most important. Delivering a strategy that is not effectively measured can create confusion or a lack of transparency that is impossible to come back from. In other words, if your strategy is set in motion but you cannot prove that it is delivering any results then it can quickly receive negative feedback from your internal stakeholders and can even be cancelled by your decision makers. If your goals cannot be demonstrably met, how will you or, perhaps more importantly, your stakeholders ever know if your strategy has been a success or how to adapt it going forwards? Everything before this point becomes utterly meaningless without ensuring that your analysis is implemented correctly and is future proofed as much as possible.

Digital marketers are fortunate (and some may say also unfortunate) to have endless tools and data at their disposal to enable full transparency. The challenges here are, therefore, not the limits of technology or visibility, but in the strategic implementation and reporting of the data that is outputted. Understanding how best to use this data and how to fit the pieces of disparate information together to form solid insights is an art form as much as a science.

'Big data' is a phrase that has been heavily used in digital marketing over recent years. This is a great way to express exactly what we are looking at here. Big data simply refers to data sets so large and complex that they are difficult to process using standard tools and techniques. It therefore also refers to being able to make smart decisions through interpretation of the full data set rather than the separate parts. The term big data was coined by NASA in 1997 when describing a problem they had with visualization. It began to be used in a wider sense from 2008 by computer scientists and has been used in digital marketing since around 2010.

Big data

'Data sets whose size is beyond the ability of typical database software tools to capture, store, manage and analyse.' (McKinsey, 2011)

We have already examined research and insight in Chapter 3 as key areas of data that will inform your strategy and will continue to influence it over time. These remain key measures of success but are unlikely to make it on to your reporting dashboards and so we will not look at those again now.

The reliability of data-based decisions

There is a great deal of data available to us and, as mentioned above, this can be a real asset to our decision making. It can, however, be dangerous if used incorrectly. There are two primary challenges that we need to be aware of: the human factor and data alignment.

The human factor

Data is in itself worthless. A simple set of information achieves nothing without some action being taken on it. Whether that action be through direct human interaction or through a human-created algorithm or formula, there is some human interaction necessary to turn the data into something actionable. This creates an opportunity for error. The human interaction is even deeper when we consider that human interaction is also necessary to set up the collection of the data in the first place. Not only could our interpretation of the data be wrong but the data itself may be wrong. For example, if we look at the implementation of a fairly standard and simple-to-use analytics tool such as Google Analytics we see four main stages where humans play a key role:

- Someone working at Google designs the product.
- Someone installs Google Analytics on their website.
- Someone sets up the preferences and reports within Google Analytics.
- Someone uses those reports to make decisions.

So the product may be perfect but the set-up may be wrong. The set-up may be fully functional but the interpretation of the reports may be wrong. Or the set-up and interpretation may be correct but there may be a glitch in the program.

Data alignment

Very few businesses rely on one data set to make decisions. It is rarely possible for one organization to look at their financial data, sales, staff numbers, marketing spend, fixed costs, investments and a great number of other data sets together in one system. This is not a technology issue but much more one of confidentiality and convenience. Managing your paid search activity in the same system that you pay your creative agency and manage your staff salaries does not make a great deal of sense. Therefore there is a very strong chance that your systems will not always agree. Even when using two very similar systems, sometimes ones produced by the same company, you will find discrepancies in the numbers. This can occur due to the definition of a term.

If, for example, we take a 'hit', how might you define that? Immediately there are two commonly used options: 1) an element of your page is loaded (eg an image); 2) someone arrives on your page.

Technically option 1 is the correct answer – a hit is when a file is downloaded – but many people still use the term 'hit' to refer to a visit. If no files other than the web page itself are downloaded when someone visits then a visit or page view is the same as a hit. There are many discrepancies between data sets that will cause your data not to match – and being aware of this is crucial.

What are analytics?

In simple terms analytics are reporting tools that allow the user to view key statistics on the performance of the item being analysed. These statistics have expanded significantly since 2005 and now include some advanced data sets such as real time, demographics, social media, attribution, multichannel and cross-device data. There are two forms of analytics, namely server based, where the web server log files are read, and tag based, where tagging code is added to the pages of the site to allow data to be collected. It is worth taking a quick look at the differences of each now.

Server-based analytics

This was the beginning of analytics and so arrived before tag-based services. Server-based analytics collects data from the log files that are kept on the server and therefore show a picture of the activity on the site. Challenges have arisen with this method since its arrival in the early 1990s. First, it only measures hits, which as we mentioned above do not show a true picture of visitors. This was addressed when page views and visits were added. Search engine spiders or robots (the methods used by search engines to crawl the internet and index websites) and other challenges such as caches then made it more difficult for server-based analytics to detect humans. This means that you may not see cached visits and may see some spider visits.

Tag-based analytics

These arrived in the mid-1990s and those of us old enough will remember seeing bright-green visit counters on the bottom of many pages. You can still find them dotted around the corners of the internet. Most of these had disappeared by 2000, or so it seemed. Instead of the graphic disappearing completely it had been replaced by a small invisible pixel, which when sent to the analytics software was able to log information about the activity on the page and behaviour of the user. This method continues to evolve but it is now the more commonly used form of web analytics as it is able to overcome some of the challenges that server-based analytics has faced. It does not, however, offer some of the solutions that server-based analytics can.

Server-based versus tag-based analytics

The advantages of server-based analytics are primarily in its integration and SEO solutions. This method uses the server logs that are already created by the company and so nothing new need be built; this also means that the company owns and retains the data at all times, which is a key consideration when buying data services from a supplier. Also, because the server-based method includes search engine spider data it can provide better SEO information than the tag-based solutions. This is because you have access to the real spider data itself rather than having limited data pulled into your tag-based software. Google Analytics, for example, is well known to have decreased its SEO analytics within its tag-based solution.

Tag-based analytics is by far the more preferable method when looking for rich user interaction data. This method enables logging of specific actions on elements within the page and gathering of advanced user data such as browser. Tag-based analytics also has the advantage of being able to count cached pages, which account for around one-third of all visits.

The most popular analytics tool has historically been Google Analytics (a tag-based solution) and it remains the leader today, primarily due to its freemium model and solid performance. There are some restrictions around what the free Google product can offer but the standard offering is robust enough for most organizations. There are still several other key players in the market and we will mention those below, as Google certainly does not have a monopoly here.

A useful case study here is Hostelworld's use of Adobe Analytics.

CASE STUDY Hostelworld

Background

Hostelworld is a market-leading booking platform focusing on worldwide hostel offerings through its website and apps in 19 languages. It focuses primarily on young people using hostels around the world. The challenge was to engage a niche audience across global markets and build a brand that delivers personalized customer journeys to next-generation travellers whilst developing a social experience and community for them.

To deliver this Hostelworld used the Adobe Experience Cloud including Adobe Advertising Cloud Search, Adobe Campaign within Adobe Marketing Cloud, and Adobe Analytics within Adobe Analytics Cloud.

Strategy

To optimize each customer's digital journey with personalized experiences, Hostelworld needed two things: insight into customer behaviour through in-depth data and tools to efficiently act on that intelligence.

Hostelworld's audience expects digital experiences that are fast, simple and personalized. Using Adobe Analytics, the company gained detailed insight into how customers used its websites and apps. Through real-time metrics, Hostelworld's marketing team learned where customers were coming from and travelling to, what information they were browsing, and their journeys through the marketing funnel.

Alongside this detail they looked at sources of traffic to determine which advertising campaigns were proving most effective and to suggest new areas where advertising could reach a hostel-friendly audience. Marketers also tested variations of copy, ads and booking funnels across multiple platforms and channels to see how they could optimize each.

The analytics data from Adobe Analytics also allowed marketers to increase the efficiency of their paid search performance. Advertising Cloud Search automatically places bids on search terms to achieve better ROI (returns on investment). This has resulted in booking costs being reduced by 20 per cent as well as improved productivity within the team.

Another benefit of using one consistent marketing tech suite is that the data from Adobe Analytics also integrates with Adobe Campaign. This has helped Hostelworld reach its young audience across a variety of digital channels. Using customer behaviour data in Analytics marketers were able to build out audience segments that Hostelworld could then use to tailor communications to reach people through any channel with the right message at the right time.

Results

The results of using this one powerful marketing suite were clear. Hostelworld saw 500 per cent higher engagement across its websites and social media activity. It experienced a 20 per cent reduction in cost per booking. One billion e-mails could be sent per year with strong click-through rates and all of this was achieved with more efficient productivity within the team.

Key lessons

Considering your technology stack and using your analytical data effectively to feed your marketing activity deliver vastly improved results across all of your activity. Adobe is one of the leaders in the space although there are others.

Tools and technology

There are many tools available to track your digital data and these can be broken down into several areas. We look at five of the most common of these here:

- web analytics;
- social analytics;
- SEO analytics;
- user experience;
- tag management.

Web analytics

What is it?

Web analytics is the tool that collects and reports on all of the key data on the performance of your website. The standard data you should expect to get from your web analytics tool includes the following:

- Page views, visits, unique visitors, bounce rate, session duration.
- New versus returning visitors: users who have visited before or not.
- Language and location: helpful for geographical purposes.
- Demographics: data on the user's high-level information such as age.

- Device type, make and model: technical data on your device hardware.
- Browser, resolution and operating system: technical data on your device software.
- Traffic source: which pages people came from.
- Keyword analysis: a review of the keywords used to reach your site.
- Goal conversion: the percentage of times that a business-defined goal is met.
- E-commerce tracking: data on user behaviour in your online shop.
- Funnel conversion: the percentage of shoppers who make it from the start to the end of your purchase journey.

How it fits into your strategy

Web analytics is vital to any digital strategy. This tool is the stalwart of your strategy, whatever your strategy may be. If you are focused on high-volume e-commerce then using real-time analytics, visitor demographics and conversion funnels are all crucial so that you can react quickly, personalize your experience for optimal conversion and monitor your sales process closely. If you are spending a great deal on digital advertising then understanding your conversion paths, attribution and traffic sources is vital to be able to improve your UX, understand which digital channels are contributing to conversion and which directly provide the traffic. If you have a content-based site then understanding what content is popular, who is reading what and on what device is essential. All of this requires web analytics. Without web analytics you are blind to the activity on your site – and without this data you cannot make the decisions you need to in order to make your strategy successful.

Social analytics

What is it?

Social analytics refers to the tools used to monitor the effectiveness of social media. There are two distinct areas of social media that can be measured and they are content and promotion. Your business may operate in one or both of these. Using social media to share engaging content is a goal of many businesses and one that can and should be monitored closely to learn how to improve future content plans. Using social to advertise your products and services to highly targeted and engaged audiences is also an increasingly common way of using the channel but one that involves very different metrics.

In order to understand how your content is resonating with your audience you need to have visibility of how users are engaging with this content, what topics are the most popular and to whom, when users engage and on what device. All of these questions are vital if you are to understand how to deliver content that will interest your customers and prospects. Your users may prefer lengthy articles or short videos, they may only consume your content at night or almost entirely on mobile devices. Your users may choose to share only very specific content types or maybe only your true brand advocates share your content. It is vital to understand this level of detail. Once you do you can make key decisions such as which content to produce and how often. This will influence how you manage resource internally and how you publish content. If your users read on their mobile devices and convert on tablets then optimizing your site for content on mobile is essential; ensuring you have a good video solution is vital if your users would benefit from video to make their decisions.

When using social media as a channel for promotion the metrics may be very different. If you are looking to improve your social footprint then you may be looking at more of the 'vanity' metrics, ie those that do not really indicate the success of an organization on social media but do look impressive to the casual viewer, such as followers. If you are looking to use social as an acquisition tool then you would also want to include clicks, visits and conversions.

Finally, you may want to measure broader metrics that are beyond your control, by which I am referring to the conversations that happen without your input. This is where social listening tools become a key part of your analytics portfolio – understanding what conversations are happening around your brand or products, your share of voice, the influence of those discussing it and the sentiment of users towards the specific conversations or your brand generally.

Some of the key metrics you should be considering here are as follows:

- Reach: the total users mentioning your brand plus their followers.
- Engagement: the people taking an action on your content.
- Average engagement rate: the average rate of people who took action versus people who saw your content.
- Impressions: the number of times your content has been seen.
- Visits: the total number of times people have been to your site/page.

- Unique visitors: the total number of individuals who have been to your site/page.
- Bounce rate: people arriving and then leaving without visiting another page.
- Click-through rate: the percentage of people who see your content and click through to the end location.
- Conversion rate: the percentage of people who buy versus those who arrived on your site or began a purchase journey.
- Sales: total number of sales (you could also split this into the separate sales channels, eg social, website, phone as a result of the activity).
- Response rate: the percentage of people who have in some way responded to your content.
- Mentions: the number of times that your brand has been mentioned.
- Followers: the number of followers you have on any or all networks.
- Buzz: combination of a number of factors that suggest how popular you are right now.
- Share of voice: the number of conversations about you versus your competition.
- Sentiment: reviewing the types of message about you for positive and negative sentiment.

How it fits into your strategy

The first point to realize here is that social analytics is important whether or not you are running social media advertising or a content plan. Even if it is not appropriate for your business to include social media within the channel mix there is still a strong chance that your brand will be mentioned or discussed there. This is of course significantly more likely if you are a B2C brand than B2B. If you are running a content strategy, as we discussed in Chapter 14, you will need to measure this via social analytics tools. If you are running advertising on social platforms then again you will need to have your measures of success defined and monitored.

Many businesses also measure the 'vanity' metrics mentioned above. You should be cautious when using these metrics for decision making or as measures of success. The caution lies in the fact that these metrics do not indicate that your content is engaging, that people are converting from your content, that you are reaching the right audience or that you have genuine followers. There are many tools and methods to grow your followers quickly but this is counter-intuitive unless done organically. Purchasing followers who have no real interest in your brand or content is akin to buying links for SEO and should be avoided. It may look impressive to the casual viewer to have 50,000 followers but if only 200 of those are genuine followers then you are disguising the true metrics and making decision making difficult for the sake of vanity.

SEO analytics

What is it?

SEO analytics is the method of tracking the signals that dictate your overall organic search performance. Without using specific tools for this purpose, you will be blind to your achievements or risks within this space. This is an area that is often overlooked or misunderstood due to the rather secretive nature of the channel. Search engines have long hidden their methods from public view and have even removed SEO metrics from analytics tools altogether. For example, Google Analytics gradually increased the percentage of 'not provided' keyword results in its organic search metrics to the point where almost nothing could be gained from looking at this data. There is more detail on this in Chapter 8. Also, simply searching Google for your site may return a ranking but this is just one ranking for one term on one day and is subject to significant change. That result may also be affected by your previous behaviour through a cookie.

Specific SEO tools are therefore needed and these can report on SEO signals. When combined these give a powerful view of your overall SEO performance and the areas to focus on to improve.

SEO metrics that can be monitored include:

- inbound links (or backlinks) and link quality;
- search visibility;
- crawl errors;
- site speed;
- broken links;
- rank tracking;

- competitor backlinks;
- brand monitoring.

How it fits into your strategy

SEO, for the vast majority of businesses, is a key channel within your strategy. If you have a website then you usually, but not always, want your site to perform well in the search results. As mentioned above, SEO can be misunderstood by all but the experienced digital marketer, and so SEO analytics tools are vital to helping you tell your story. Reporting on how the content that you produce, and design changes that you make, are affecting your performance are vital to gaining investment into the channel. Similarly to social media analytics – the other often misunderstood channel – you need to be wary of vanity metrics. The cry from the boardroom is often 'Make us number one on Google' but this is not necessarily the aim. Number one on what terms? For how long? And it may not even be possible if the wider business is not willing or able to create the content or link profile necessary to achieve this. Using the above metrics and tools will help to focus minds on the results of one of the most cost-effective channels for generating traffic to your site.

User experience (UX) tools

What is it?

UX tools include everything from ensuring that the user is having a pleasant experience to optimizing conversion, and more. The tools in this area are varied and can offer a great deal of insight on behaviours. Some of the outputs are less quantifiable than the other analytics tools as they will show only the behaviour not the cause or intent. For example, if you are viewing a heatmap of user behaviour and you see that your new homepage design has led to more users focusing on your secondary content, and fewer on your primary content, then you can decide that the change has had a negative effect and choose to revert the design to the previous version. You will not, however, know whether this was caused by the new content that you have released, the colours, layout or even macro factors such as what is in the news. You also will not know what the users intended when they arrived. Perhaps the new design performs better for different organic keywords and so you are now attracting a different user group to your site and they are more interested in the secondary content.

UX tools give you the opportunity to test different theories and optimize towards these to create the best possible outcome for the user and your goals.

How it fits into your strategy

UX analytics is vital to your strategy as it offers something that none of the other analytics tools can. Traditional analytics can provide a great deal of data for interpretation but UX analytics can display real user journeys, funnels and behaviours. This gives you a fresh perspective on the same data and enables you to gain rich insights into what users really think of your site and how they interact.

Tag management

What is it?

Tag management is a solution that is implemented by many larger organizations in order to make the implementation of other systems easier and to solve some issues that tags create. Tags are pieces of code that you put into your website code in order to fulfil certain tasks such as monitoring traffic or understanding visitor data. Tag management is therefore not a pure analytics tool itself but is worth looking at alongside the above tools, as it should be considered simultaneously.

When tags are called upon by the browser (or 'fired') they can cause a number of issues.

These include:

- Changes to a page could result in a tag no longer functioning correctly.

- Some older tags will fire one after the other rather than asynchronously (see Figure 19.1), which can slow down a site, especially if any of these tags have errors in them.

- Adding new tags to a site will normally involve IT resource, which can very often be difficult to get, especially at short notice.

Synchronous and asynchronous tagging are two different methods of tags firing. Synchronous tagging is where tags fire one after the other and this can result in site delays. Asynchronous tags fire simultaneously and as such are able to speed up site performance.

Figure 19.1   An example of asynchronous tagging

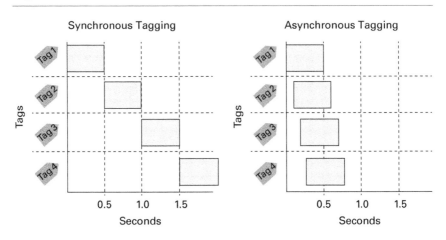

Tag management offers a solution to these problems by offering a simple interface where anyone, usually a marketing professional rather than IT professional, can manage the tags themselves. The tag management product hosts all the tags together and dynamically manages which tags need to fire and when. Marketers can then add, edit or remove tags as needed. This is a significant advantage and one that is becoming more in demand as the need for a greater range of tags increases.

How it fits into your strategy

As mentioned above, tag management is a solution that, as well as solving some issues that tags create, also puts the power to manage tags in the hands of the marketers. This frees up much-needed resource in the technology or IT department and gives the marketing department the ability to manage the digital strategy much more closely and respond to the demands of improved analytics, programmatic marketing and other tag-based solutions in a more agile fashion.

What to look for when selecting a partner

Integration is an important factor. We have already mentioned data discrepancies, above, and so ensuring that your choice of analytics tool will fit with your established systems is a key consideration and should be discussed with your potential and existing suppliers. As we have already looked at, privacy and data collection is a sensitive area and one that is highly regulated (consider the GDPR in Europe, 2018). You should be comfortable that your supplier is adhering to any relevant laws and regulations on this.

Future proofing is important. For example, if your chosen tool is free to use then does it have any restrictions around traffic volumes or any other metrics? If so, then would you expect to exceed these in the next three to five years? If the answer to this question is yes, then you must consider whether this is affordable and whether this is the most effective solution to implement. Changing technology in the future could be difficult and may result in a loss of data.

Is your chosen supplier a reliable one? Some companies have been providing their services for many years or are part of a long-established group that is highly unlikely to go out of business. However, as is the nature of the digital world, some of the most innovative new solutions are offered by young companies. Not seizing these opportunities may result in a loss of competitive advantage, but they do present a risk if the business is not successful in the long term, and protecting yourself for this is worth considering.

Performance can vary greatly and so ensuring that you have adequate service level agreements (SLAs) in place with the supplier is important. Should you expect a customer service agent to answer your call quickly, then this needs to be stated. You may also require the service to have downtime of no more than 0.1 per cent, and other considerations.

Data ownership is another important consideration. We mentioned above that an advantage of server-based analytics is that you own the data. Most analytics solutions now are tag based, which means you may not own what you consider to be your data (see tag-based analytics above). You should investigate this thoroughly and consider your position carefully.

There are many suppliers that offer the above analytics platforms. You should ensure you conduct your own research but here are some you may want to consider:

Web analytics

- Google
- Adobe
- Webtrends
- IBM

Social analytics

- Facebook Insights
- Twitter Analytics
- Brandwatch

- Salesforce Marketing Cloud
- Sprout Social
- Snaplytics
- Iconosquare
- Buzzsumo

SEO analytics

- Searchmetrics Suite
- Moz
- Cognitive SEO
- Majestic SEO
- SEMRush
- Google Search Console

UX tools

- Optimizely
- Usabilla
- Verify
- Appsee

Keep in mind that the above tools may improve, decline or be stopped altogether and new entrants will change the market. These are not recommendations but instead a view of some successful suppliers at the time of publishing.

Attribution modelling

Attribution modelling gives marketers the ability to see what effect different components of their campaigns have on their customers and therefore how valuable they are. This can be measured within a channel, which in the case of display might be used to make sure that an awareness campaign is being delivered to people who are mostly new customers. Cross-channel attribution, which is more commonly implemented by advertisers, looks at the interaction between people and their exposure and/or interactions with each element of the digital mix. This provides a picture of how each channel is playing its part and therefore how valuable or efficient each channel is compared to its peers.

Advertisers use attribution modelling to place a more accurate worth on any channel or activity. Having this information available also allows advertisers to know where to place budget more accurately (planning). There are two key variations of attribution – data-driven attribution and rule-based attribution. The differences are the methodology used to define how credit is awarded to each channel for the part it plays in a sale (or other campaign goal) compared to the other channels involved. Rule-based attribution is the simpler version and while still very important does sometimes require a certain amount of trial and error to determine that best set of rules and variations of reporting needed to give a picture of campaign activity. Rules-based attribution is very similar to 'path to conversion' reporting. Rules-based attribution will vary slightly depending on the provider of the service, but generally there are several default reports that advertisers use to get an understanding. It is commonplace for a combination of these to be used at the same time. These reports look at placing credit for conversion in the following ways:

- The *linear* model might be used if your strategy is designed to maintain contact with potential customers and keep the product fresh in the consumer's mind. This might be an especially useful way of measuring success for a product that has a prolonged research phase or for an advertiser with products in a very competitive space. The linear attribution model will place equal credit for all of the channels.

- The *first interaction* model can help you to understand which channels create initial awareness for your brand or product. All the credit is given to the channel that is first that is seen by any user. Therefore this is a useful report to run on a strategy that has a primary objective of awareness.

- The *position-based* model is far more useful in giving insight into how channels can be used to adjust credit for different parts of the customer journey, such as early interactions that create awareness and late interactions that close sales. When you are trying to raise awareness of a product but also make sales with a limited budget, this can be helpful in giving credit only to those channels that do exactly that.

- A *custom attribution model* potentially becomes very useful to a marketer who has used a combination of the above models to understand their activity and has a framework that they fully understand. Their framework will account for how valuable any one element of activity is over its peers most of the time. The model can be used to provide a good sense-check of their ongoing marketing activity. With the implementation of a custom rule-based attribution model the nuances of any marketing strategy are better accounted for.

As may be apparent from comparing the common rule-based attribution models, a marketer will have to run these models in conjunction with each other and often run a set of the models for each element of the activity running, whether that be different sites that adverts are placed on or, more likely in the case of programmatic executions, the different strategies and campaign elements, eg awareness, action and retargeting strategies. This can prove quite lengthy and, although rule-based attribution represents a vitally important step forward in allowing advertisers to understand consumer behaviour in a multichannel world, it is still quite assumptive and therefore does not provide perfect measurement of how budget is deployed. On the other hand, data-driven attribution looks to solve that issue entirely. The companies that provide this service collect all possible campaign and site data from an advertiser and use a mathematical model to analyse the importance of each touchpoint. The algorithms they use to do this are their proprietary-developed intellectual property and as such are closely guarded secrets. However, enough about their methods can be explained for a decision on which supplier to select.

Fundamentally, every user journey and touchpoint of paid (and non-paid) media are assessed against all other customer journeys and a set of algorithms determine how effective a contribution the different campaign and marketing components contribute – thus allowing advertisers and marketers to assess the performance of individual components and work out the best way to deploy future budgets.

Ultimately, attribution modelling allows marketers a robust as possible way to avoid channel conflict. Savvy marketers have always looked at activity holistically but the available data often forces them, often inadvertently, to put their channels into conflict, looking at the pricing and values of channels individually and not at how they interact together and the effect that they have on each other.

Reporting

All of these analytics tools are incredibly powerful and give you the data you need to report on the success of your digital strategy, but ultimately they are worthless if not pulled together into a strong reporting format and process. In order to enlighten yourself and your stakeholders on the progress you are making, and to see the challenges that you face, a strong dashboard is necessary and this will need to be appropriate to your goals as well as your stakeholders' objectives, which may necessitate different versions. There are two primary areas to consider when building your reporting: the data and the presentation.

Data

The data you use, no matter from which source, must be tailored to the audience that will be consuming it. This means understanding the needs of your audience and also their knowledge of digital. The focus of your content providers will be on the engagement in their content and which themes are gaining the most interest. An important measure of this may be bounce rate, but if your content providers are not digital savvy then they may not understand what this metric means. Having this perspective is crucial to ensure that your reports resonate with the end user and enable you to tell your story to a receptive audience.

As well as tailoring your reports for your audience, you will also need to ensure that your strategy is represented. If you have implemented a digital marketing strategy that focuses heavily on organic search then this should feature in all reports. How is your content featuring in the organic rankings? How have your new designs improved site audit results? What SEO signals have been created by your social strategy? Ensure that you align the reports with your goals as well as those of your audience or your story will be incomplete. How often you produce and circulate these reports also needs consideration. Producing reports can take time, and automation should be considered where possible. Many of the above tools have options to deal with this. Also there will be meetings in your business that demand reports, but no reporting should be produced without robust data available. You should never compromise the quality of the report simply to meet a meeting timescale, or you can do serious harm to your story.

One key element to build into your reports is how you will measure success. For example, are you comparing against sales targets or historical achievements? When comparing against historical data there are a number of common comparisons but each of these has its disadvantages, which you must be aware of:

- *Year on year (YoY)*: comparison with last year's results can be useful in showing growth over time and also ensures that any seasonal differences are almost eliminated. It does not, however, give true visibility of changes in market conditions since 12 months ago, which in many industries can be vast.

- *Month on month (MoM)*: this can be useful for reporting against budgets and any growth or decline over the year. It does not, however, account for seasonal changes. In many industries, for example, January will always be stronger than December or vice versa, so this really tells us very little.

- *Week on week (WoW)*: this can show very dynamic and recent fluctuations in data, which can be useful in seeing where changes have had an impact but it also means that many other factors will be playing a part in the fluctuations, and so pulling the data apart into actionable insights can be difficult.

Finally, considering predictive analysis is important. Using the data to report historically is useful but using the data to predict what will be coming is far more powerful. Forecasting should be a key part of your reporting processes and you should be able to make recommendations to the business on what your stakeholders can be doing to capitalize on the trends you are seeing. Hindsight by itself offers little value.

Presentation

When producing your reports, presentation can be just as important as the data itself. Ensuring that your audience can immediately understand what they see, what it means to them and what actions they can take from it is vital to taking your stakeholders on the journey with you. In order to do this you should always keep the following principles (consider this a checklist) at the front of your mind:

- *Tell a story.* Every good story has a beginning, a middle and an end. Your report should be no different. Not just a collection of numbers but a narrative about why I should believe your message. These three stages can be defined in the following three simple questions: What are we trying to achieve? Did we achieve it? What do we do next? If your dashboard can do this then you will have a strong start.

- *So what?* This is a question you should be asking yourself all the time. We achieved 10 per cent conversion rate this January. So what? Last year we only achieved 9 per cent. So what? So we have increased by 1 per cent, a gain of over 10 per cent. So what? Market conditions were difficult so this increase actually represents a significant gain. You can go on for some time with this challenging question, but ultimately this means you will always have a strong output from your data. Commentary is important in a dashboard to show that you understand and are acting on the data you have, so ensure you ask the 'so what?' question at all times.

- *Keep it simple.* This is always a good principle in marketing. Never assume knowledge or that what is obvious to you is obvious to anyone else. Really challenge yourself to create something that everyone will understand. This does not mean you need to dumb down the content but that you need to communicate it clearly. Remember that you are deep in the knowledge whereas your audience may not understand the context. Keep the graphs simple, the data clear and the commentary sharp and to the point.

- *Graphics.* Using graphics to bring data to life is a very strong way of communicating your message, especially when dealing with time frames. Trends can be absorbed much faster and easier by the human brain with the use of graphics than through numbers or words.

- *Label it up.* Ensure you label everything clearly. It is easy to forget to add the axis to the chart or to label whether you are working in GBP or USD. Incorrect labelling can lead to incorrect assumptions, which can prove costly if not discovered before decisions are made.

- *Check, check and check again.* Finally, it is obvious – but always check your data. The number of reports produced with faulty data, incorrect labelling or unrealistic assumptions is astounding. It is easily done as reports often evolve over a period of time before being circulated so always check, check and check again. It is also often worth having an independent person to check, as fresh eyes can often spot the mistakes that you may miss.

There are many tools now available to help with data visualization. Platforms such as Qlik Sense, Tableau and Google Charts offer simple ways to display data in interactive and beautiful formats that are easy for anyone to understand. The outputs are only as good as the inputs, of course, so ensure your data is accurate, but this can be far more effective than an Excel or PowerPoint format. It is also useful for digital marketers to show that they are using the latest digital platforms.

Summary

In this chapter we examined how the data landscape has evolved, with big data becoming a more common challenge for businesses. We looked at how data needs to be managed and interpreted carefully due to the issues that can be presented through the human factor and through data alignment. We reviewed analytics and the key areas that these tools cover, as well as the metrics you should expect to review from each. We also looked at some potential suppliers, but there are many more available and so you should conduct your own research before making any decisions. Finally, we looked at reporting and how turning your data and analytics into meaningful dashboards is vital if you are to take your stakeholders on your journey with you. In the next and final chapter we look at how to present your strategy to your decision makers to ensure you gain the approval and support you need to deliver a world-class digital marketing strategy for your organization.

Chapter checklist

- The data landscape ☐
- The reliability of data-based decisions ☐
- What are analytics? ☐
- Tools and technology ☐
- Attribution modelling ☐
- Reporting ☐

Further reading

- *On big data:*
  Marr, B (2015) *Big Data: Using smart big data, analytics and metrics to make better decisions and improve performance,* John Wiley & Sons
- *On web analytics*:
  Kaushik, A (2009) *Web Analytics 2.0*, Sybex. In his book Avanish covers web analytics in a great deal of depth and so this is a very useful read for anyone who will be using analytics in their strategy, which is most of us.
  Sharma, H (2018) *Maths and Stats for Web Analytics and Conversion Optimization*, Blurb

- *On a broader view of marketing metrics*:
  Davis, J A (2013) *Measuring Marketing: 110+ key metrics every marketer needs*, John Wiley & Sons. This is recommended if you want to gain a broad understanding of the key metrics for marketing as a whole, rather than specific digital marketing.

- *On social media analytics:*
  Bali, R and Sarkar, D (2017) *Learning Social Media Analytics with R: Transform data from social media platforms into actionable business insights*, Packt Publishing

References

McKinsey (2011) [accessed 1 November 2015] Big Data: The Next Frontier for Innovation, Competition and Productivity [Online] http://www.mckinsey.com/insights/business_technology/big_data_the_next_frontier_for_innovation

An implementation guide is available at:
www.koganpage.com/DigitalMarketingStrategy/2

PART FIVE
Tailoring your final digital marketing strategy

Putting together your digital marketing strategy 20

What we will cover in this chapter

This chapter looks at how we pull together all of the elements we have discussed throughout this book into one robust, future-proofed and documented strategy. We will structure this in the way that is most effective to tell your story and most logical to help you plan out the delivery as smoothly as possible.

Chapter goals

By the end of this chapter you should have a clear view of how to apply the theory and how to turn the wealth of information in the digital marketing field into a story that you can communicate effectively, both within your company and with investors or other external stakeholders.

Where to start

Throughout this book we have looked at a diverse range of areas that make up digital marketing from planning and regulations to channel optimization and technology. Whether you are building your first digital strategy, developing a transformation project or looking to refine your existing strategy, the following steps will take you through how best to construct the final documented strategy itself.

At this point you should know your audience, competitive landscape, brand, proposition and goals. You should understand the relevant business and planning models that will help you create the framework. You should understand consumer trends and the technology landscape. You should appreciate the possibilities in digital and how each area affects the rest of the ecosystem. You should know what you want to measure and have a view of how you could approach that. You should also have some ideas of how your content strategy could play out or improve. Now you need to knit this together into a powerful strategy. But where do you start?

If you have the above pieces of the puzzle in place you have the 'Why'. If you don't, you should go back and put these in place before you read further. You now need the 'What' and 'How', which will in turn dictate the 'When'. Building out this detailed strategy will help you significantly in the implementation. In this chapter we will therefore look at how we pull together the elements of your strategy that we have discussed in this book to create one integrated strategy that is smart, cohesive and robust.

It is important to keep in mind throughout this chapter that the focus here is on how you build your strategy, not on how you put it into place. That is equally crucial, of course, but this book is not intended to be a 'how to' guide for implementation as there are plenty of resources online and agencies that can help you with this.

To build an effective strategy it is helpful to break it down into stages or phases. Each stage runs through a number of tasks that take your strategy to the next level. As with each step of a journey, this helps you and your stakeholders understand how your strategy will move forwards in an organized and methodical manner. We will therefore break down the build of your strategy into six stages. If you have existing digital marketing activity you may well recognize one of these phases as where your business is on the journey, and you could potentially pick up from there.

Stage one: assessment

This stage happens before your strategy starts to take shape. Alongside the areas you should already understand, you also need to ensure your background work is done. Much of this was discussed in the early chapters of this book.

Cultural assessment

Understand the culture of your business. Is it sales-focused or brand-focused? Is it a creative organization or analytical? Is the company a risk-taker or focused on brand safety? These factors amongst others will determine how you approach and position your strategy to your internal audience.

Leadership buy-in (and regular check-ins)

Engage your leadership team early to ensure they are aware of what you are doing and can line up their teams behind you to ensure you have the support you need to implement this.

Technology assessment

You need to understand your technology stack. Do you have any marketing technology in place such as a CMS, marketing automation suite, document management system, analytics platform, social management tools, SEO tools etc? Also, what is your wider tech landscape – your server status and speed, coding skills within the organization, app performance and reviews?

Budget

You may need to complete your strategy to justify your budget or you may know your budget at this stage. If you don't know your budget then you will need to have some high-level conversations with whomever controls the purse strings to get a rough guide to enable you to build a sensible strategy, or your final strategy is at risk of being too bold or not bold enough.

Resource

Review your team and any resources across the business that are needed to deliver this. Do you have the volume and quality of resource you need to deliver your strategy and is it set up in the optimal way? If not you will need to consider recruitment, training, perhaps even redundancies or restructures.

Stakeholder and working group set-up

At this stage you should also establish any working groups with key internal stakeholders to give them the chance to feed in their thoughts and experiences. You will not think of everything and your business partners will be crucial in delivering the best possible outcome. They will also be big supporters of your strategy if you are solving their problems.

Stage two: the foundations

This is the first stage of constructing your strategy. Here we look at the pieces you need to have in place before you can start to promote your business heavily. For example, sending consumers to a poor website is going to damage your results in the short term and your branding in the long term. Launching a campaign without the supporting customer service in place will result in complaints that will escalate quickly.

Customer service

The first area to assess is customer service. Why? Because once you start to promote your business you open yourself up for customers to contact you via digital with questions and complaints, and you cannot then take time to construct your service plans. See Chapter 18 for more detail.

SMS messaging

As we have discussed, consumers are increasingly using messaging for direct communications of every type. You should look at the technology and process for this early on in your strategy. Chapter 12 contains the detail you need.

Historic performance

If your company is not a brand new start-up then you should have some historic data. That may be some social media posts, content engagement or sophisticated campaigns. It may only be offline marketing data or sales conversion figures. Whatever you have you should conduct a detailed analysis of performance to find any trends that will be relevant to inform your strategy and help predict performance.

Targeting and segmentation

You should already know your audience but here you need to consider exactly who they are and how you find them. How will you target them across the various channels you employ and how will you effectively segment your data. Will you be able to target people by job title on LinkedIn or use programmatic display to find them? What search terms are relevant? Will you customize your website to account for the various segments? Refer to Chapter 1 for more information.

Regulations

It is crucial that you understand the regulatory environment. You may have legal and compliance advisors in your business who can help you with this. This can help you understand the requirements in your industry but you also need to understand marketing regulations. Privacy and data protection, the GDPR, accessibility and other relevant terms that will affect your messages, channels, data collection and controls, for example. This is discussed in Chapter 5.

Data strategy

Keeping the regulations in mind, you need to build a data strategy. How will you collect and retain the data? What will you do to cleanse and maintain the data on a regular basis? Who will own it and how will you connect your data sets together? How will you resolve data conflicts, such as if your internal sales numbers don't match those provided by an affiliate? How will you get your single customer view in place to enable the best possible, client-centric decision making? We looked at data in Chapter 19.

Attribution strategy

You also need to establish at this stage what your preferred attribution strategy will be. Do you favour pure last-click attribution? If your strategy is very broad and complex perhaps you need to weight it more evenly across the journey? Either way, you need to establish this now. This is discussed in Chapter 19.

Targets

You know your goals but what are your exact targets? You need to set specific targets for your activity now. What numbers do you aim to achieve? Consider sales, conversion rates, cost per acquisition, content engagement levels, retention, issue resolution speed and the other metrics we have discussed throughout the book.

Retention strategy

If you are attracting clients you need to know how you will retain them in advance. You must not fall into the trap that many organizations do of waiting until there is a problem before building a retention strategy or it will be too late. This is discussed in detail in Chapter 17.

Content strategy

Before you can make your social media or SEO strategies effective, have your website rich and keep clients informed across multiple channels, you need a content strategy so you must establish this early on. Chapter 14 is important to understand here.

Partnerships

If there are partnership opportunities then discussions will take time and should begin early in your strategy.

Website

No marketing can happen until you have a destination for the consumer to visit. Your website needs to be developed with a responsive vision, appropriate analytics, clearly thought-through journeys and ideally personalization. This should include flexibility and platforms such as a CMS to enable quick content delivery and the many other areas we have discussed throughout the book to maximize SEO, experience and conversion. Ensure you have understood Chapter 16 for this.

Analytics

As well as adding the appropriate tagging to your site, you need to ensure your analytics platform is customized with appropriate goals and reports are built and standardized at this stage to ensure your data is correctly collected from day one as this can be difficult or impossible to go back and fix. See Chapter 19 for the detail.

SEO fundamentals

Ensure you consider the SEO triangle at this stage. Does your site plan include strong SEO principles such as hierarchy, content, speed etc? See Chapter 8 for the detail here.

Social foundations

You should plan your social presence now. You can link to your website and should launch the relevant channels. You do not need to be everywhere, only where your audience may be. Consider opening branded channels, individual channels for staff if they have external profiles. Consider how your content plays out and differentiates across them. See Chapter 11 for more information.

Reporting dashboards

Now that you have your website, analytics, social media plans, SEO, retention and content plans, you need to build a dashboard that your stakeholders will buy in to that clearly tracks latest results and progress over time (consider 13 months rolling timelines) to be able to report progress once your strategy launches.

Stage three: sophistication

We have now planned the foundations. We have the destinations planned and we know how we will plan and manage our content. We know whom we are targeting and how we attract and retain customers. Yet our strategy is still fairly basic. Chances are that at least some of our competitors are more sophisticated. To really win we need to become much smarter. This is where we move to stage three.

Data collection, append, cleanse

Ensure that the data you have is in a fit state. Without good-quality and complete data sets as well as the correct processes in place throughout the entire organization, your sophistication stage will quickly fall apart. You should take the time to cleanse your data to ensure accuracy, append missing data to your data sets, train your staff and build or rebuild your systems to make this possible. This also includes ensuring you have the relevant marketing permissions and, ideally, a preference centre in place to enable the best possible personalization of your communication strategy. Consider using third parties to help with this.

Cultural considerations

A 'one size fits all' strategy, as we have discussed throughout the book, is not good enough. If your organization works across multiple territories you must consider this as it includes languages, culture, pricing, payment methods, distribution channels and a great deal more. This can be intensive work and using local experts is crucial, but the work can save embarrassing and damaging issues, create seismic shifts in performance and enable you to beat the competition. Keep in mind that cultures don't just change by country but also by regions within countries, by religious beliefs, by gender and much more.

Localization

Consider your local strategy. If you have stores, for example, you need to ensure they are SEO optimized. Local strategy is becoming increasingly important as most search engines, social networks and other digital platforms continue to focus on relevancy.

Personalization

Everyone on this planet is different. The expectation for businesses to know individuals has grown enormously, as we discussed in Chapter 15. Use your data and consider AI to build unique experience across your platforms and you will see improvements across all of your metrics.

Channels

You now know what you plan to say, how you say it and what your targets are. You should apply your knowledge of the channels from Chapters 8 to 11 to decide how you best set up your channel strategy. Are all of these channels relevant and how do they integrate with each other? Also, how do they integrate with the offline channels, for example ensuring your paid search is performing with strength when your television commercials are running? This is a big part of your planning phase with a great deal of detail. Do not rush this.

Communications strategy, CRM

Plan your comms strategy. You know what content you are producing and what channels you have available so now you should decide what you will send, to whom and how frequently. Your preference centre plans should be built in here as well, alongside your personalization and e-mail marketing. Chapter 17 can aid you here.

E-mail and automation

Look at your e-mail channel. Your comms strategy is in place so what platform do you need to deliver this effectively? Refer to Chapter 12 for more detail here.

Stage four: formalize

We now have a clear strategy that has been built on solid data and knowledge, has strong foundations and is sophisticated and future proofed. This now needs to be documented and communicated if it is going to be embedded within the organization, which is essential if it is going to reach its maximum potential.

Strategy and transformation documentation

Document your strategy. All the hard work you have done above should come together into a document or a series of documents. You must clearly lay out what you are trying to achieve, how you will achieve that over what time frame and at what cost. You may wish to compile a detailed written document for the teams that will be heavily involved in the implementation including processes and diagrams. This will also help with briefing suppliers and selecting platforms. For your senior stakeholders and decision makers, however, you are more likely to want to produce a high-level visual presentation. Storytelling remains, in my view, the most powerful tool at a human's disposal. Do not underestimate the power of bringing your story to life and, if you are unsure of the support you will get, find a storyteller who can help you bring this to life. I have created templates that are available from **www.koganpage.com/DigitalMarketingStrategy/2**

Disseminate, educate, convince

In 2015, I developed the 6S Framework for presenting to decision makers. Below is a high-level view of this.

The 6S Framework

- **S**ynopsis: what's the answer?
  - Executive summary.
- **S**cene setting: why are we doing this?
  - Reminder of the goals and targets.
  - Background.
  - Company history.
  - Competitors.
  - Market.
  - Consumer/customer.
  - Approach.
  - Assumptions.
  - Expectations.
  - Contents and what is coming next.
- **S**tory: what are we doing and why? Should I agree?
  - Channels.
  - Website.
  - Brand impact.
  - Resource.
  - Suppliers and partners.
- **S**ums: how much does it cost?
  - Financial plans.
- **S**teps: how and when does this happen?
  - Clear action plan.
  - Timescales.
  - Responsibilities.
- **S**urprise! What about...?
  - Be prepared for questions.

Before beginning your presentation, however, it is important to understand the psychology of our decision makers. Figure 20.1 below is helpful and you will probably recognize your audience as fitting into one of these boxes.

Figure 20.1 Types of decision making

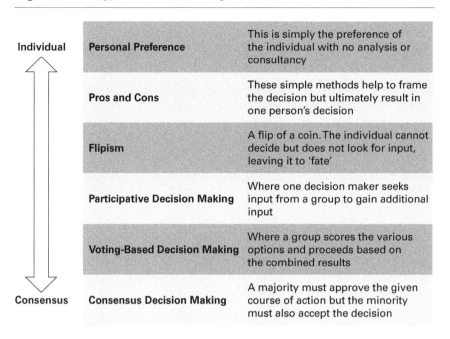

Individual	Personal Preference	This is simply the preference of the individual with no analysis or consultancy
	Pros and Cons	These simple methods help to frame the decision but ultimately result in one person's decision
	Flipism	A flip of a coin. The individual cannot decide but does not look for input, leaving it to 'fate'
	Participative Decision Making	Where one decision maker seeks input from a group to gain additional input
	Voting-Based Decision Making	Where a group scores the various options and proceeds based on the combined results
Consensus	Consensus Decision Making	A majority must approve the given course of action but the minority must also accept the decision

If you have built a robust strategy by following the above steps and you use the 6S Framework, positioning your story effectively for the psychology of your decision makers, then you have given yourself the strongest chance of having your strategy ratified and you can move to implementation.

Stage five: continuous improvement

Now you are live. Your strategy is working and everyone has bought into it. Congratulations. But I'm afraid I have bad news. You can't relax. Your strategic planning never ends. I can guarantee you only one result of your strategy, and that is that some of it will be wrong. No matter how smart you have been, there will be some assumptions or tests that simply won't work out as you hoped. As a result you will need to adjust your plans. New technology will arrive; consumer trends will change; the world economy may shift. All of this means you need to stay agile.

Review your strategy annually. Your channel management and the day-to-day tactical implementation will, of course, be in a constant state of review through your daily tracking, weekly reporting, monthly dashboards and quarterly reviews, but your actual strategy itself also needs to stay flexible. Therefore, you should take the time once a year to review it, understand how the landscape has changed and work through whether it is still appropriate to continue along the chosen path for the remainder of the strategy, be it three or five years, or whether it is appropriate to make changes. Do not let pride get in the way here. You must be willing to change – that is essential to success in digital marketing. A strategy that is no longer relevant will not become more relevant if you leave it alone.

Depending on the complexity of your strategy, implementation can be the hardest stage but, as any successful entrepreneur or angel investor will tell you, an idea without action will never be more than an idea. The greatest strategy ever written is worth nothing if it is never implemented.

Summary

The above steps will give you an effective guide to the process of constructing your strategy and the detail throughout the book gives you enough information to build out each channel and process. The channels and digital landscape change continuously so do use third parties, your analytics and insight platforms and the market to keep yourself up to speed.

We have discussed throughout the book that digital is an ecosystem. You cannot implement some of this without considering the rest. As part of this, your organization also needs to be lined up. An organization that works in silos will never deliver its best results and there are still far too many of these. If this is you then I strongly encourage you to break the silos down.

It is an exciting time to be working in this field and as technologies such as AI, IoT, VR and AR, amongst many more, continue to move at pace, the opportunities for delivering exciting, smart digital strategies are growing all the time. You must not be swept up in the excitement though. Keep your discipline and focus on what is important for your business and your customers, and implement these technologies as appropriate.

Finally, I wish you the best of luck. Whether you are learning about digital marketing, implementing your first strategy or reviewing your existing strategy, I hope this book is a useful guide and tool for this process. If you need any further assistance with your digital strategy or would like to discuss speaking or training opportunities, don't hesitate to reach out to me. My contact details are in 'About the author' at the beginning of the book.

I hope to be reading about your award-winning strategy in the near future.

Further reading

- *On decision making*:

  Hardman, D (2009) *Judgment and Decision Making: Psychological perspectives*, Blackwell. This includes some fantastic insights into the psychology of this interesting field.

- *On project management*:

  Newton, R (2016) *Project Management Step by Step: How to plan and manage a highly successful project*, 2nd edn, Pearson

- *On effective presentations*:

  Ledden, E (2017) *The Presentation Book: How to create it, shape it and deliver it! Improve your presentation skills now*, 2nd edn, Pearson Business

INDEX

Note: Numbers, acronyms, 'Mc' and '+' within main headings are filed as spelt out. '#' is ignored in filing order. Page locators in *italics* denote information contained within a figure or table.